ECE/TIM/SP/21

United Nations Economic Commission for Europe/
Food and Agriculture Organization of the United Nations

UNECE

F A O
FIAT PANIS

Timber Section, Geneva, Switzerland

Geneva Timber and Forest Study Paper 21

FOREST PRODUCTS ANNUAL MARKET REVIEW 2005-2006

UNITED NATIONS
New York and Geneva, 2006

NOTE

The designations employed and the presentation of material in this publication do not imply the expression of any opinion whatsoever on the part of the secretariat of the United Nations concerning the legal status of any country, territory, city or area, or of its authorities, or concerning the delimitation of its frontiers or boundaries.

Please note that the Timber Bulletin series has been completely discontinued. The present publication will from now on be issued under the Geneva Timber and Forest Study Paper series.

ABSTRACT

The UNECE/FAO *Forest Products Annual Market Review, 2005-2006* provides general and statistical information on forest products markets and related policies in the UN Economic Commission for Europe region (Europe, North America and the Commonwealth of Independent States). The *Annual Market Review* begins with an overview chapter, followed by a description of government and industry policies affecting forest products markets. After a description of the economic situation and construction-related demand in the region, five chapters based on annual country-supplied statistics, describe: wood raw materials, sawn softwood, sawn hardwood, wood-based panels, and paper and paperboard. Additional chapters discuss markets for wood energy, certified forest products, value-added wood products and tropical timber. In each chapter, production, trade and consumption are analysed and relevant material on specific markets is included. Tables and graphs provided throughout the text present summary information. Supplementary statistical tables may be found on the Market Information Service website within the UNECE Timber Committee and FAO European Forestry Commission website.

ECE/TIM/SP/21

UNITED NATIONS PUBLICATIONS
Sales No. E.06.II.E.11
ISBN 92-1-116945-3
ISSN 1020-2269

PREFACE

The United Nations Economic Commission for Europe strives to foster sustainable economic growth in its member countries, in particular through policy relevant analysis at the sectoral level. The *Forest Products Annual Market Review, 2005-2006* contributes to this objective by analysing forest product market developments and the government and industry policies that drive them, and thereby draws the attention of Governments, industry and other stakeholders to their policy options. The *Review* addresses these issues in a perspective of sustainable development and pays particular attention to the links between sectors. The links of the forest products markets to energy, climate change and globalization feature prominently in this issue of the *Review*.

As the UNECE region is the main producer, consumer and exporter of forest products in the world, Governments, industry and other stakeholders have a responsibility to promote sustainable forest management, both inside and outside the region. Through their public procurement policies, several Governments in the region are taking measures to ensure that wood and paper products purchased by public bodies stem from sustainable, and especially legal, sources. Industry associations and individual corporations are also establishing green, environmentally oriented purchasing policies. These procurement policies and their effects on sustainable forest management and markets for wood and paper products are a theme in this issue of the *Review* and the subject of a policy forum during the UNECE Timber Committee session in October 2006.

The *Review* is produced within the integrated programme of work of the UNECE Timber Committee and the FAO European Forestry Commission. It is based on statistics supplied by official country statistical correspondents and is the earliest comprehensive analysis of the sector available each year for the UNECE region. It is a key background document for the annual Timber Committee Market Discussions to be held in October 2006.

I would like to express my appreciation to our partners in FAO and to the 40 experts and partners who have worked directly to produce this *Review*. The information base was provided thanks to over 100 contributors of information and statistics. I take this opportunity to express my sincere gratitude to all those who contributed, directly and indirectly, to preparing this *Forest Products Annual Market Review, 2005-2006*.

The Review is intended for government policymakers and market specialists in the sector, as well as in other sectors. I hope it will achieve its objectives of providing a factual and neutral analysis of market and policy developments and providing a stimulus for meaningful policy discussion in international forums.

Marek Belka
Executive Secretary
United Nations Economic Commission for Europe

FOREWORD

By the Leader of the UNECE/FAO Team of Specialists on Forest Products Markets and Marketing

The UNECE region grows more wood than it harvests but market demand is not keeping pace with surplus supply. This presents opportunities for sustainable market development that would help the region's economies. To be sustainable, forest products markets, like forest management, must be built on three pillars: environmental, social and economic.

The UNECE/FAO Team of Specialists on Forest Products Markets and Marketing advises the UNECE Timber Committee and the FAO European Forestry Commission on forest products markets structures, policies and opportunities in the UNECE region in the context of these three pillars. The members of the Team are authors, contributors and reviewers of the *Forest Products Annual Market Review, 2005-2006*.

To ensure that purchases of wood and paper products originate from both legal and sustainable sources, Governments are establishing procurement policies, while companies and forest-sector associations are creating corporate social responsibility programmes. These policies and their effects on sustainable forest management and markets for wood and paper products are key themes in this *Review*. Also featuring is a policy forum held during the annual UNECE Timber Committee session in October 2005. The *Review* examines China's forest products trade and its influence on markets in the UNECE region – which will also be the theme at the Timber Committee's forthcoming market discussions on 3 and 4 October.

The *Review* analyses market and policy developments in the light of environmental, social and economic conditions. It is based on first-available statistics supplied by official country correspondents and is the first comprehensive analysis available each year for the UNECE region. It is comprehensive, covering all primary wood processing and value-added wood products sectors.

In addition to providing information to participants at the Timber Committee market discussions, this *Review* is a valuable resource for market specialists, Government policymakers and other forest sector stakeholders. It supports UNECE and FAO priorities by providing an objective analysis of market and policy developments and a stimulus for meaningful policy discussion in international forums.

This issue of the *Review* highlights the following policy issues:
- Emerging markets for wood products and implications for the global forest sector
- Forest law enforcement, governance and trade and initiatives to retain forestland
- Policies promoting the sound use of wood
- Climate change policy
- Wood energy promotion policies
- Initiatives aimed at increasing global competitiveness in wood and wood products markets
- Trade policy and tariff and non-tariff barriers
- Emergence of China as a major player in the wood products manufacturing arena.

I wish to express my appreciation to the Team members, the secretariat review team and to all the other persons who contributed information and statistics. I believe that this *Forest Products Annual Market Review* is a unique source of information for Governments, industry, educators and other stakeholders throughout the region and in the global forest products community.

Richard Vlosky

Dr. Richard Vlosky
Leader of the UNECE/FAO Team of Specialists
on Forest Products Markets and Marketing

CONTENTS

LIST OF TABLES

LIST OF GRAPHS

ACKNOWLEDGEMENTS

On behalf of the Geneva-based Review Team, the UNECE Timber Committee and the FAO European Forestry Commission, it is an honour to thank all the people who contributed directly or indirectly to the production of the *Forest Products Annual Market Review, 2005-2006*. While we mention some people below, we simultaneously acknowledge their associates, organizations, companies or institutions that facilitated contributions of their time and travel.

In addition to people mentioned below, numerous others helped on the *Review* and their names are included in the following list of contributors. The analysis is based on statistics received from official country correspondents, who are also listed. Some information in the chapter on certified forest products is from the Timber Committee and European Forestry Commission Network of Officially Nominated Country Correspondents on Certified Forest Products Markets and Certification of Sustainable Forest Management. Our sincere appreciation goes to these people without whose efforts made it possible to produce the *Review*.

In order of chapter number, we first acknowledge the external authors and their collaborators, then all those who helped from the secretariat.

The policy chapter was written by Jim Bowyer, Professor Emeritis, Department of Bio-based Products, University of Minnesota, and Director of Responsible Materials Program, Dovetail Partners, US. His experience was supported by a new author, Helmuth Resch, Emeritus Professor, University of Natural Resources, Austria. Dr. Bowyer is a member of the UNECE/FAO Team of Specialists on Forest Products Markets and Marketing (ToSFPM&M). Working with these experts was intellectually stimulating and we thank them.

We appreciate the continued contributions of Dieter Hesse, Senior Economic Affairs Officer, UNECE, who analyzed the economic framework for market developments. Al Schuler, Research Economist, Northeast Forest Experiment Station, USDA Forest Service, and Craig Adair, Director, Market Research, APA–The Engineered Wood Association, US, wrote the construction section in the economic overview chapter. Dr. Schuler also is a ToSFPM&M member. They again wrote the section on engineered wood products markets in the value-added wood products chapter. The first part of the value-added products chapter was written by Tapani Pahkasalo, Market Analyst, Savcor Indufor Oy, Finland. Jukka Tissari, Head, Business Intelligence and Market Research, Savcor Indufor, assisted him. In the *Review*, the analysis of primary-processed products is complemented with indications of demand from secondary-processed products through the valuable insight of these authors.

Håkan Ekström, President, Wood Resources International, brings forward a wealth of experience when again analyzing wood raw materials. He is Editor-in-Chief of *Wood Resource Quarterly* and the *North American Wood Fiber Review*, two publications tracking worldwide wood fibre markets and prices. Mr. Ekström, a member of the ToSFPM&M, consulted with other experts and incorporated their contributions.

Our thanks for the sawn softwood analysis goes first to its coordinator, Russell Taylor, President, International WOOD MARKETS Group Inc., Canada. Nikolai Burdin, Director, OAO NIPIEIlesprom, Russia, wrote the Russian analysis. Arvydas Lebedys, Forestry Officer—Statistics, FAO, contributed information about Baltic markets; Jarno Seppälä, Consultant, Pöyry Forest Industry Consulting, Finland, wrote the western European analysis for the first time. Mr. Taylor and Dr. Burdin are members of the ToSFPM&M. We thank all of them for their rich analysis of sawn softwood markets.

We would also like to thank Rod Wiles and Rupert Oliver, both from Emerging Markets Office, Forest Industries Intelligence Limited who produced the sawn hardwood analysis. Both are members of the ToSFPM&M. We are truly grateful that production of the chapter is again possible thanks to our continued collaboration with the American Hardwood Export Council (AHEC). Cooperative efforts between Mr. David Venables, European Director of AHEC, and the secretariat, continue to be mutually rewarding.

Ivan Eastin, Director, Center for International Trade in Forest Products, University of Washington, produced the North American analysis and coordinated the chapter's production. Bénédicte Hendrickx, Economic Advisor, European Panel Federation, analyzed the European panel markets. They had input on the Russian market from Dr. Burdin. We thank all these authors, and their contributors, and look forward to continued cooperative efforts.

Once again four authors performed the paper, paperboard and woodpulp market analysis: Peter J. Ince, Research Forester, USDA Forest Service, US Forest Products Laboratory (and chapter coordinator); Professor Eduard L. Akim, PhD, Saint Petersburg State Technological University of Plant Polymers and the All-Russian Research Institute of Pulp and Paper Industry; Bernard Lombard, Trade and Competitiveness Director, Confederation of European Paper Industries (CEPI) with statistical assistance by Eric Kilby, CEPI; and by Tomas Parik, Managing Director, Wood and

Paper A.S. Dr. Ince works in the Timber Demand and Technology Assessment Research Work Unit led by Ken Skog, Forest Products Laboratory, USDA Forest Service, whom we would also like to thank for enabling this continued cooperation. Both Dr. Ince and Professor Akim are members of the ToSFPM&M, and Professor Akim is the Deputy Leader.

Once again we appreciate the collaboration with Florian Kraxner and his co-authors. An expert on certified forest products (CFPs) he was joined by Eric Hansen, Professor, Forest Products Marketing, Corvallis, Oregon, US, who was the first author of the CFP chapter. He is also a member of the ToSFPM&M. They were joined by Toshiaki Owari, Professor, Forest Business and Management, University of Tokyo, who shared his understandings of Asian markets.

Our colleagues in ITTO: Steve Johnson, Statistician and Economist, Jairo Castaño, Market Information Service Coordinator, and new this year, Jean-Christophe Claudon, based their tropical timber analysis on the ITTO *Annual Review and Assessment of the World Timber Situation 2005*. Drs. Castaño and Johnson are also members of the ToSFPM&M.

As in previous years, we benefited by having two capable assistants during the *Review* production, Pauliina Liekoski and Matti Toivio. Both masters students at the University of Helsinki's Department of Forest Economics, they conducted market research and produced all the graphics. In addition they revised our *Graphics Production System*, *Review Production Manual*, *Review Planning System* and websites associated with the *Review*. These assistants are critical to the timely production of the publication and the effort is mutually advantageous. Their internships were facilitated thanks to Heikki Juslin, Professor, and Tomi Riini, Assistant, Forest Products Marketing, Department of Forest Economics, University of Helsinki.

This year's *Review* was produced with direct input by 40 people. Ed Pepke (UNECE/FAO Timber Section) led the project. The individual chapters had the following lead authors: 1. Ed Pepke; 2. Jim Bowyer and Helmuth Resch; 3. Dieter Hesse, Al Schuler; 4. Håkan Ekström; 5. Nikolai Burdin, Arvydas Lebedys, Jarno Seppälä and Russ Taylor; 6. Rod Wiles and Rupert Oliver; 7. Ivan Eastin, Bénédicte Hendrickx and Nikolai Burdin; 8. Peter Ince, Eduard Akim, Bernard Lombard and Thomas Parik; 10. Florian Kraxner, Eric Hansen and Toshiaki Owari; 11. Tapani Pahkasalo and Craig Adair; 12. Steve Johnson, Michael Adams, Jairo Castaño and Jean-Christophe Claudon.

Alex McCusker (UNECE/FAO Timber Section) collected, validated and produced the statistics. Ronald Jansen, United Nations Statistics Division, provided the latest forest products trade statistics from Comtrade and Bruce Michie, Senior Researcher, EFI, validated the trade data and produced the database for trade flow graphs and tables. Thanks to them all for the most up-to-date, global, statistical database possible.

Maria Levina (UNECE/FAO Timber Section) was responsible for the publication layout for the first time. Cynthia de Castro, (UNECE/FAO Timber Section) performed all administrative duties. Sefora Kifle (UNECE/FAO Timber Section) prepared price data and supported authors with documents and journals. Barbara Hall, Consultant, was the principal copy editor. Christina O'Shaughnessy (Editor, Trade Development and Timber Division) also did some copyediting and proofreading. Yves Clopt (UNECE Graphic Design Unit) designed the new cover. Thanks to all of them.

Initial technical reviews were done by Ed Pepke, Douglas Clark and Kit Prins (UNECE/FAO Timber Section). Florian Steierer (UNECE/FAO Timber Section) also reviewed several chapters. We appreciate the second reviews from the Forest Products and Economics Division of the FAO Forestry Department by Osamu Hashiramoto.

This draft manuscript was completed on 25 July 2006. It is a true pleasure to personally thank all members of the Team, and the many other contributors, for their devoted efforts in producing this year's *Forest Products Annual Market Review*.

Ed Pepke
Forest Products Marketing Specialist
UNECE/FAO Timber Section
Trade and Timber Division
United Nations Economic Commission for Europe
Palais des Nations
CH - 1211 Geneva 10, Switzerland
E-mail: info.timber@unece.org

CONTRIBUTORS TO THE PUBLICATION

The secretariat would like to express our sincere appreciation for the information and assistance received from the following people in preparation of the *Forest Products Annual Market Review*. The base data for the *Review* were supplied by country statistical correspondents, who are acknowledged in a separate listing. We regret any omissions.

Martti Aarne, Finnish Forest Research Institute, Finland

Craig Adair, APA – The Wood Engineered Association, United States

Eduard L. Akim, Saint Petersburg State Technological University of Plant Polimers, Russian Federation

Florian Borlea, Forest Research and Management Institute, Romania

Jim Bowyer, University of Minnesota, United States

Michael Buckley, World Hardwoods, United Kingdom

Nikolai Burdin, OAO NIPIEIlesprom, Russia

Jairo Castaño, International Tropical Timber Organization, Japan

Jean Christophe Claudon, International Tropical Timber Organization, Japan

Roger Cooper, University of Wales, United Kingdom

Guillaume Daelmans, Fédération Belge du Commerce d'Importation du Bois, Belgium

Pierre-Marie Desclos, Forest Products Consultant, Italy

Ralf Dümmer, Ernährungwirtschaft, Germany

Ivan Eastin, Center for International Trade in Forest Products, University of Washington, United States

Håkan Ekström, Wood Resources International, United States

Carl-Éric Guertin, Quebec Wood Export Bureau, Canada

Ben Gunneberg, Pan European Forest Certification Council, Luxembourg

Riitta Hänninen, Finnish Forest Research Institute, Finland

Eric Hansen, Oregon State University, United States

Osamu Hashiramoto, Forestry Department, FAO, Italy

Dieter Hesse, UNECE, Switzerland

Bengt Hillring, Swedish University of Agricultural Sciences, Sweden

Peter Ince, USDA Forest Service, United States

Filip de Jaeger, CEI-Bois and European Federation of the Parquet Industry, Belgium

Hans Jansen, UNECE, Switzerland

Ronald Jansen, UN Statistics Division, United States

Bénédicte Hendrickx, European Panel Federation, Belgium

Heikki Juslin, University of Helsinki, Finland

Emiko Kato, Japan Wood-Products Information & Research Center, Japan

Eric Kilby, CEPI, Belgium

Robert Kozak, University of British Columbia, Canada

Florian Kraxner, International Institute for Applied Systems Analysis, Austria

Arvydas Lebedys, FAO, Italy

Nico Leek, Stichting Bos en Hout, Netherlands

Pauliina Liekoski, University of Helsinki, Finland

Fengming Lin, Chinese Academy of Forestry, China

Bernard Lombard, CEPI, Belgium

Elina Maki-Simola, Eurostat, Luxembourg

Bruce Michie, European Forest Institute, Finland

CTS Nair, Forestry Department, FAO, Italy

Sten Nilsson, International Institute for Applied Systems Analysis, Austria

Rupert Oliver, Forest Industries Intelligence Limited, United Kingdom

Lars-Göran Olsson, Swedish Wood Association, Sweden

Olle Olsson, Swedish University of Agricultural Sciences, Sweden

Toshiaki Owari, University of Tokyo, Japan

Heikki Pajuoja, Metsäteho, Finland

Tapani Pahkasalo, Savcor Indufor, Finland

Tomás Parik, Wood and Paper, A.S., Czech Republic

Joanna Pikul, Wood Technology Institute, Poland

Ewald Rametsteiner, Institute of Forest Sector Policy and Economics, Austria

Birger Rausche, Federal Ministry of Consumer Protection, Food and Agriculture, Germany

Helmuth Resch, Universtiy of Natural Resources, Austria

Tomi Rinne, University of Helsinki, Finland

Al Schuler, USDA Forest Service, United States

Jarno Seppälä, Pöyry Forest Industry Consulting, Finland

Yrjö Sevolo, Finnish Forest Research Institute, Finland

Markku Simula, Ardot Oy, Finland

Ken Skog, USDA Forest Service, United States

Xiufang Sun, Forest Trends, China

Patricia Sundberg, Nordic Timber Council AB, Sweden

Oleksandr Svirchevskyy, UNECE, Switzerland

Russell Taylor, R.E. Taylor & Associates, Ltd., Canada

Jukka Tissari, International Trade Center, Switzerland

Matti Toivio, University of Helsinki, Finland

David Venables, American Hardwood Export Council, United Kingdom

Darius Vizlenskas, State Forest Service, Lithuania

Nelson Y. S. Wong, International Forest List, Malaysia

Roderick Wiles, Forest Industries Intelligence Limited, United Kingdom

STATISTICAL CORRESPONDENTS

The national statistical correspondents listed below are the key suppliers of data for this publication. We are grateful for their essential contribution and their significant efforts in collecting and preparing the data. Complete contact information for the correspondents is provided in the publication *Forest Products Statistics*.[1]

Ashot Ananyan, National Statistical Service, Armenia

Djanbulat Baijumanov, National Statistical Committee, Kyrgyzstan

Ramazan Bali, Ministry of Environment and Forestry, Turkey

Anna Margret Björnsdottir, Statistics Iceland

Aija Budreiko, Ministry of Agriculture, Latvia

Nikolai Burdin, OAO NIPIEIlesprom, Russian Federation

Josefa Carvalho, Direcção Geral dos Recursos Florestais, Portugal

Lydia Denisova, Agency on Statistics of the Republic of Kazakhstan

Jiri Dobias, Ministry of Agriculture, Czech Republic

Mira Dojcinovska, State Statistical Office, The former Yugoslav Republic of Macedonia

Alain Dupont, Institut National des Statistiques, Belgium

Simon Gillam, Forestry Commission, United Kingdom

Branko Glavonjic, Belgrade State University, Serbia

Hanne Haanaes, Statistics Norway - Statistisk sentralbyrå, Norway

Johannes Hangler, Federal Ministry of Agriculture, Forestry, Environment and Water Management, Austria

Eugene Hendrick, COFORD (National Council for Forest R&D), Ireland

James L. Howard, USDA Forest Service, United States

Aristides Ioannou, Ministry of Agriculture, Natural Resources and Environment, Cyprus

Constanta Istratescu, National Institute of Wood, Romania

Surendra Joshi, National Board of Forestry, Sweden

Nico A. Leek, Probos (formerly Stichting Bos en Hout (SBH)), Netherlands

Angelo Mariano, Ministry of Agricultural and Forest Policies, Italy

Anthony Mifsud, Agricultural Research and Development Centre, Malta

Zdenko Milinovic, Agency for Statistics, Bosnia and Herzegovina

Michel Morel, Ministère de l'Agriculture, de l'Alimentation, de la Pêche et des Affaires Rurales, France

Darko Motik, University of Zagreb - Faculty of Forestry, Croatia

Mika Mustonen, Forest Research Institute, Finland

Yuri M. Ostapchuk, State Committee on Statistics of Ukraine

Andras Pluzsik, State Forest Service, Hungary

Birger Rausche, Federal Ministry of Food, Agriculture and Consumer Protection, Germany

Annie Savoie, Natural Resources Canada, Canada

Václav Stránský, Ministry of Agriculture, Czech Republic

Wladyslaw Strykowski, Wood Technology Institute, Poland

Rafael S. Suleymanov, State Statistical Committee, Azerbaijan

Roman Svitok, National Forest Centre, Slovakia

Irena Tomsic, Statistical Office, Slovenia

---

[1] *Forest Products Statistics* is available at: www.unece.org/trade/timber/mis/fp-stats.htm

Mati Valgepea, Center of Forest Protection and Silviculture, Estonia
Roberto Vallejo Bombín, Ministry of Environment, Spain
Darius Vizlenskas, State Forest Survey Service, Lithuania
David Walker, Federal Office for the Environment, Switzerland
Frank Wolter, Forest Administration of Luxembourg

DATA SOURCES

The data on which the *Forest Products Annual Market Review* is based are collected from official national correspondents[2] through the FAO/UNECE/Eurostat/ITTO Joint Forest Sector Questionnaire, distributed in April 2006. Within the 56-country UNECE region, data for the 29 EU and EFTA countries are collected and validated by Eurostat, and for other UNECE countries by UNECE/FAO Geneva.

The statistics for this *Review* are from the TIMBER database system. As the database is continually being updated, any one publication's analysis is only a snapshot of the database at that particular time. The database and questionnaires are in a state of permanent development. Data quality differs between countries, products and years. Improvement of data quality is a continuing task of the secretariat, paying special attention to the EECCA and south eastern European countries. With our partner organizations and national correspondents, we strongly believe that the quality of the international statistical base for analysis of the forest products sector is steadily improving. Our goal is to have a single, complete, current database, validated by national correspondents, with the same figures available from FAO in Rome, Eurostat in Luxembourg, ITTO in Yokohama and UNECE/FAO in Geneva. We are convinced that the data set used in the *Review* is the best available anywhere as of July 2006. The data appearing in this publication form only a small part of the total data available. *Forest Products Statistics* will include all of the data available for the years 2001-2005. The TIMBER database is available on the website of the joint Timber Committee and European Forestry Commission at www.unece.org/trade/timber/mis.htm

The secretariat is grateful that correspondents provided actual statistics for 2005 and, in the absence of formal statistics, their best estimates. Therefore all statistics for 2005 are provisional and subject to confirmation next year. The responsibility for national data lies with the national correspondents. The official data supplied by the correspondents account for the great majority of records. In some cases, where no data were supplied, or when data were confidential, the secretariat has estimated figures to keep region and product aggregations comparable and to maintain comparability over time. Estimations are flagged within this publication, but only for products at the lowest level of aggregation.

Despite the best efforts of all concerned, a number of significant problems remain. Chief among these problems are differing definitions, especially when these are not mentioned, and unrecorded removals and production. In certain cases, for example woodfuel removals, the officially reported data can be only 20% of actual figures. Conversions into the standard units used here are also not necessarily done in a consistent manner.

In addition to the official statistics received by questionnaire, trade association and government statistics are used to complete the analysis for 2005 and early 2006. Supplementary information came from experts, including national statistical correspondents, trade journals and internet sites. Most of these sources are cited where they occur in the text, at the end of the chapters, on the list of contributors and in the annex reference list.

EXPLANATORY NOTES

"Apparent consumption" is calculated by adding a country's production to imports and subtracting exports. Apparent consumption volumes are not adjusted for levels of stocks.

"Net trade" is the balance of exports and imports and is positive for net exports, i.e. when exports exceed imports, and is negative for net imports, i.e. when imports exceed exports. Trade data for the twenty-five European Union countries include intra-EU trade, which is often estimated by the countries. Export data usually include re-exports. Subregional trade aggregates in tables include trade occurring between countries of the sub-region.

For a breakdown of the regions please see the map in the annex. References to EU refer to the 25 countries members of the EU in 2005. The term EECCA refers to the 12 countries of the former Soviet Union previously referred to as CIS.

The term "softwood" is used synonymously with "coniferous". "Hardwood" is used synonymously with "non-coniferous" or "broadleaved". More definitions appear in the electronic annex.

All references to "ton" or "tons" in this text represent the metric unit of 1,000 kilograms (kg).

The use of the term "oven-dry" in this text is used in relation to the weight of a product in a completely dry state, e.g. an oven-dry metric ton of wood fibre means 1,000 kg of wood fibre containing no moisture at all.

---

[2] Correspondents are listed with their complete contact details in "Forest Products Statistics, 2001-2005".

SYMBOLS AND ABBREVIATIONS USED

(Infrequently used abbreviations spelled out in the text may not be listed again here.)

…	not available
€	euro
$	United States dollar unless otherwise specified
ATFS	American Tree Farm System
B.C.	British Columbia, Canada
BJC	builders' joinery and carpentry
CFP	certified forest product
CIS	Commonwealth of Independent States
CO_2	carbon dioxide
CoC	Chain-of-custody
CSA	Canadian Standards Association
ECB	European Central Bank
EECCA	Eastern Europe, Caucasus and Central Asia subregion (see annex for 12 CIS countries)
EFSOS	European Forest Sector Outlook Study
EFTA	European Free Trade Association
EQ	equivalent of wood in the rough
EU	European Union
EWPs	engineered wood products
FDI	foreign direct investment
FSC	Forest Stewardship Council
GDP	gross domestic product
GHG	greenhouse gas
GWh	giga watt hour
ha	hectare
IMF	International Monetary Fund
ITTO	International Tropical timber Organization
kWh	kilowatt hour
LCA	life cycle assessment
LSI	life cycle inventory
LVL	laminated veneer lumber
m.t.	metric ton
m^2	square metre
m^3	cubic metre
MDF	medium density fibreboard
NAFTA	North American Free Trade Agreement
NGO	non governmental organization
OSB	oriented strand board
PEFC	Programme for the Endorsement of Forest Certification Schemes
PJ	peta joule
PoC	Province of China
PPP	public procurement policies
SAR	Hong Kong Special Administrative Region of China
SFI	Sustainable Forestry Initiative
SFM	sustainable forest management
STEM	Swedish Energy Agency
VAT	value-added tax
VAWPs	value-added wood products

Chapter 1

Government procurement and corporate social responsibility policies influencing UNECE region forest products markets:
Overview of forest products markets and policies, 2005-2006

Highlights

- Government procurement polices and corporate social responsibility policies are new drivers for ensuring the legality and sustainability of the source of wood and paper products in the UNECE region.

- UNECE region forest products markets climbed slowly to record levels in 2005 as demand from US housing and European construction stimulated production and trade.

- China has become the world's largest log importer, producing primary and secondary processed products for domestic and export markets; Chinese exports compete with UNECE region producers.

- Wood energy received a boost from record high oil prices and the policies that Governments initiated to promote renewable energy sources and to mitigate climate change.

- Storms in Sweden and the United States in 2005 devastated forests but buoyant markets, aided by the need of reconstruction, absorbed the increased production of wood products.

- The United States – Canada Softwood Lumber Agreement was to end in July 2006, restoring $4 billion in duties collected from Canadian sawnwood exporters, and laying out a new seven-year framework for sawnwood trade.

- Illegal logging remains a critical issue in the forest sector, and both industry and Governments are enacting policies to combat illegal practices domestically and to stop imports of illegal wood products; one major step was the signing of the St. Petersburg Declaration at the Ministerial Conference on Forest Law Enforcement and Governance in 2005.

- Central and eastern European countries and Russia continue to accelerate out of the socio-economic transition period with increased exports, including value-added wood products.

- Engineered wood products, which are environmentally friendly and efficiently produced and employed, continued to make inroads into traditional wood products markets and fend off competition for non-wood substitutes.

1.1 Forest products market and policy developments, 2005-2006

This chapter provides an overview of forest products markets and policy developments in the UNECE region, and for the basis of analysis, its three subregions: Europe, North America and Eastern Europe, Caucasus and Central Asia (EECCA).[3] The chapter first presents the findings of this year's analysis, and then summarizes the key developments for each market segment. As the chapter can bring forward only some of the main developments, readers are encouraged to find further market and policy details in the following 11 chapters of the *Forest Products Annual Market Review, 2005-2006* (*Review*) and in its electronic annexes of statistical tables available on the UNECE Timber Committee and FAO European Forestry Commission website.[4] The issue of China's forest products market developments is woven throughout the chapters in this *Review*. The theme of the annual Timber Committee Market Discussions is "China's forest products trade influences on UNECE region markets" on 3 and 4 October 2006.

The second chapter, "Forest product market and policy interactions, 2005-2006", analyses the following policies, not all of which are summarized in this chapter:

- Emerging markets for wood products and implication for the global forestry sector.

- Forest law enforcement, governance and trade and initiatives to retain forestland.

- Policies promoting the sound use of wood.

- Climate change.

- Wood energy promotion policies.

- Initiatives aimed at increasing global competitiveness in wood and wood products markets and overall performance of the sector.

- Trade policy and tariff and non-tariff barriers.

1.1.1 UNECE region development

1.1.1.1 Consumption of forest products

For the UNECE region in 2005, consumption of forest products advanced by 1% to a new record level (table 1.1.1). However, some market sectors and some subregions were stronger by far. Wood-based panels consumption rose the most, by 4.5 million m³, an increase of 3.3% from 2004 (graph 1.1.1). Sawnwood, like structural panels, was driven by record high housing starts in North America and buoyant housing markets in

Europe, resulting in a consumption increase of 3.6 million m³, an increase of 1.3%. In contrast, region-wide paper and paperboard consumption was stable, but this disguises a serious downturn in North America by 2.4%. Paper and paperboard consumption advanced in both other subregions, Europe and the EECCA.

GRAPH 1.1.1

Consumption by wood products sector in the UNECE region, 2001-2005

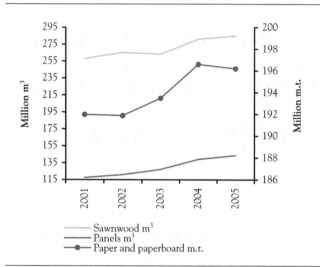

Source: UNECE/FAO TIMBER database, 2006.

The EECCA region continues to rebound from the 1990s transition period, and in many product sectors has expanded production and imports beyond pre-1989 levels. While consumption remains low compared to the other two subregions, it is rising faster. EECCA's consumption rise appears to have been diminished due to continuing decreases in sawnwood consumption. However, from the sawn softwood chapter analysis, part of the explanation of the decrease could be underreporting of small- and medium-sized sawmills for local consumption.

1.1.1.2 Demand drivers

The demand drivers behind the wood and paper products consumption increases in 2005 were:

- Favourable macroeconomic conditions, which are expected to continue in 2006.

- US housing starts, which reached a 30-year high in 2005 at 2.1 million units; however, rising mortgage rates should dampen housing construction in 2006.

- The upward trend in European new residential construction, both western and eastern, over the last three years, which may moderate as a result of rising interest rates.

- China's rapid economic expansion, which has become a major engine of global growth, and which

---

[3] The name "Eastern Europe, Caucasus and Central Asia" is a new UNECE term introduced this year in place of the Commonwealth of Independent States (CIS). It is comprised of the same 12 countries (see annex for list of countries).

[4] www.unece.org/trade/timber/mis/fpama.htm.

TABLE 1.1.1

Apparent consumption of sawnwood[1], wood-based panels,[2] and paper and paperboard in UNECE region, 2001-2005

	Thousand	2001	2002	2003	2004	2005	Change 2004 to 2005	
							Volume	%
Europe								
Sawnwood	m³	107 386	107 807	110 692	114 233	117 806	3 573	3.1
Wood-based panels	m³	54 676	54 255	56 526	63 637	65 843	2 206	3.5
Paper and paperboard	m.t.	89 311	88 842	90 323	90 898	92 263	1 364	1.5
Total	m³ EQ[3]	562 065	560 473	573 742	592 738	606 608	13 871	2.3
of which: EU25								
Sawnwood	m³	94 992	93 905	96 471	99 249	101 812	2 564	2.6
Wood-based panels	m³	49 772	48 660	49 981	55 873	56 516	643	1.2
Paper and paperboard	m.t.	82 754	81 730	83 092	83 622	84 424	802	1.0
Total	m³ EQ[3]	512 157	505 168	516 004	531 673	539 521	7 849	1.5
EECCA								
Sawnwood	m³	15 364	13 226	12 396	11 990	10 363	-1 627	-13.6
Wood-based panels	m³	5 998	6 702	8 165	9 104	10 713	1 609	17.7
Paper and paperboard	m.t.	5 144	5 698	6 421	6 964	7 506	542	7.8
Total	m³ EQ[3]	51 617	51 201	54 664	57 358	59 165	1 807	3.2
North America								
Sawnwood	m³	135 484	144 148	140 129	155 120	156 804	1 684	1.1
Wood-based panels	m³	56 893	60 106	62 580	66 522	67 240	718	1.1
Paper and paperboard	m.t.	97 542	97 401	96 726	98 751	96 390	-2 361	-2.4
Total	m³ EQ[3]	638 470	656 995	652 237	689 393	685 234	-4 159	-0.6
UNECE region								
Sawnwood	m³	258 233	265 181	263 217	281 343	284 973	3 630	1.3
Wood-based panels	m³	117 567	121 064	127 271	139 263	143 796	4 533	3.3
Paper and paperboard	m.t.	191 997	191 940	193 470	196 613	196 158	-455	-0.2
Total	m³ EQ[3]	1 252 152	1 268 668	1 280 643	1 339 488	1 351 007	11 519	0.9

Notes: 1/ Excluding sleepers, 2/ Excluding veneer sheets, 3/ Equivalent of wood in the rough. 1 m³ of sawnwood and wood-based panels = 1.6 m³ EQ[3], 1 m.t. paper = 3.39 m³ EQ[3]

Source: UNECE/FAO TIMBER database, 2006.

is forecast to continue in 2006 with GDP growth of nearly 10%, generating strong import demand for oil and raw materials, including wood.

- Public procurement policies by Governments and other public bodies, both national and sub-national, which have resulted in more interest in certified forest products (CFPs) and consumers following Governments' lead in some countries.

- Corporate social responsibility policies, which have also generated demand for CFPs.

1.1.1.3 The China factor

The China factor has entered all equations. China is now the hottest forest products market in the world, and therefore mentioned frequently throughout this *Review*. Other sectors are experiencing similar developments in China, for example, metals and energy. A combination of reduced domestic harvests for flood control and increased production for domestic and export markets has resulted in China becoming the world's greatest importer of wood raw materials, specifically sawlogs and veneer logs (graph 1.1.2). China has long been the world leader in tropical log imports, but imports of temperate logs, especially from across the border in Russia, have escalated in the last few years. Imports of high-value temperate hardwood sawlogs and veneer logs from the UNECE region have also increased rapidly, with the result of rising hardwood log prices in the United States and Europe.

GRAPH 1.1.2

Chinese wood products imports and exports, 1997-2005

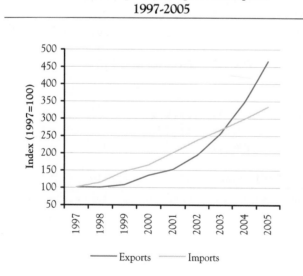

Source: White et al, from Chinese Customs Statistics, 2006.

China has systematically reduced imports of primary-processed wood products such as sawnwood, panels and veneer, and established domestic production based on imported logs and chips. Despite raw material imports, China is competitive due to relatively low labour and manufacturing costs. Domestic consumption of value-added wood products, for example, furniture and flooring, is increasing together with a rise in the standard of living, but much of the production is exported to the United States and the EU. China's relatively weak currency is another advantage for exporters.

Concerning China's rapid rise, two sides should be considered. Using furniture as an example, China's wood products exports to the United States have escalated by 1,000% in value since 1997. US furniture manufacturing has declined, together with employment and related demand for sawn hardwood, veneer and cut-to-size dimension stock. However, anticipating even greater Chinese imports, some US furniture manufacturers have established lower cost production in China while maintaining their more valuable asset – their domestic marketing channels; others shut down completely. Some sawn hardwood and hardwood dimension manufacturers have successfully exported to China, but others went out of business. Furniture buyers, importers, middlemen, retailers and consumers are purchasing more and more competitively priced Chinese furniture.

This scenario is repeating itself with other products and with other countries, for example, from imported veneer logs, China is exporting plywood to the United States and the EU. Other primary products, or semi-manufactured products such as mouldings, are also starting to flow out of China. The pattern of exports based on imported raw material is repeating itself in other low-cost Asian countries, such as Viet Nam. Further, it is forecast to occur in another high-population, low-cost country, India.

One sector not currently impacted by Chinese exports is pulp, paper and paperboard. China's domestic consumption is rising in this sector, along with domestic manufacturing. Paper products are made from imported chips and pulp, and huge volumes of recovered paper and paperboard are shipped from North America and Europe. While not impacted by China's exports, their imports of virgin and recovered fibre are resulting in rising prices. This is advantageous to spur recycling of used paper and paperboard in UNECE member countries, while impacting profitability of other users of this same fibre furnish in the UNECE region.

1.1.1.4 Public procurement and corporate social responsibility policies

Another thread followed throughout this *Review* is the market effects of public procurement policies. This issue is linked to the 5 October 2006 policy forum on "Public Procurement Policies for Wood and Paper Products and their Impacts on Sustainable Forest Management and Market Developments". In particular, in western Europe and the United States, and outside of the UNECE region in Japan, Governments are implementing procurement policies to ensure their wood and paper product purchases are from legal and sustainable sources.

Companies and trade associations are establishing environmentally friendly policies, for example, for their purchases of wood and paper products. This is not simply a marketing campaign, but rather a long-term commitment to buy and sell products that are legally and sustainably produced. They realize that using sustainably produced, recyclable wood and paper products reduces the ecological footprint of their operations; in other words, they not only do less damage to the environment, but they actually promote healthy forests. Companies and countries should use more forest products in an efficient, sustainable manner.

FIGURE 1.1.1

Nordic forest

Source: Nordic Timber Council, 2006.

The vast majority of forest-based industries have always realized the long-term need for sustainable forestry, and balanced growth and harvests, especially in their local forests. However, global trade means purchases from areas where harvesting might not be legal and sustainable. Environmental non-governmental organizations continue to highlight illegal logging and unsustainable forest management. Whether reactive or proactive, corporations and associations are implementing policies.

In June 2006, the International Council of Forest and Paper Associations signed an agreement on sustainability, committing to sustainable development and to working with other stakeholders to ensure that environmental, social and economic benefits of natural resources are available to current and future generations. The industry vowed to continuously promote sustainable forest management worldwide by:

- combating illegal logging;
- supporting recovery of paper and wood products;
- ensuring that its activities respect the environment;

- improving the resources on which the industry depends;
- creating solutions to global climate change and energy supply;
- investing in workers and communities.

One spin-off from public procurement policies and corporate social responsibility policies will be to gradually inform consumers about the benefits of green purchasing and, it is hoped, to boost confidence in buying wood and paper products. Consumers throughout the chain will eventually be more aware of the sources of their purchases of wood and paper products.

1.1.1.5 Wood energy interactions

Oil prices hit a record $75 per barrel as the *Review* went to press. Combined with the need to reduce greenhouse gas emissions, Governments are promoting alternative energy sources, including biofuels, as renewable forms of energy for sustainable development and energy security. Biomass energy policies set targets at the regional, national and EU levels. Considerable investment is being made throughout UNECE countries in alternative energy R&D and implementation for all scales of installations.

Wood-based fuels are readily available in the UNECE region in both processed and unprocessed forms, making them the most promising biofuel for the present and the future. For the first time the *Review* has a chapter dedicated to wood energy markets and policies.

Although woodfuels account for only 7% of the world's total energy supply, they are extremely important in some countries. Developing countries consume over three quarters of the world's woodfuels, which in turn accounts for 15% of their total primary energy consumption. The remaining quarter is used in developed countries where it accounts for only 2% of total energy consumption (FAO, 2006a). However, these figures underestimate the more efficient consumption of wood-based fuels within the wood industry, including recovered wood. In the UNECE region, considerable unaccounted volumes of wood are burned for heat and electricity.

The importance of wood energy also varies considerably in developed countries. In Europe, for instance, the growing amount of woodfuels used in Belgium, France and Germany is small compared to Finland, Sweden and Austria where woodfuels provide up to 17 % of the national energy demand. The economics of wood burning are often improved by the use of carbon credits under the Kyoto Protocol. In some countries, major traditional wood industries are developing profit centres based on wood energy, using their strengths in such areas as logistics and industrial scale wood handling. New energy markets for small-diameter timber and forest residues, including stumps in some areas, have been economically advantageous for forest owners where markets exist.

Government instruments to promote woodfuel development, production and consumption include various forms of assistance for research and development, tax incentives, subsidized loans, capital subsidies, energy taxes, market liberalization, information campaigns, training and standards (FAO, 2006a).

However, there is another side to the promotion of wood energy: the effects on availability of wood for traditional wood processing industries, especially panel and pulp manufacturers. They see the competition for their raw material as an economic threat and have established policies to promote the highest value of wood and wood residues. With rising transportation fuel costs, the hauling radius is getting smaller, and with large scale fixed investments in either a panel or pulpmill, the local competition for raw material can have negative consequences on profitability.

1.1.1.6 Climate change

The most important development in mitigation of climate change in 2005 was when the Kyoto Protocol went into effect after Russia's ratification. In line with the treaty obligations, Governments in Europe and Russia are enacting policies for sequestering carbon and mitigating climate change. Most European countries have a climate change strategy taking into account the structure of their greenhouse gas emissions and their potential to reduce emissions and increase carbon sequestration. Despite the continued reluctance of the current US Government to address the climate change issue, there are indications that a number of States are prepared to act independently of the Federal Government to adopt specific binding targets for reducing greenhouse gas emissions.

The Kyoto Protocol has fundamentally changed the framework conditions, such as the need for rigorous and formal accounting of carbon flows, the assignment of a monetary value to carbon emissions through emissions trading, and the possibility to offset carbon emissions in one country by reductions in another. Consequences of these changes are being felt in the marketplace, for instance, in increased stimulus for wood energy. Forest sector and climate change policies overlap on carbon sequestration in forest biomass, use of renewable wood energies and carbon storage in forest products.

In May 2006, the European Forestry Commission discussed the consequences of the entry into force of the Kyoto Protocol for Europe's forests. The Commission stated that developments regarding the Kyoto Protocol offered the sector major challenges and opportunities that must be addressed in a proactive and cross-sectoral manner (FAO Forestry, 2006b). The Commission concluded, *inter alia*, that a major forestry contribution to climate change mitigation in Europe would be made through sustainable forest management, including the production and use of wood, and that profound long-term changes were to be expected from the fact that an ecological service, carbon sequestration, has been assigned a monetary value.

1.1.1.7 Competitiveness of the forest sector

In both Europe and North America the forest-based industries are working together with research and Governments to improve the competitiveness of the entire sector. The *European Technology Platforms* are a proactive approach to the competition of market globalization. The *Technology Platform of the European Forest-Based Sector* (FTP) is organized with the cooperation of the European Confederation of Woodworking Industries, the Confederation of European Forest Owners, and the Confederation of European Paper Industries, together with additional support from different stakeholders.

FIGURE 1.1.2

Wooden home promotion

Source: Nordic Timber Council, 2006.

The premise of the FTP is that the European primary wood processing industry must work with considerably increased material efficiency and lower energy consumption. To this end, research is necessary in order to develop advanced, safe technologies and production processes across integrated production chains that will allow the flexible primary and secondary processing of a wider range of wood products. The result would be innovative wood-based products targeted not only for traditional applications in wood and paper markets of construction, insulation, furniture, packaging and specialty papers, but also for many uses outside the wood sector, including vehicles, textiles, medical, electronics and food.

In January 2005, a leading group of forest sector experts, as well as authorities of the European Commission, approved the sector's *Vision for 2030*: "It comprises a competitive, knowledge-based industry that fosters the extended use of renewable forest resources. It strives to ensure its societal contribution in the context of a bio-based, customer-driven and globally competitive European economy" (European Commission, 2004).

From the above initiatives in Europe, the *Strategic Research Agenda* was launched in mid-2006. Its approach envisages entirely new forest-based value chains, some founded on a zero-waste, "bio-refinery" concept. The Agenda's impetus stems from demands for the increased production of bio-fuels combined with comprehensive use of renewable raw materials, meriting an integrated production of pulp, energy and chemicals from wood. The processing could occur first in combined manufacturing of chemical pulp, bio-fuels and various base chemicals. The second stage would then be with other forest and manufacturing residues not integrated with pulp production.

There are similar national, state, and provincial initiatives in North America, including the *Agenda 2020 Technical Alliance* programme, a joint research initiative of the US Department of Energy and the American Forest & Paper Association, with similar goals as the European Forest-Based Technology Platform. The Agenda 2020 technology portfolio is organized around seven core technology platforms including advancement of the forest bio-refinery, nanotechnology for the forest products industry, breakthrough manufacturing technologies, next-generation fibre recovery and utilization, and enhancement of environmental performance.

1.1.1.8 UNECE region in a global context

The UNECE region is the main consumer and producer of forest products in the world, and as such has a lead responsibility in assuring their sustainable production from forests in and outside the region. In terms of consumption, the UNECE region's share of world consumption ranges from 80% for industrial roundwood to 55% for paper and paperboard (graph 1.1.3).

GRAPH 1.1.3

UNECE region's share of world consumption of primary forest products, 2005

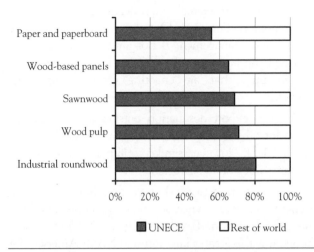

Note: UNECE region in 2005, world in 2004 (most current statistics).
Sources: UNECE/FAO TIMBER database, FAO statistics, 2006.

With the themes of purchasing policies and of competitiveness running through this *Review*, the region's share of imports and exports becomes important. Most forest products are traded within the 3 subregions, and secondly between subregions (graph 1.1.4).

GRAPH 1.1.4

Imports of primary and secondary forest products by subregion, 2004

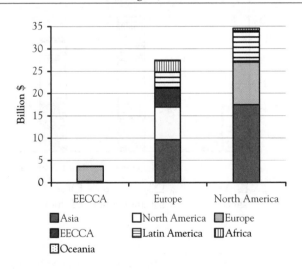

Note: Intra regional trade excluded, e.g. between European countries.
Source: UN COMTRADE/EFI, 2006.

The volume of imports from outside the UNECE region is smaller: significant suppliers to Europe and North America are Latin America and Asia (as well as Africa, but only to Europe). The EECCA has relatively small imports, for example high quality grades of paper. The imports by Europe and North America from regions where forest management is not always sustainable has increased the attention of importers, both Government and industry, that are enacting green procurement policies.

A main export destination outside of the UNECE region for all three subregions is Asia, especially China (graph 1.1.5). However, similar to imports, most exports are from subregion to subregion.

The relation between Europe and North America changes completely when secondary processed products enter the equation. Based on primary products alone, Europe was the greater importer and North America the greater exporter in 2004. But when higher value products are included, however, Europe becomes a greater exporter than North America. This occurs because tremendous volumes of value-added wood products were imported by the United States, especially from Asia, Europe and Latin America, exactly the reverse the scenario from only primary products.

GRAPH 1.1.5

Exports of primary and secondary forest products by subregion, 2004

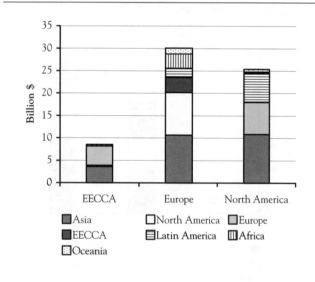

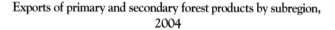

Note: Intra regional trade excluded, e.g. between European countries.

Source: UN COMTRADE/EFI, 2006.

The relative position of different regions of the world has changed significantly over the past 10 to 15 years. In particular, two subregions, Europe and North America have exchanged their net trade positions for forest products (including secondary processed wood and paper products, which are increasingly important).

The UNECE subregions' trade balance can be compared to other continents. Europe and the EECCA together have been leading the world in exports over the last decade, while the massive decrease in US exports has steadily brought down the North and Central America subregion, making it a net importer over the last five years. The FAO European Forestry Commission explored the trends at the May 2006 session, based on a secretariat note on *Progress Towards Sustainable Management in Europe* (FAO, 2006e).

North and Central America (a FAO subregion), which used to be the world's largest net exporter, has become one of the two major net importers (with Asia): the chief reason has been the booming US domestic market which has attracted offshore suppliers (Canada remains the major source of US imports, but has reduced exports abroad). In the last ten years, the subregion has moved from being a net exporter of about $15 billion per year to a net importer of about the same value.

Europe, including Russia, which was a minor net importer in the early 1990s, has become the largest net exporting subregion with exports of primary processed products to all parts of the world, such as sawnwood, as well as value-added products (graph 1.1.6). The competitive advantage of European producers seems to reside in strong marketing, product development and sophisticated process technology.

GRAPH 1.1.6

Global net trade by region, 1990-2004

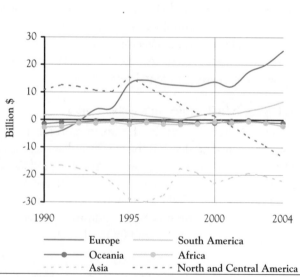

Notes: Forest products include primary, secondary and non-wood. For this graph only, Europe includes Russia and Asia includes the other 11 EECCA countries.

Source: FAO Forestry, 2006c.

The EECCA subregion is currently exporting one third of its harvest as roundwood, yet sawnwood exports continue to increase. On the other hand, some panels (particle board) and value-added products are mainly consumed domestically and not exported. However, approximately 60% of plywood production is exported primarily to Europe and Asia.

The raw material source of the UNECE region's exports is changing dramatically. Fifteen years ago it was the heavily forested subregions that were the largest exporters in the world, e.g. North America and the former USSR. But now North American exports have changed, despite an increase in standing timber volumes and forested area. The United States had drastically reduced primary and secondary processed wood products exports, originally for lack of resource availability when harvests from the national forests slowed for environmental reasons, and in recent years because raw material, labour and manufacturing costs became too high compared to competitors. China is the best example where export success no longer depends on domestic forest resources – their growing exports are based on imported raw materials.

FIGURE 1.1.3

Modern wooden townhouses

Source: Nordic Timber Council, 2006.

2006 marks 15 years of the transition process from a centrally planned to a market economy. The FAO European Forestry Commission discussed the changes in forest products markets in central and eastern European and the EECCA at the May 2006 session. Transition had, and is still having, tremendous impacts throughout the forest sectors in those countries and for their competitors in the wood and paper marketplace. It is appropriate to note here the main developments over the period in forest products markets and trade:

- Consumption of forest products has risen steeply in the eight former transition countries that are now members of the EU, driven by increased prosperity and strong demand for housing and furnishings.

- Trade patterns have changed significantly, with increased exports of (roundwood and sawnwood) by a few countries (Baltic countries, more recently Romania and Ukraine), increased imports of pulp and paper, especially in Poland and Ukraine, and increased exports of further processed products, notably furniture, from a few countries, notably Poland.

- Obsolete wood processing capacity has been closed, but others started with investments in large, modern, often export oriented mills.

- Employment in all parts of the sector has decreased, exacerbating general problems of rural unemployment or underemployment.

- A number of central and eastern European countries have made great strides in value-added processing, thereby achieving the advantages of distinguishing products from primary commodities such as sawnwood and panels (graph 1.1.7)

GRAPH 1.1.7

Net trade of secondary wood products in selected central and eastern European transition countries, 2000-2004

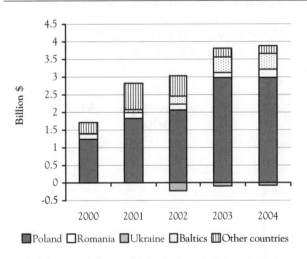

Note: Secondary processing produces value-added products including furniture, cabinetry, millwork and joinery.
Source: FAO Forestry, 2006d.

Russia and the other countries in the EECCA went though a tough transition slump, but production and exports are rebounding (graph 1.1.8). Investment capital, both foreign and domestic, is more available, along with manufacturing technology and equipment. Costs remain relatively low for labour and manufacturing, including energy.

While the region's trade balance is generally positive, net trade of panels continued to decline in 2005 (graph 1.1.9). Increasing volumes of panels are imported by the United States and the EU from outside the region, especially from South America, Oceania and most recently from China.

GRAPH 1.1.8

Exports of primary wood products in the UNECE region, 2001-2005

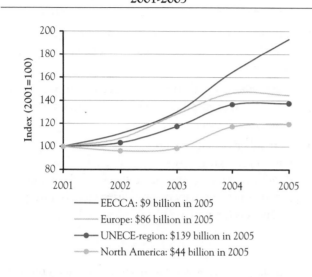

Note: Primary wood products include roundwood, sanwnwood, panels, woodpulp and paper and paperboard.

Source: UNECE/FAO TIMBER database, 2006.

GRAPH 1.1.9

UNECE region's trade balance of primary forest products, 2001-2005

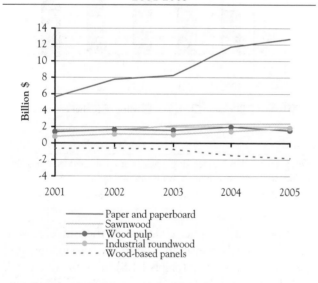

Source: UNECE/FAO TIMBER database, 2006.

1.1.2 Europe subregion developments

2005 started with a major storm in the Baltic Sea region, which resulted in great damage to Sweden's forests. Most of the over 60 million m³ of damaged timber was harvested and processed by mid-2006. Fortunately, sawnwood markets were strong in 2005, and with competitive pricing and favourable exchange rates, Swedish forest owners and sawmillers found buyers.

Sweden's surplus sawnwood also found markets due to a major production downturn in the other major Nordic producer, Finland. A labour dispute shut down Finnish pulp and paper mills during the summer of 2005, which had far reaching consequences, both geographically as well as throughout the wood industries. It well illustrates the interdependency of the forest and forest industries sector. Pulp mills not only run on pulpwood and recycled fibre, but also on clean pulp chips produced as a by-product of sawmilling. As 30% of a sawmill's revenue can come from by-products, they are essential to profitability, especially as mills produce considerable volumes of residues. Without a market for the chips, sawmills closed, not only in Finland, but also those across the Baltic Sea region that had pulp chip contracts with Finnish pulpmills.

These two unrelated events actually had a concurrent interaction on European markets and on European export destinations such as the United States and Japan. They well illustrate both the fragility of the markets and their resilience to both natural and manmade calamities. As mentioned in the *Review* in 2000, following the two hurricanes in Europe yielding a year's harvest in only three days, the interval of the storms is getting shorter and causing increasingly greater damage. For this and other reasons, Governments are enacting climate change policies.

1.1.3 EECCA subregion developments

The forest products market situation of the EECCA subregion continued to improve in 2005. Exports of primary products, especially roundwood, continued increasing steeply, reaching over 48 million m³ for Russia, a record level, which was two times greater than any other country in the UNECE region. This means a loss of potential value-added through primary and further processing, an idea that has not, however, escaped the various levels of the Russian Government as well as industry associations. Rises in roundwood export taxes in 2005 were an incentive for increased domestic processing, but possibly a stimulus to illegal exports.

Given the relative economic and political stability achieved in Russia and the currency revaluation of 1998, foreign investors have been attracted by various government incentives. Foreign direct investment is increasing, which is one reason for the record high Russian production of sawn softwood and panels.

Some important recent policy developments of 2005-2006 in Russia that had impacts on the forest sector include:

- ratification of the Kyoto Protocol by Russia which allowed it to come into force;

- continued debate on a new forest code and possible private ownership of forests and privatization of forest-based industries;

- recognition that illegal logging accounts for approximately 10% of legal harvests.

1.1.4 North America subregion developments

US housing starts have increased approximately 5% each year since 2000, to reach 2.1 million units in 2005; this single development had ramifications throughout the UNECE region. These wood-framed houses, which have been getting larger, required record levels of sawn softwood (109.5 million m³) and structural panels (44.4 million m³). North American production could not satisfy demand and European exports to the United States registered new highs. Imports from outside the UNECE region of structural sawnwood and panels were also at maximum levels.

There were important associated demands for interior building components, doors, windows and flooring, as well as furniture and cabinetry. Overseas producers capitalized on the US demand and their competitive costs to export higher value-added wood products. This resulted in reducing US production of cabinets and furniture, with an associated decreased demand for fine hardwoods and non-structural panels. US duties on both structural wood product imports and furniture imports have not stemmed the flow.

FIGURE 1.1.4

Furniture frame from engineered wood products

Source: APA - The Engineered Wood Products Association, 2006.

The US housing cycle peaked late in 2005 and new housing construction is forecast to decline in 2006 to under 1.8 million units through 2007. Sawnwood and

structural panel consumption will be negatively impacted in 2006 and 2007, as well as joinery and interior wood products. Not only is this is a significant concern for Canadian and US producers, but also for exporters in Europe and from around the world. As a result, the boom years for sawnwood demand and prices since mid-2003 in North America appear to be over, and prices have already quickly eroded starting in the second quarter, 2006.

As this *Review* goes to press, negotiations have produced a possible end to the long-running United States – Canada sawn softwood trade dispute. In mid-2005 countervailing and anti-dumping duties on Canadian sawn softwood totalled 21%, down from 27.2% in 2002. After four years of litigation through the North America Free Trade Agreement and the World Trade Organization, the new agreement would result in seven years of stability, a strictly controlled market share and a return of the over $4 billion in duties paid during the course of the disagreement, 80% of which would go back to Canada.

In autumn 2005, southeastern United States was hit by Hurricane Katrina, causing damage to 50 million m³ of timber, equivalent to 80% of an annual harvest in the area. Prices of sawnwood and panels for reconstruction shot up with demand as millions of homes and buildings were rebuilt.

As of 2006 in British Columbia, Canada, the mountain pine beetle infestation has affected 8 million hectares of mature lodgepole pine. With 400 million m³ of standing timber in need of salvage, the Provincial Government has nearly doubled the allowable cut and provided incentives for establishing forest-based industries. In Ontario and Quebec, Provincial Governments have reduced the annual allowable cut by 20% for sustainability concerns. To compensate the crisis for the industry, the Provincial Governments are offering a variety of assistance programmes, from reduced stumpage fees to financing for mill upgrades.

1.2 Market sector developments

1.2.1 Wood raw materials

Record production of primary wood products drove demand for removals of roundwood in the UNECE region to new heights for the fifth consecutive year. Strong production of sawnwood and demand from the panel, pulp and energy producers meant that production of chips and other by-products also rose. The greatest increases came from the EECCA subregion, where Russia and other countries have found ready markets for roundwood, especially in Europe and China. Both Europeans and Chinese have invested in facilities to advance both roundwood and sawnwood exports to their countries. Russia exported over a third of its harvests in

2005. With higher demand in North America and Europe, combined with higher transportation costs, wood fibre prices rose for both roundwood and chips. Roundwood prices also rose in Brazil due to transport costs.

The hurricanes in Sweden and the United States caused considerable damage to forests, as mentioned above. Partly due to the additional 60 million m³ damaged by the storm in Sweden, and partly due to the downturn in US production, softwood removals in Europe now exceed those of the United States for the first time since 2000 (the year of clean-up following major windstorms across western Europe).

Illegal logging exists to various extents, usually less than 1% of harvests, in most countries in the UNECE region.[5] However, the Russian Government estimates that 10% of fellings are illegal. Another study estimated a higher percentage, up to 20% (Wood Resources International LLC and Seneca Creek Associates, 2004). On the basis of these two estimates, the volume of illegal logging in Russia ranges from 15 to 30 million m³. Many countries in the EECCA subregion, and some in the Europe subregion, experience considerable illegal logging in the form of firewood cutting, often with a root cause of poverty.

1.2.2 Wood energy

Driven by record high fossil fuel prices and government policies to increase production and use of renewable fuels, the trade of woodfuels is developing across the UNECE region. Relatively low transportation costs by sea make long-distance shipping economically feasible, for example, from Russia to Sweden, or in some cases, from South America to Europe. Conversely, high road transportation costs limit the radius of profitability. Nevertheless, wood energy plants need not be massive, and small- to medium-sized installations near a forest resource can and do serve local demand for heat and power.

While the centre of woodfuel consumption is currently in the Nordic countries, Austria and in North America, Government policies with the objective to raise woodfuels production and consumption are having the desired effect in other countries, such as France and Germany. Firewood consumption by individuals is widespread across the UNECE region, although it is rarely burned in efficient furnaces, leading to loss of potential heat as well as potential health problems. Proven economical technology is available for small- to

medium-sized, wood-fired district heating systems where wood is combusted efficiently.

Sweden is an example of how policy measures, such as carbon dioxide taxes and funding for conversion to woodfuels, have created a strong market that draws wood and other biomass fuels from across Europe and even from North America and the EECCA. Pelletizing wood residues raises their caloric value, allows them to be easily conveyed, and increases their economical transport distance. Sweden is by far the largest consumer of pellets in Europe, and thus achieves some economies of scale for pellet costs. The production of pellets is increasing, along with their market share.

Traditional wood industries, especially panel and pulp manufacturers, are highly concerned about competition for their raw material resource, as noted above.

1.2.3 Sawn softwood

Sawn softwood consumption was at record levels in North America and Europe. With the storm in Sweden, the high demand was fortunate timing as Sweden's production increased by 1.1 million m³ to reach a new high of 17.8 million m³. Two-thirds of production was exported, or nearly 12 million m³.

Another Nordic country, Finland, experienced greatly different market events. A nearly two-month labour dispute in 2005 at pulp and paper mills disrupted sawmills. Dependent on pulpmills for sawmill chip by-products, sawmills also shut down in Finland, as well as in other supplying countries. Finland's sawnwood production predictably fell in 2005, but the extent of the decline, by 1.3 million m³, was unexpected. Surprisingly, Finland, the third largest producer in Europe behind Germany and Sweden, imported 450,000 m³ of sawnwood. Benefiting from new sawmill investments, Germany increased production by 2.6 million m³ per year, reaching a record 21.0 million m³.

European exports to the United States were also at a new record level, not only from Nordic countries, but also from central and eastern Europe. Canada remains by far the largest supplier to the US market, despite constraints by the United States – Canada Softwood Lumber Agreement. At the time this *Review* went to press, there were signs of a new agreement that would establish a seven-year framework for cross-border sawn softwood trade. The long-running trade disagreement generated $4 billion in duties, 80% of which would be returned to Canada under the new agreement.

1.2.4 Sawn hardwood

In contrast to softwood, sawn hardwood consumption decreased in the UNECE region in 2005, primarily because of the decline in furniture and cabinetry manufacturing. Imports of lower cost value-added

---

[5] Findings of the Joint UNECE/FAO Workshop on Illegal Logging and Trade of Illegally Derived Forest Products in the UNECE Region, 2004. Documentation available at: www.unece.org/trade/timber/docs/sem/2004-1/sem-2004-1.htm.

hardwood products are increasing and disrupting the traditional hardwood trade. Production, consumption and prices fell. Some sawn hardwood processors have been progressive and set up manufacturing plants in low-cost countries such as China. Western European manufacturers used to look to eastern Europe for lower manufacturing costs, but now are looking further east to Asia. A structural change is taking place in the hardwood sector.

One growing market for hardwoods is for parquet and laminate floorings. Promotion of the beauty of wooden floors has been successful, supported by the health benefits of wood flooring in comparison to other floor coverings.

1.2.5 Panels

Favourable demand for panels came both from new construction and renovation for structural panels, and from the associated demand for mouldings, millwork and furniture for those houses and buildings. European, North American and EECCA production were all at record high levels in 2005, as were exports. The United States continues to import increasing volumes of panels from offshore, although there have been tariffs to control some countries' imports, for example, Brazil.

Despite the healthy market situation, the European Panel Federation and its members remain vigilant over rising wood raw material costs, as well as soaring costs for transportation and petroleum-based resins. Their raw material comes from both virgin and recycled fibres, and together the costs have increased regularly over the last five years (graph 1.2.1).

1.2.6 Paper, paperboard and woodpulp

North America's pulp and paper industry took a downturn in 2005 as demand dropped and Canadian producers suffered from a stronger Canadian dollar. This decrease in consumption by 2.4% opposed the general trend foreseen by the recent *European Forest Sector Outlook Study*, which forecast continued long-term growth (UNECE/FAO, 2005). Production fell while in Europe and Russia, production continues to rise. As in other sectors, public purchasing policies for paper and paperboard have favoured products with some percentage of recycled fibre content, and some large paper consumers, such as Time Inc., have demanded that all paper comes from forests certified for sustainable forest management.

European pulp and paper manufacturers are also concerned about the long-term availability of affordable wood fibre. The new EU Renewable Energy Policy in 2005 is a source of concern for the Confederation of the European Paper Industries (CEPI). They believe the policy and countries' subsidies to the wood energy sector create unfair competition for the paper industry's main raw material. CEPI is responding through a Renewable Energy Sources Working Group, which provided their input to the EU Biomass Action Plan in 2005.

1.2.7 Certified forest products

The area of certified forest area leaped by 12% over the last year, reaching 270 million hectares by mid-2006. This equals 7% of the global forest area, but remains confined to temperate and boreal forests, amounting to 85% in the UNECE region (58% in North America and 29% in western Europe).

GRAPH 1.2.1

European panel manufacturers wood costs, 2002-2006

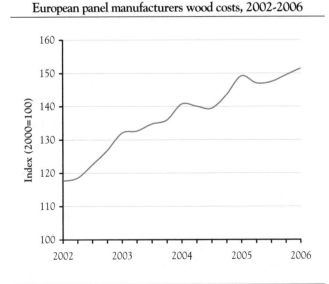

GRAPH 1.2.2

Certified forest area worldwide, 1998-2006

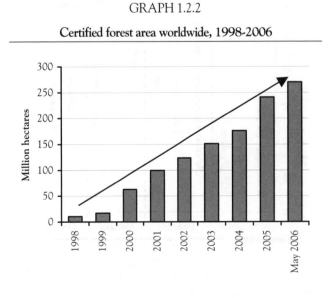

Source: European Panel Federation, 2006.

Sources: Individual certification systems, country correspondents and Canadian Sustainable Forestry Certification Coalition, 2006.

A small but growing portion is in tropical forests, for which certification was initially started to curb deforestation and promote sustainable forest management.

Government and industry policies for procurement of legal and sustainably produced wood and paper products are driving certification. The EU Action Plan for Forest Law Enforcement, Governance and Trade may also promote certification.

Some rivalry between certification systems means that the two major systems do not envisage mutual recognition despite the preference for this option from the wood industry and mid-chain wholesalers and retailers. As a result, some public and private forests are being certified by multiple systems.

1.2.8 Value-added wood products

Value-added wood products trade continued to grow in 2005, in part driven by successful economic development policies to promote secondary processing of sawnwood, veneer and panels. US imports of furniture grew by 11% in 2005, reaching a record $16.1 billion, more than the next four of the top five furniture importers together. Italy remains the world's largest furniture exporter, but with a downturn in 2005, it could be surpassed by China in the next year if trends continue at the same rate.

Engineered wood products, such as I-beams and laminated veneer lumber (LVL), are consistently gaining market share at the expense of traditional wood products on the life cycle curve (graph 1.2.3)

GRAPH 1.2.3

Wood products and their competitors' life cycles, 2006

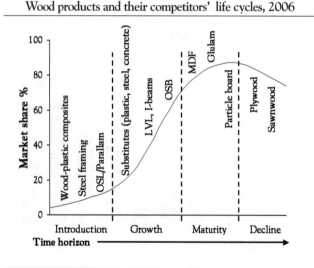

Note: OSL and Parallam are oriented strand lumber (sawnwood).
Source: USDA Forest Service, 2006.

1.2.9 Tropical timber

Public procurement policies in importing countries were affecting tropical timber exports as evidenced by the International Tropical Timber Organization's (ITTO) Market Discussion in June 2006. A study by ITTO found that less than 5% of tropical forests are managed sustainably, leading some tropical countries to certify their forests' sustainable management to maintain exports to environmentally sensitive markets (ITTO, 2006). Economic development policies in tropical countries continue to successfully promote production and export of value-added products, as opposed to primary wood products. In general, tropical timber markets improved in terms of production and trade in 2005, and prices rose.

China remains by far the world's largest log importing country; however, it is decreasing tropical log imports in favour of temperate logs from the EECCA region. Formerly a major plywood importer, China's plywood imports are only 25% of previous levels as veneer log imports – both softwood and hardwood, temperate and tropical – are processed into plywood. The Chinese Government promotes domestic plywood production to boost employment and offset reduced domestic log supplies, through a variety of policies, including tariffs.

1.3 References

Canadian Sustainable Forestry Certification Coalition. 2006. Available at: www.sfms.com

European Commission, 2004. Vision 2030 A technology platform initiative by the European forest-based-sector. European Commission Directorate-General for Research, Information and Communication Unit, Brussels, Belgium.

FAO Forestry, 2006a. Cross Sectoral Approach to Forest Sector Issues: Wood Energy, Implications of Kyoto Protocol; and Cooperation on Forest Fires. European Forestry Commission session document FO: EFC/2006/4 Rev.1. Available at: www.unece.org/trade/ timber/efc/33efc_zvolen/EFC_2006_4_Rev1Cross_sec toralapproach.pdf

FAO Forestry. 2006b. Woodfuels website. Available at: http://www.fao.org/forestry/foris/webview/forestry2/ind ex.jsp?siteId=3281&sitetreeId=14067&langId=1&geo Id=0

FAO Forestry. 2006c. 15 Years of Economies in Transition: Lessons Learned and Challenges Ahead for the Forestry Sector. European Forestry Commission session document FO:EFC/2006/2.1. Available at: www.unece.org/trade/timber

FAO Forestry. 2006d. Progress Towards Sustainable Management in Europe. Discussion report for the FAO European Forestry Commission session, Zvolen,

Slovakia. Available at:www.unece.org/trade/timber/efc/33efc_zvolen/zvolen_2006May.htm

FAO Forestry. 2006e. State of the World's Forests 2005. Available at: ftp://ftp.fao.org/docrep/fao/007/y5574e/y5574e10.pdf

ITTO. 2006. Status of Tropical Forest Management 2005. Available at: www.itto.or.jp

UNECE/FAO. 2004. Joint UNECE/FAO Workshop on Illegal Logging and Trade of Illegally Derived Forest Products in the UNECE Region. Documentation available at: www.unece.org/trade/timber/docs/sem/2004-1/sem-2004-1.htm

UNECE/FAO. 2005. European Forest Sector Outlook Study. ECE/TIM/SP/20. Geneva, Switzerland. Available at: www.unece.org/trade/timber

White, A., Sun, X., Canby, K., Xu, J., Barr, C., Katsigris, E., Bull, G., Cossalter, C. & Nilsson, S. 2006. China and the Global Market for Forest Products: Transforming Trade to Benefit Forests and Livelihoods. Washington, D.C., US, Forest Trends Organization. Available via: www.forest-trends.org

Wood Resources International LLC and Seneca Creek Associates. 2004. Illegal Logging and Global Wood Markets: The Competitive Impacts on the U.S. Wood Products Industry. Study conducted for the American Forest & Paper Association. Washington D.C. Available at: www.afandpa.org

Chapter 2
Policy issues related to forest products markets in 2005 and 2006[6]

Highlights

- As part of a continuing trend that has policy implications for forests worldwide, Chinese imports of wood continued to rise in 2005, with the volume of imports more than tripling since 1997.

- Since 1997 the export value of forest products from China increased from $4 billion to $17 billion, a period in which imports of Chinese wood products rose nearly 1,000% in the United States and 800% in the EU – in response, the United States and the EU took protective trade measures against some products.

- The Ministerial Conference on Forest Law Enforcement and Governance in November 2005 marked the signing of the St. Petersburg Declaration, an international agreement intended to stem illegal logging and related trade.

- A recent trend of sales of large tracts of US industry-owned forestland to investment groups is raising concerns about implications for the future on forestland and growth of conservation easement programmes.

- Life-cycle assessment of alternative building products has now gained the attention of the forest products industry, with life-cycle inventory findings widely promoted by industry associations.

- Recovery and reuse of construction timbers and other types of wood products for raw material and energy have gained the attention of Governments and niche market suppliers in the private sector, although further research and development of logistic channels will be needed to increase the use of recovered wood.

- In the United States, initiatives to combat climate change continue to emerge, including efforts on the part of clusters of States to act independently of the Federal Government and to force federal action.

- Research and development in support of biomass energy development is proceeding rapidly with the private sector pointing to its need for secure supplies of woody biomass and to avoid government policies that could divert wood from higher value-added uses.

- The long-standing sawn softwood dispute between Canada and the United States appears to have been resolved.

- Market growth of engineered wood products is robust in North America and Europe.

---

[6] By Dr. Jim L. Bowyer, Dovetail Partners Inc. and University of Minnesota, and Dr. Helmuth Resch, University of Natural Resources.

Secretariat introduction

Forest products markets are not only affected by internal and external market forces, but also by government policies and trade association policies. Especially in this chapter, but also throughout, the *Forest Products Annual Market Review* analyses policies that influence the production, trade and consumption of forest products. New technological advances can extend the range of options available to policy-makers, manufacturers and marketers.

The authors' choices of policy issues in the chapter are those that are most influencing markets in the UNECE region. While many of these issues were discussed last year, they merit further consideration this year due to new developments. For example, the rapid pace of developments in China's wood and wood products trade merit further elaboration, especially as some new trade restrictions have been imposed by importing countries' Governments. China's consumption, production and trade are spurred by economic development policies, and are increasingly affecting the UNECE region forests and markets, both positively and negatively. The authors will present the policy issues analysed in this chapter at the 3-4 October 2006 Timber Committee Market Discussions. One theme of this *Review* and of the Market Discussions will be China's impact on UNECE region wood products markets.

The secretariat would like to express its sincere appreciation to Dr. Jim Bowyer,[7] Director of the Responsible Materials Program, Dovetail Partners Inc., and Professor Emeritus, Department of Bio-based Products, University of Minnesota, USA, who was again the lead author this year. Although having formally retired from the University this year, he remains active internationally in forest products marketing and policies. We welcome Dr. Helmuth Resch, Emeritus Professor,[8] University of Natural Resources and Applied Life Sciences, Vienna, Austria, who co-authored the chapter based on his wealth of experience in this field.

2.1 Chapter overview

This chapter focuses on the principal policies that influence markets for forest products, on the market forces most influential in driving change in established

---

[7] Dr. Jim L. Bowyer, Director of the Responsible Materials Program, Dovetail Partners Inc., 4801 N. Hwy 61, Ste. 108, White Bear Lake, Minnesota 55110, USA and Professor Emeritus, Department of Bio-based Products, University of Minnesota, USA, tel: +1 651 762 4007, fax: +1 651 762 9642, e-mail: jimbowyer@comcast.net, www.dovetailinc.org.

[8] Dr. Helmuth Resch, Emeritus Professor, University of Natural Resources, Gregor Mendel Str. 33, A-1180 Vienna, Austria, tel: +43 147654 4254, fax: +431 476 544 295, e-mail: resch@boku.ac.at, www.boku.ac.at.

global markets and in public policy, and on new and emerging technologies that are likely to impact both markets and forest-related policy (figure 2.1.1).

Issues included in the chapter:

• Emerging markets for wood products and implications for the global forest sector.

• Forest law enforcement, governance and trade and initiatives to retain forestland.

• Policies promoting the sound use of wood

• Climate change policy.

• Wood energy promotion policies.

• Research and development policies.

• Initiatives aimed at increasing global competitiveness in wood and wood products markets, and overall performance of the sector.

• Trade policy and tariff and non-tariff barriers.

FIGURE 2.1.1

Policy and market interactions

Source: UNECE, 2006.

2.2 Emerging markets for wood products and implications for the global forestry sector

2.2.1 *China on the rise*

Any discussion of emerging markets for wood products and of developments that will impact the global forestry sector must begin with recent and ongoing developments in China – developments that are based in part on unsustainably and illegally harvested timber, and that are encouraged by wood products consumption in the United States, the EU and Japan. As noted in the policy chapter of last year's *Review*, China has within an extremely short time frame established itself as a major player in the global forest products sector. New information provides evidence of continued rapid growth in 2005 and an indication that recent trends may continue for some time to come. Among the findings of White *et al.* (2006) are that:

- During the period 1997-2005 the value of China's wood raw materials and wood products imports rose from $6.4 billion to $16.4 billion and the volume more than tripled to over 133 million m³ of roundwood equivalent (graph 2.2.1).

- During the period 1997-2005 the export value of wood products from China increased from $3.5 billion to $16.2 billion (graph 2.2.2). The value of US imports of Chinese wood products have increased nearly 1,000% since 1997, while imports of such goods by the EU have risen almost 800%, led by the United Kingdom, Germany and the Netherlands.

- China is now the world's leading importer of industrial roundwood.

- Domestic consumption of paper and paperboard within China grew by an average of 9.6% per year between 1990 and 2003.

- China is now the second largest producer of paper and paperboard in the world, with most of its production for domestic consumption.

- Chinese imports of Russian logs have increased 21 times since 1997, from 0.95 million m³ to 20 million m³ in 2005.

- China has rapidly shifted from being a net importer of wood products to a net exporter. China imports low value raw materials used in manufacturing higher value-added products that are sold in export markets, a trend that is likely to continue at least in the mid-term.

Thus far, policy responses of UNECE countries to China's forest industry growth have been limited to initiatives designed to stem growth of wood products imports from China (see section 2.9). In the near future, policy analysts may face increasing pressure to address the impact of increasing imports on the health of rural, wood industry-dependent communities.

The shift within China from forest products importer to exporter is illustrated with examples from the plywood and paper industries. For example, as recently as the late 1990s, China was an importer of large quantities of plywood. Subsequently, however, net imports shifted to raw logs and barely processed wood to supply a fast-growing domestic plywood industry, with domestic

production increasing from 2.6 to 21.0 million m³ during the period 1994-2004. China became a net exporter of plywood in 2001, with large impacts on plywood producers in other countries, especially Brazil, Indonesia and Malaysia. Thus far, Chinese plywood production has had little impact on softwood plywood producers in the UNECE countries. This may change, however, as the quality of China's plywood increases.

GRAPH 2.2.1

China's forest product import trends, 1997-2005

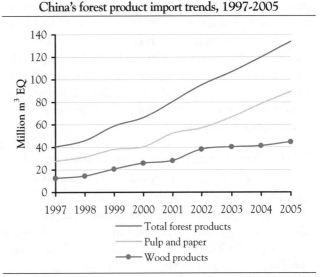

Note: Volumes in roundwood equivalent. For wood products the Chinese Customs Statistics correspond to FAOSTAT; however, for pulp and paper the Chinese statistics are higher. Wood products include logs, sawnwood, plywood, wood chips, fibre board, veneer and particle board.

Source: White *et al*, from Chinese Customs Statistics, 2006.

GRAPH 2.2.2

China's forest product exports by country, 1997-2005

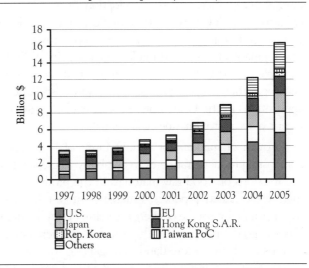

Source: White *et al*, from Chinese Customs Statistics, 2006.

A similar trend can be seen in paper. In 1997 China's imports of paper were reportedly 70% greater than its imports of pulp as measured by roundwood equivalents.

Just two years later, imports of paper and pulp were equal. Today, pulp imports far exceed imports of paper. Unlike wood products, most of the paper produced is for domestic consumption.

The fast-changing situation in China is seen by some as a harbinger of change that will soon encompass India and other developing countries. For example, consumption trends that are likely to foreshadow a wood deficit in India suggest the possibility of net wood imports of 20 to 70 million m^3 by 2020. All of these developments present what Michael Jenkins, President of Forest Trends, and David Kaimowitz, former Director General of CIFOR, describe as a wake-up call for the global forestry community that demands a strong leadership role on the part of producing and consuming countries alike to address issues related to sustainable forestry and conservation and to the future of timber-dependent communities worldwide.

2.2.2 New products drive export market growth

In recent years a high-value niche market for laminated timbers has developed in east Asia. In Japan, for example, glue laminated beams now comprise over 60% of the posts and beams used in traditional housing construction. Changes to the Japanese Agricultural Standard for such products opened this export area. Markets for engineered wood products are also expanding within Europe, where products such as laminated veneer lumber (LVL), Parallam, wooden I-beams, and similar products are finding increased acceptance. Such products now represent 35% of the floor joist market as well as large segments of the header and beam market in the United States and Canada (BIS, 2005).

Now a new family of engineered composites is gaining market acceptance. Trends in adoption of wood-plastic composites (WPC) in North America, and to a lesser extent in Europe, may presage new opportunities for development of expanded markets globally. In 2005, for example, 700,000 tons of WPC were used for exterior decking, other construction products, and miscellaneous applications in the United States, with market growth in recent years approximating 20% annually.

Growth of markets for various forms of wood-based composite products translates to an ability to use smaller-size fractions of wood raw materials in the production of high value added products. Emerging interest in using wood as a major source of energy has similar implications. From a policy perspective, the effect is to increase the options available to forestland managers, to increase the potential for economic harvest and use of small trees (including potential future sawtimber trees), and to increase pressures for unsustainable harvest levels. The changes may require new forest management policies and regulations to ensure sound practices.

2.2.3 UNECE countries dominant in global wood products production and trade

Despite the increasing presence of China in global markets, the production of industrial roundwood, sawnwood, panels, paper products and pulp in the UNECE region – consisting of Europe, eastern Europe, Caucasus and Central Asia,[9] and North America – reached shares of 82%, 73%, 63%, 66% and 77%, respectively, of world production in 2004. In recent years, overall consumption of forest products within Europe has reached record levels. Production in the EU-25 is also robust with increases from 2003 to 2004 of 2.2% to 6.7% for a range of key forest products (UNECE/FAO, 2005a). Thus, at the global level, Europe remains a significant exporter of forest products, accounting for approximately half of global forest products exports by value. Europe's wood products exports were twice the value of North America's in 2004. Trade in sawnwood and wood-based panels is almost balanced. However, while Europe imports significant amounts of wood pulp, it exports a far greater value of paper and paperboard. In general, but with great variation by subregion, exports have increased more than imports for most products over the last four decades.

2.3 Forest law enforcement, governance and trade and initiatives to retain forestland

Illegal logging was the focus of the November 2005 Ministerial Conference on Forest Law Enforcement and Governance (FLEG) held in St. Petersburg, Russia. Countries discussed differences between poverty-driven and commercial illegal logging, and considered measures that both timber- exporting and importing countries could take to help stem the problem. The Conference ended with the adoption of the St. Petersburg Declaration, a measure that pledges high-level political support for efforts to strengthen national capacities in countries plagued by illegal logging, and a commitment to monitoring, assessment, technology transfer and information-sharing focused on the illegal timber trade. Approaches ranging from improved law enforcement and anti-corruption activity to strengthening of forest policy and focusing on causes of rural poverty are all addressed in the declaration. Signatories included Russia, 18 of the EU-25 countries, most of the countries of eastern Europe, Canada, China, Japan, Mongolia, Norway, Switzerland, the United States and the European Commission. A follow-up meeting is planned for 2015.

The St. Petersburg Conference followed by one month a meeting of the EU Agricultural and Fisheries Council in which unanimous agreement was reached on

---

[9] Eastern Europe, Caucasus and Central Asia (EECCA) is the new UNECE term for 12 countries of the Commonwealth of Independent States (CIS).

a regulation establishing a forest law enforcement governance and trade (FLEGT) licensing requirement for imports of timber into EU countries. To be implemented on a voluntary basis, the programme will require documentation for all imported timber designated for free circulation that attests to legal harvesting and legal import in accordance with existing national laws (Council of the European Union, 2005).

With regard to forest governance, perhaps the greatest change is occurring in Russia, where federal forestry reforms are currently under consideration. While forests remain federally owned, control over their use has effectively shifted in recent decades to regional Governments. One result of this shift is that local Governments have become empowered to make demands on timber companies to pursue "socially responsible policies" such as construction of heating facilities for local communities. Now, the Duma, the Russian Parliament, is considering a draft of a new forest code that would reform the management of Russia's forestry resources. Legislation in 2004 served to move control of forests back to federal agencies. The new code reflects a "business first" philosophy. One provision calls for introduction of auctions to sell forest tracts to the highest bidder, whether from inside or outside a particular region. As currently written, forests adjacent to urban areas, lakes and rivers would also be subject to the auction sales requirement, eliminating local zoning restrictions. Local communities, NGOs and various activists are opposing many such provisions (Lankina, 2006).

In the United States, a dramatic turn of events in the forestry arena has taken place in recent years with the sell-off of large tracts of forest industry-owned timberland, spurred by pressures to increase profitability. Mirroring the trend in sales of industry-owned forestland is the growth of timber investment management organizations (TIMOs) and real estate investment trusts (REITs) that have together increased ownership of forestland at rates exceeding 20% annually since the late 1980s. Spurred by concern over the possible long-term implications of shifts in ownership and by rapid expansion of second home development within forested areas (development that is expected to impact over 18 million hectares of private forestland by 2030), a new approach to protection of forestland has emerged within the United States – the conservation easement (Stein *et al.*, 2005; Fernholz *et al.*, 2006). A conservation easement is a tool that restricts land use conversion in exchange for a one-time payment, yet allows landowners to continue activities that fit their ownership objectives. An easement might allow continued forest management (perhaps with the caveat that lands be certified by the Forest Stewardship Council [FSC] or the Sustainable Forestry Initiative [SFI]), but prohibit subdivision and second home development. Governmental and non-governmental organizations alike

are involved in the purchase of conservation easements. A governmental programme that operates in cooperation with individual States is the Forest Legacy Program of the US Forest Service. Under this programme the Forest Service and State-level interests identify lands to be enrolled, and then federal funds, matched by at least 25 per cent non-federal funds, are used to finance purchase; State Governments often provide the matching funds. The extent of forestlands enrolled in conservation easement programmes has risen sharply over the past decade, with two to three million hectares of forestland now under easement agreements. From a policy perspective, there is some concern that conservation easements enacted in perpetuity or for long time periods may limit options for future generations to deal with situations that cannot be foreseen today.

2.4 Policies promoting the sound use of wood

2.4.1 *Encouraging wider use of LCI/LCA in environmental assessment of construction materials*

Armed with findings of research groups around the world, forest-based industries in western Europe and North America are publicizing significant CO_2 savings that can be made by using timber in the construction of housing and other buildings, both in terms of embodied energy and in-use energy efficiency. While there are different wood-frame and solid timber structures across Europe, generally, higher wood content relates to lower embodied energy of the building. For example, a brick-faced wood frame house in England was found to save 1.55 tons of CO_2 per 50 m^2 wall, compared with brick and block, while facing the timber frame with softwood weatherboarding could increase savings of up to 3.45 tons of CO_2 (CEI-Bois, 2005). Thus, such a house could save around 5 tons of CO_2 (equivalent to driving 23,000 km in a 1.4 litre car) even before its lower heating costs are considered.

Similar results have been obtained in the United States, where wood-frame construction dominates residential home building. A comprehensive report issued in late 2005 by the Consortium on Research for Renewable Industrial Materials (CORRIM) found differences in embodied energy and global warming potential of 67% and 157%, respectively, when comparing wood and steel framing in floor and roof assemblies. Differences in air and water emissions, again lower for wood framing, are 85% and 312%. Large differences were also found in a comparison of wood and concrete construction.

2.4.2 Building rating systems

The UK-based Building Research Establishment (BRE) released a new EcoHomes buildings rating system in April 2006. The new system gives preference to wood over non-wood building materials based on the stated recognition that "responsibly sourced timber products are arguably the most renewable and lowest impact construction material in common use". The use of wood certified by the SFI is given preference (BRE, 2006). Previously, the highest rating in all BRE programmes was given to wood certified under the FSC programme.

The US-based Leadership in Energy and Environmental Design (LEED) programme uses a point system in rating buildings, with points awarded in a number of environmentally related categories, including site factors, water efficiency, materials and resources, and indoor air quality. Within the materials and resources category are provisions intended to promote the sound use of building materials. Examples of such provisions are provided by LEED that recognizes: (a) advanced framing techniques that serve to minimize the quantity of framing materials used; (b) minimization of the use of wood and other materials for strictly aesthetic purposes; (c) reduction of construction waste; (d) use of materials with recycled content; and (e) the use of certified wood and wood products. To date, the use of only FSC - certified wood is recognized, although consideration is currently being given to acceptance of other certification programmes, and certification is not required for any material other than wood.

The LEED programme is controversial within the United States because development of its standards is not scientifically based. As a result, various industries, including the wood products industry, have formed a *North American Coalition on Green Building*, which is intended to "foster greater participation in the green building market by creating a credible, science-based programme that employs life cycle assessment (LCA) and life cycle inventory (LCI) methodology." It is too early to tell what impact the new coalition may have within North American markets.

2.4.3 Wood recycling

Recycling of used construction timbers is a relatively recent procedure, and recovered wood products are now considered a new material resource. Developing recycling channels is thought not only to contribute to the overall sustainability of the European woodworking and furniture industry, but also to prolong the carbon fixation benefits inherent in wood. However, logistics for the collection, sorting and cleaning of previously used wood materials will have to be improved, and detection methods for chemical compounds in wood products will be needed.

The lifetime of wood in buildings depends on regional practices and local circumstances, such as climate conditions. After many decades or even centuries of use, wooden beams can be re-used, either intact or re-sized, in new buildings. Reclaimed wood, such as sawnwood, flooring and furniture parts, is often highly valued for its character and patina. Some specialist companies collect used wood in order to manufacture instruments such as violins, pianos and flutes, so that they will have the same sound quality as historical pieces. One interesting approach has been taken by the city of Vienna, Austria, which has made an inventory of its urban wood resources and is actively involving industry, architects and builders in developing a strategy to optimize the life cycle of wooden building materials and extend re-use and recycling. A recent study demonstrated that of 44,000 tons of building and demolition wood, over half could be re-used, 6,700 tons as sawnwood and beams and 16,000 tons recycled into wood-based panels, with much of the remaining material potentially useful for energy generation and other applications (CEI-Bois, 2005).

Across Europe, efforts are made to develop markets and new products for recovered wood, including wood-plastic composites (WPC), animal bedding, mulch for pathways and playgrounds, charcoal and compost. However, the production of wood-based panels, mainly particle board, is a main outlet and expected to continue to grow using increasing amounts of recovered wood. The proportion of sawmill by-products used in the production of particle board has risen from one third in 1970 to over 75% today. In North America, sawmill residues commonly go to either particle board or paper manufacture, depending upon the region and proximity of production facilities. The relative amounts of raw material used vary greatly depending on the local availability of wood resources. In southern Europe, some companies may use up to 100% of sawmill by-products and recovered wood because of the scarcity of forests. To ensure that recovered wood-based panels are safe and environmentally friendly, the European Panel Federation has issued quality standards limiting the amount of impurities.

2.4.4 Paper recycling

The EU *Vision for 2030* (European Commission, 2005a) expects significant benefits from streamlined paper recycling because recycled paper is now one of the main raw material sources for paper products in Europe. With a goal of increasing the use of recovered fibre (a growing challenge as the proportion of recovered fibre increases), it is recognized that industry needs to develop more sophisticated collection systems to further boost the availability of recovered paper. New processing technologies and criteria in product design to facilitate the use of recycled fibre for high value-added paper grades are also needed, as is development of new applications for recovered inorganic materials that cannot be used for paper.

2.5 Climate change policy

2.5.1 *General developments in 2004 and 2005*

The Kyoto Protocol went into effect in 2005 after Russia ratified the treaty, and this was discussed in detail in last year's *Review*. Governments in Europe and Russia are enacting policies to respond to their obligations for sequestering carbon and mitigating climate change. Most European countries have already drawn up a climate change strategy. The features of the strategy depend on, for instance, the amount of greenhouse gas (GHG) emissions to be reduced (and the extent to which the targets have been reached since the base year of 1990), the political will to achieve those commitments, as well as the efficiency of present energy use. The logic of the Kyoto Protocol means that they will seek to reduce emissions in those areas where there are the greatest potential gains.

Among many other complex choices, countries must decide how much priority to give to biomass and forest-related measures to reduce emissions, and what policy instruments to use to achieve these objectives. This will depend notably on the amount of land under forest cover, the potential of conversion to forest, the potential supply of wood and biomass energy, domestic or imported, the size of wood processing industries etc., and may well vary widely between countries.

The main areas of intersection between forest-sector policy and climate-change policy are carbon sequestration in forest biomass, use of renewable energies, notably wood, to replace fossil fuels, for heat, electricity and, possibly in the future, transport fuel, carbon storage in forest products and replacement of energy-intensive, non-renewable raw materials by renewable and environment friendly materials.

With the coming into force of the Kyoto Protocol, the framework conditions have changed in some fundamental ways, such as the necessity for rigid and formal accounting for carbon flows, the assignment of a monetary value to carbon emissions through emissions trading, and the possibility to offset carbon emissions in one country by reductions in another. The consequences of these changes are not yet clear, but they are already being felt in the marketplace, for instance in increased stimulus for wood energy (see chapter 9).

In May 2006, the European Forestry Commission discussed the consequences of the entry into force of the Kyoto Protocol for Europe's forests. The Commission stated that developments regarding the Kyoto Protocol offered the sector major challenges and opportunities that must be addressed in a proactive and cross-sectoral manner (FAO European Forestry Commission, 2006a). The issues identified by the Commission were:

- "Some countries had opted to account for forest management under article 3.4 of the Kyoto Protocol, in the expectation of increased revenue from these activities, or as a "safety net" to achieve national commitments, while others had opted not to do so;
- Some countries which had opted to include forest management under article 3.4 had decided to manage the credits centrally, while others were seeking ways to assign them to forest owners;
- A major forestry contribution to climate change mitigation in Europe would be made through sustainable forest management, including by producing and using wood;
- New scenarios predict significant temperature and precipitation changes for Europe. These will present new opportunities for forests in some areas of Europe, while they compound the vulnerability of forests in others;
- Profound long-term changes were to be expected from the fact that an ecological service, carbon sequestration, has been assigned a monetary value. The full implications of this were not yet apparent, especially as the likely price range and market size for carbon were still uncertain".

Despite the continued reluctance of the current United States Government to address the climate change issue, there are indications that a number of States are prepared to act independently of the Federal Government to adopt specific binding targets for reducing greenhouse gas emissions. In 2005, for example, it was announced that 11 northeastern States, brought together by the Governor of New York, would work together to create a market-based emissions trading system linked to emissions caps for electricity-generating companies.

In an unrelated development, California legislators in September 2004 adopted greenhouse gas regulations that called for a 30% reduction in emissions by 2026, primarily through tougher requirements on vehicle manufacturers to raise vehicle efficiency. Eleven other States and two Canadian provinces subsequently indicated their intent to follow California's lead in defiance of protests from automakers and warnings from Washington that State regulations would not be allowed to supersede Federal law. A Federal Court of Appeals ruled in favour of the Federal Government. Then, in late April 2006, ten States, including New York, California, Oregon, Wisconsin, Maine and Massachusetts, and several NGOs filed suit against the Federal Government over its decision to not regulate CO_2 as a contributor to global warming and with the objective of establishing the Clean Air Act as a platform for combating global warming (Barrett, 2006). Should the States prevail, it would be a significant boost for biomass energy development.

State-led initiatives to reduce carbon emissions include concerted action to develop renewable energy, including biomass energy. A number of the States participating in the April 2006 suit against the Federal Government are national leaders in biomass energy development. California and Oregon, for example, are both aggressively pursuing development of forest-based bio-energy industries, with Oregon focusing on the use of forest thinnings as a source of bio-fuel. It appears likely that Maine, already a national leader in producing bio-energy, will be the venue for the country's first full forest biorefinery.

2.5.2 Forest-based carbon sinks and carbon trading

In contrast to the role of forests as a net source of greenhouse gases in most parts of the world, Europe's forests are a large net sink and thus demonstrate the potential of forests to mitigate climate change via carbon sequestration (FAO European Forestry Commission, 2006b). From 1990 to 2005, European forests sequestered an amount of CO_2 in their biomass approximately twice the 5% emissions requirements of the Kyoto Protocol. However, Europe's production of greenhouse gases from fossil fuel consumption dwarfs the role of its forests as carbon sinks.

European countries are tackling their obligations via different policy approaches in the forest sector. For example, Ireland developed a National Allocation Plan for the Kyoto phase of the EC Emissions Trading Scheme in 2005, setting the overall amount of allocations to the trading sector at 23,014 million tons of CO_2 per year. One priority in Ireland is carbon sequestration through plantations. A basic assumption is the sequestration of over 2 million tons of CO_2 per year over the first five years contributed by forests planted since 1990. The estimates were derived in late 2005 by means of a computer model and were based on levels of afforestation from 1990 to the end of 2012. For the period from 2008 to 2012, 14,000 hectares of new forests are to be planted each year. The estimated cost of carbon dioxide purchases would then amount to about $20 (€15) per ton and forestry would contribute over $38 (€30) million per year (COFORD, 2006).

In the Netherlands, however, the focus is more on the use of biomass fuels for electricity generation. There is a goal for afforestation for carbon sequestration, but its effects will not be significant, as land for plantations in the Netherlands is scarce and expensive. The Netherlands has stressed energy transition to renewable sources, and, in particular, ambitious targets have been set for the share of sustainable biomass in total energy consumption.

There is a policy of replacing coal by biomass at power plants, and as domestic biomass supply is limited, the country is becoming a significant importer of biomass. Another pillar of the Dutch climate change policy is using the Kyoto "flexible mechanisms" (Clean Development Mechanism and Joint Implementation) to support GHG emission reduction or carbon sequestration projects in other countries, notably Bulgaria and Romania, some of which concern biomass and forestry.

A number of countries, including France, Switzerland and Germany, informed the European Forestry Commission that they would start accounting for "forest management" under article 3.4 of the Kyoto Protocol, presumably as this would provide a supplementary income stream for forest owners unable to market all their wood. However, other countries, including ones with major forest industries such as Finland, Sweden and Austria, have decided not to account for forest management under item 3.4. They believe that this would provide a perverse incentive by encouraging carbon sequestration rather than wood supply for raw material and energy uses, both of which they consider to be more positive for climate change than carbon sequestration.

The Chicago Climate Exchange (CCX), the first greenhouse gas emissions trading programme in North America, announced in 2005 that it would extend and expand the programme through 2010. The exchange currently has 100 members, including municipalities, manufacturers and business entities. Among the metropolitan areas represented are Chicago, Illinois; Oakland, California; Portland, Oregon; and Boulder, Colorado. Aracruz Cellulose in Vitória, Brazil is the first Latin American corporation to commit to the CCX emissions reduction schedule. To put the Chicago effort into perspective, some 13,000 companies in Europe are required to limit emissions of greenhouse gases.

A development that clouds the future of carbon trading was the April 2006 plunge in the value of carbon credits traded on the European Climate Exchange. The more than 50% drop in share value was blamed on lower than expected emissions in Spain and France that served to release large numbers of carbon credits, combined with the issuance of too many carbon credits across Europe (Wynn, 2006).

2.6 Wood energy promotion

Governments are showing increasing interest in promoting alternative, renewable forms of energy to promote sustainable development and energy security (figure 2.6.1). As a result, biomass energy targets have been set and biomass energy policies drawn up at the regional, national and EU levels. Considerable investment is being made throughout UNECE countries in alternative energy research and technology development. Alternative energy technologies are now evolving rapidly, including technologies for production of biomass energy for small-, medium- and large-scale installations.

FIGURE 2.6.1

Biomass energy

Source: A. Korotkov, 2006.

An animated policy debate is under way, focusing on how to achieve the national and EU biomass energy targets in an efficient and effective way, and without excessive market distortion. It tries to reconcile the competing interests of stakeholders:

- energy consumers
- forest owners, who welcome a new strong demand for wood
- industries that use wood as raw material.

Some industries, especially panel and pulp and paper, have noted reduced availability and higher prices of their core raw material as a result of competition from energy users.

In May 2006, the European Forestry Commission also discussed these issues. It looked for ways in which sustainable forest management can contribute to solving societal problems such as global warming and the growing need for alternative energy sources. It was also seeking ways to enhance cooperation between the energy and forest sectors (European Forestry Commission report, 2006).

The Commission identified these consequences of strong energy demand and higher prices for wood fuels:

- "Stronger prices and higher volumes of wood fuels were strengthening the economic viability of forestry in many areas;

- Current monitoring of developments in this field was unsatisfactory due to incomplete and inconsistent information;

- Forest sector institutions should take the lead in demonstrating the desirability of wood energy, for instance by using wood fuels in their buildings;

- Several countries reported that biomass energy targets had been developed in consultation with forest sector policy makers and that consequently forest plans and targets were being modified;.

- Forest policy needs to ensure that the growing public information needs are met in a consistent and proactive way about wood as an energy source, sustainability of sources and environmentally friendly heating systems;

- Fast-growing wood fuel consumption should be maintained within sustainability limits;

- In southern Europe, demand for wood energy could promote clearance of undergrowth and other forest fuel, thus reducing the risk of forest fires;

- Competition for wood between the forest products and energy sectors should be further discussed".

Faced with the strong competition for wood supplies by energy users, industry leaders on both sides of the Atlantic have pointed out that to realize the full potential of forests, including use of forest biomass for products, energy and biochemicals, a balanced and stable supply of wood is required. They also note that the wood industries themselves are major users of biomass energy, covering internal heat energy demands for pulp and paper manufacturing, drying of sawnwood, veneer and chips, and for pressing of panels and sheets. Industry generates energy from timber fractions that cannot be converted to products, and is increasingly selling heat or power to local communities or the public grid. Further, the recently enacted programmes providing subsidies to power plants that combust biomass for energy threaten this long-standing leadership position in development of bio-energy. They consider unfair the resulting competition between publicly subsidized entities and plants that use such raw material for products, such as composition boards and pulp, as well as those that produce energy for internal use.

A contrasting point of view is that many conventional forest industries and forest management itself also receive subsidies and fiscal incentives from a wide variety of sources in many countries. In some European countries, carbon taxes or similar instruments favour renewable over non-renewable energy sources. In a 2005 report published by the United States-based American Forest & Paper Association, it was noted that energy production using pulpwood is competitive or nearly competitive with new coal energy production in four of seven States studied (South Carolina, Maine, Florida and Georgia), and would become competitive in two of the other States (Texas and Wisconsin), with subsidies as low as 0.9-1.3 cents/kWh. The report concluded that subsidies should be used cautiously, either in the form of public funds for capacity investment or direct subsidy per unit of energy produced, to avoid injury to existing industries.

There is a strong and growing use of economic and fiscal incentives for renewable energy. For instance, in the United States, efforts are currently under way at the Federal level to expand the existing 0.9 cent/kWh tax credit for biomass energy to include forest-derived biomass. Subsidies currently apply only to closed-loop biomass systems (i.e. to dedicated energy plantations). The issue is complicated by the fact that subsidies will likely be needed to support open-loop systems; for example forest thinnings-to-energy proposals in the western United States, where forest thinning is needed to reduce catastrophic fire risks.

Some industry associations, especially panel and pulp and paper, maintain that forest-based materials should effectively apply the "cascading principle", where the structural properties of the wood are first used to create new products, recovered materials are used for recycled products, and eventually, material not economically viable for recycling is used for energy.

The other viewpoint is that maintaining open competition on price between wood-consuming sectors (e.g. energy and traditional wood consumers) is desirable, when this has been adjusted to take account of overall social priorities, such as renewability and security of energy supply.

There is significant potential for research and development in the wood energy field: for instance, the EU *Vision for 2030* – with one lead slogan of "Moving Europe with the help of bio-fuels" – sees a reduction in the dependence on oil and gas through the production of advanced bio-fuels that are expected to form an integral part of the forest-based sector and create significant new business opportunities. Research is focused on direct conversion of biomass into bio-fuels such as ethanol, with feedstocks to be obtained from manufacturing plants, forests and tree plantations. It is envisioned that in generating new products of higher added value, sorting and recovery operations of feed streams will also derive fibre and feed stock. Bio-fuels may also be produced from already isolated fractions of wood such as lignin in a bio-refinery. The overall efficiency of bio-fuel production from forest biomass may be enhanced by integrating its energy system with that of other already existing industrial processes.

2.7 Research and development

From a policy perspective, new research directions will require either new investment in research and development or significant redirection of current research, or both. As reported last year, the need for new research investment coincides with a significant decline in wood utilization research on the part of Federal Government laboratories, industry and a number of universities. A positive development is marked increases in federal competitive grants funding in a few key areas, and especially those related to bio-fuels and biochemicals development.

The EU established the *European Technology Platforms* to provide a framework for stakeholders, led by industry, to define research and development (R&D) priorities across a broad range of industries. The *Technology Platform of the European Forest-Based Sector* is organized with cooperation by the European Confederation of Woodworking Industries, the Confederation of European Forest Owners, and the Confederation of European Paper Industries. A wide range of different stakeholders supports it. It aims at establishing and implementing the sector's R&D roadmap for the future. In January 2005, a leading group of the forest-based sector, in cooperation with companies, universities, research institutes, associations, national support groups and experts, as well as authorities of the European Commission, approved the sector's *Vision for 2030*: "It comprises a competitive, knowledge-based industry that fosters the extended use of renewable forest resources. It strives to ensure its societal contribution in the context of a bio-based, customer-driven and globally competitive European economy" (European Commission, 2005b).

The vision is to lead to major contributions to society: through the development of new and innovative products tailored to consumer needs; management of sustainable forests; reduction of environmental impacts; resistance against climate change and its effects; reduction of Europe's dependence on oil; participation in Europe's strategy for growth and jobs; and sustenance of employment, especially in rural areas.

There is demand for higher added-value products in existing product segments and a need for the development of entirely new uses of wood as a raw material, as well as a more active engagement in the bio-energy field. Indeed, "green" chemicals, novel composites, and the non-wood values of European forests have already been identified as product opportunities. New concepts are hoped for that use wood to mitigate climate change as all wood products "lock up" carbon. Wood can contribute also by providing substitutes for non-renewable materials in sectors such as packaging, fuels, chemicals and construction.

The resulting *Strategic Research Agenda*[10] has now been established and its implementation was officially launched at an international conference in Austria in May 2006. It is an ambitious undertaking, as it deals with five areas, sometimes overlapping:

- Development of innovative products for changing markets and customer needs.

- Development of intelligent and efficient manufacturing processes, including reduced energy consumption.

- Enhancing availability and use of forest biomass for products and energy.

- Meeting the multifunctional demands on forest resources and their sustainable management.

- The sector in a societal perspective.

The European effort mirrors similar national, State, and provincial initiatives in the United States and Canada. The Agenda 2020 Technical Alliance programme, a joint research initiative of the US Department of Energy and the American Forest & Paper Association, has goals nearly identical to those of the European Forest-Based Technology Platform. The Agenda 2020 technology portfolio is organized around seven core technology platforms including advancement of the forest bio-refinery, nanotechnology for the forest products industry, breakthrough manufacturing technologies, next generation fibre recovery and utilization, and enhancement of environmental performance.

2.8 Initiatives aimed at increasing global competitiveness in wood and wood products markets, and overall performance of the sector

In recent decades, sawnwood production has changed significantly across both Europe and North America, with changes in sawmilling equipment that processes smaller diameter logs at higher speeds. In western Europe, sawnwood export has been emphasized by Sweden, Finland, Austria, and to some extent Germany, with the bulk of products exported to America and, to a lesser extent, Asia and the Middle East. However, eastern Europe holds certain comparative advantages in sawnwood production drawing new investments for sawmills into areas such as the Carpathian Mountains.

In order to meet global competition, the *European Technology Platforms* included the observation that the European primary wood processing industry would have to work with considerably increased material efficiency and lower energy consumption. Research to develop advanced technologies is recommended to develop

innovative and safe production processes across integrated production chains that will allow the flexible production of a wider range of wood products. Specifically, advanced sorting and grading systems for roundwood, processed materials, and final products have potential for optimizing material efficiency and making production more reliable. Technologies for producing new panel-type products and three-dimensional materials also have promise. Improved processing techniques can also be adapted to the specific requirements of novel products, enhancing material efficiency. The speed of production will also have to increase considerably and specific energy consumption can be reduced through the introduction of new concepts such as techniques to make wood drying faster and of higher quality.

Potential for substantial improvement is also seen in the secondary wood processing arena, especially through incorporation of advanced predictive tools in conjunction with novel quality assessment techniques; advances in these areas could lead to more efficient wood use and improved product characteristics. New functionalities could also be created by reengineering particles, flakes, veneers, and sawn timber, as well as by chemical, thermal or mechanical modification. In this regard, development is envisioned of new wood-based composites and materials with specific, tailor-made properties and functionalities, through exploitation of the unique physical and chemical characteristics of wood and its components. This new generation of composite materials will be manufactured exclusively or partially from wood particles, fibres, fibre fragments, cellulose or hemicelluloses, and from enhancement of these elements through application of advanced technologies including nanotechnology. These new wood-based products are targeted not only for traditional applications in wood and paper markets of construction, insulation, furniture, packaging, and specialty papers, but also for many uses outside the wood sector, including vehicles, textiles, medical, electronics and food.

The *Strategic Research Agenda* envisages entirely new forest-based value chains founded on a zero-waste, "bio-refinery" concept. Demands for the increased production of bio-fuels and overall use of renewable raw materials merit a fully integrated production of pulp, energy and chemicals from wood. A key element here is the close integration of chemical pulp manufacture and the optimized production of bio-fuels and different base chemicals. New systems need to be developed for the separation and refining of organic substances and fibres from wood and pulping waste streams. The integrated production of clean bio-fuels from spent pulping liquors will also be an important outcome. Similar processes are to be developed and demonstrated for the handling of different forest residues, bark and other materials not integrated with pulp production.

---

[10] www.forestplatform.org

2.9 Trade policy and tariff and non-tariff barriers

The long-standing US-Canadian sawn softwood trade dispute entered a new phase in April 2006, when officials from both countries announced a tentative seven-year agreement that would revoke sawnwood duties and end ongoing litigation. The pact calls for elimination of duties when the composite sawn softwood price exceeds US$355. Below this level, taxes would be re-imposed according to a tiered system linked to price and export volume. Eighty per cent of sawnwood duties collected to date by the United States would be returned to Canadian producers (Random Lengths, 2006a, 2006b). The apparent agreement follows a series of actions in the World Trade Organization (WTO) over the past year in which judgements alternately favoured the United States and Canada (Canada Foreign Affairs, 2006). While the latest development is promising, it is expected to take two to three months to iron out the details. The delay brings to mind December 2003, when an agreement in principle to end the dispute was announced only days before both parties abandoned negotiations (CBC News, 2006).

Although anti-dumping duties of up to 198% on US imports of Chinese bedroom furniture remain in force, generating almost $117 million in 2005, US imports of Chinese wood bedroom furniture nonetheless increased in 2005, rising by more than 15% over 2004 levels. In addition, US imports of Chinese wood furniture overall have continued a sharp upward trend, as have imports of wood furniture, including wood bedroom furniture from Vietnam, Taiwan and several other nations (Piland, 2005). In late 2005 and early 2006, similar trends have triggered calls from industry associations in Canada, Germany and Italy for imposition of duties on Chinese imports of upholstered and other furniture (Won, 2005; Minder, 2006).

2.10 References

Anon. 2006a. United States, Canada tentatively agree to lumber deal. Eugene, Oregon, USA, Random Lengths Publications. April 27.

Anon. 2006b. Details of tentative lumber deal outlined. Eugene, Oregon, USA, Random Lengths Publications. April 28.

American Forest & Paper Association. 2005. Biomass Study – Final Report. Washington, D.C., USA. American Forest & Paper Association. December 6.

Barrett, D. 2006. 10 states sue EPA over global warming. Associated Press, April 27. Available at: www.cbsnews.com/stories/2006/04/27/tech/main1553 669.shtml?CMP=ILC-SearchStories

BIS. 2005. Structural Engineered Wood Products in the Pacific Rim and Europe: 2005-2010. North Sydney NSW, Australia, BIS, Shrapnel Business Research and Forecasting. August.

BREEAM. 2006. EcoHomes 2006: The Environmental Rating System for Homes. EcoHomes Guidance. Issue 1.1. U.K. Foundation for the Built Environment, Building Research Establishment Environmental Assessment Method. April. Available at: www.breeam.org/pdf/EcoHomes2006Guidance_v1_1_April2006.pdf

Canada Department of Foreign Affairs and International Trade. 2006. Softwood lumber: Canada wins appeal at WTO. News Release no. 36, April 13. Available at: w01.international.gc.ca/minpub/Publication.asp?publi cation_id=383869&Language=E.

CBC News. 2006. Softwood lumber dispute. Canada Broadcasting Corporation, April 13. Available at: www.cbc.ca/news/background/softwood_lumber

CEI-Bois. 2005. Roadmap 2010. Handbook "Tackle climate chance: use wood" Part 2. European Confederation of Woodworking Industries. Brussels

Council of the EU. 2005. Forest Law Enforcement, Governance and Trade. Press Release No. 258, Agriculture and Fisheries Council, Luxembourg, October 25.

European Commission, 2004. Vision 2030 A technology platform initiative by the European forest based-sector. European Commission Directorate-General for Research, Information and Communication Unit, Brussels, Belgium.

European Commission. 2005a. Networking of national research programmes in the European Research Area. European Commission, Directorate-General for Research, Brussels, Belgium.

European Commission. 2005b. Innovative and sustainable use of forest resources – Vision 2030. European Commission, Directorate-General for Research Directorate B. Brussels, Belgium.

European Confederation of Woodworking Industries. 2005. Forest-Based Sector Technology Platform, 2005: Innovative and sustainable use of forest resources. Brussels, Belgium.

FAO European Forestry Commission. 2006a. 33rd Session, Zvolen, Slovakia, 23-26 May. Report of the FAO European Forestry Commission Session, 26 June.

FAO European Forestry Commission. 2006b. 33rd Session, Zvolen, Slovakia, 23-26 May. Cross sectoral approach to forest sector issues: Wood energy, implications of Kyoto Protocol and coordination on forest fires. FO:EFC/2006/4 Rev.1, 23 May.

Fernholz, K., Howe, J. & Bowyer, J. 2006. Conservation easements to protect working forests. Dovetail Partners, Inc., Feb. 23.

Available at: www.dovetailinc.org/documents/Dovetail
Easements0206_000.pdf

Lankina, T. 2006. Karelians Denounce Federal Forestry
Reforms. Russian Regional Report, Vol.11,5.

Minder, R. 2006. EU furniture makers seek curbs on
cheap imports. London: Financial Times, March 07.
Available at: us.ft.com/ftsuperpage/superpage.php?new
s_id=fto030720061718259948.

North American Coalition on Green Building. 2006.
Available at: www.apawood.org/pdfs/unmanaged/
CoalitionOnePager.pdf

Perez-Garcia, J., Lippke, B., Briggs, D., Wilson, J., Bowyer,
J. & Meil, J. 2005. The Environmental Performance
of Renewable Building Materials in the Context of
Residential Construction. Wood and Fibre Science,
Vol. 37, CORRIM Special Issue, pp. 3-17.

Piland, J. 2005. Duties curb China's wood bedroom
imports. Wood and Wood Products 80(6). Available
at: www.iswonline.com/wwp/200506/soi_resfurn.cfm

Stein, S., McRoberts, R., Alig, R., Nelson, M., Theobold,
D., Eley, M., Dechter, M. & Carr, M. 2005. Forests on
the Edge – Housing Development on America's
Private Forests. USDA Forest Service, PNW-GTR-
636. May. Available at: www.fs.fed.us/projects/fote/rep
orts/fote-6-9-05.pdf

Teislev, B. 2002: Wood-Chips Gasifier Combined
Heat and Power. Esbjerg, Denmark, Babcock &
Wilcox Vølund R&D Centre.

UNECE/FAO. 2005a. Forest Products Annual Market
Review, 2004-2005. Timber Bulletin Vol. LVIII.

UNECE/FAO. 2005b. European Forest Sector Outlook
Study, 1960-2000-2020. Main Report. Geneva,
Switzerland, United Nations Economic Commission
for Europe, and Rome, Italy, the Food and Agriculture
Organization of the United Nations.

US Department of Energy/American Forest & Paper
Association. 2006. Agenda 2020 Technology
Alliance. Available at: www.agenda2020.org

White, A., Sun, X., Canby, K., Xu, J., Barr, C., Katsigris,
E., Bull, G., Cossalter, C. and & Nilsson, S. 2006.
China and the Global Market for Forest Products:
Transforming Trade to Benefit Forests and
Livelihoods. Washington, D.C., USA, Forest Trends.

Won, S. 2005. Furniture makers seek duty on China
imports. Toronto, Canada, Globe and Mail,
November 2. Available at: www.theglobeandmail.com
/servlet/Page/document/v5/templates/hub

Wynn, G. 2006. CO_2 market on brink as price continues
to slide. Reuters, April 28. Available at:
www.planetark.org/dailynewsstory.cfm/newsid/36175/s
tory.htm

Chapter 3
Record North American housing market slows in 2006: Economic developments influencing forest products markets, 2005-2006[11]

Highlights

- Favourable macroeconomic conditions for forest products markets in 2005 are expected to continue in 2006.

- Low interest rates, favourable business profitability and increases in asset prices supported cyclical growth forces and offset the dampening economic effects of higher energy prices.

- Economic growth will slow slightly in North America in 2006, but will continue to be more robust than in the euro area where moderate growth in western Europe masks ongoing dynamic expansion in eastern European economies.

- High global demand for oil and high oil prices will support growth in Russia and other net energy-exporting countries.

- China's rapid economic expansion, which has become a major engine of global growth, is forecast to continue in 2006 with GDP growth of nearly 10%, generating strong import demand for oil and raw materials, including wood.

- US housing starts reached a 30-year high in 2005 at 2.1 million units, but rising mortgage rates should dampen housing construction in 2006.

- The upward trend in European new residential construction of the last three years may moderate as a result of rising interest rates.

- Construction activity has been stronger in central and eastern European countries than in western Europe and this is not expected to change.

- The ongoing robust expansion of output in the North American manufacturing sector is expected to strengthen both the non-residential building and non-building construction in the subregion.

- Price increases for building materials in North America moderated in 2005 despite the continuing strong housing market, reflecting better availability of building materials with increased domestic production and offshore imports.

---

[11] By Mr. Dieter Hesse, UNECE, Dr. Al Schuler, USDA Forest Service and Mr. Craig Adair, APA-The Engineered Wood Association.

Secretariat introduction

The secretariat of the UNECE/FAO Timber Section appreciates the continuing collaboration with Mr. Dieter Hesse,[12] Senior Economic Affairs Officer, UNECE, who contributed the macroeconomic overview in the first section of this chapter. This overview sets the stage for the market sector analyses in the following chapters and is equally appreciated by delegates at the annual Timber Committee Market Discussions.

We also wish to express our thanks, once again, to Dr. Al Schuler,[13] Research Economist, US Department of Agriculture, Forest Service, and Mr. Craig Adair,[14] Director, Market Research, APA–The Engineered Wood Products Association, for the analysis in the second section of this chapter, focusing on construction developments. Construction of houses and non-residential buildings creates demand for structural wood products as well as for value-added wood products.

3.1 Economic developments

3.1.1 *Economic developments in 2005*

3.1.1.1 *Global context*

The global macroeconomic context for forest product markets was favourable in 2005. World output increased by 4.8% in 2005, underpinned by a solid expansion of world trade. The global expansion in 2005 took place against the background of high and volatile oil prices and strong increases in non-fuel commodity prices. Global financial market conditions have remained conducive to economic growth, and despite a progressive tightening of monetary policy in the United States, long-term interest rates have remained at unusually low levels. Interest rate spreads for emerging markets have also stayed close to historic lows. Inflationary pressures have remained benign.

Growth has become more broadly based across the major regions during 2005. Current projections are for the world economy to continue expanding at a robust rate of

somewhat less than 5% in 2006.[15] The United States is set to remain a major driver of international economic activity, which, in addition, is also supported by strengthening growth forces in Japan and the euro area. Economic growth is expected to remain strong in the emerging market economies of eastern Europe, Caucasus and central and eastern Asia, and Latin America. The latter region benefited from low lending rates in international financial markets and strong growth in revenues from exports of raw materials.

The continued dynamic economic performance of China stands out among the east Asian emerging market economies. Real GDP is forecast to increase by 9.5% in 2006, only slightly down from nearly 10% in the previous year. The buoyancy of the Chinese economy is reflected in strong import demand for oil and raw materials (including timber) and a rising trade surplus. There will also be continued strong growth in India, averaging 7.3% in 2006.

Major downside risks to the favourable global outlook are related to developments in the oil markets, where geopolitical uncertainties have led to considerable price volatility, and the continued increase in the US current account deficit. In mid-2006 the international oil price for light sweet crude was slightly over $70 per barrel. Another source of uncertainty is the development of real long-term interest rates, which could adversely affect housing markets in the United States as well as a number of European countries. There are also concerns that further increases in energy prices may eventually drive up consumer price inflation, leading to a more pronounced tightening of monetary policy than currently expected.

The dollar appreciated by approximately 12% against the euro and 14.5% against the yen between January 2005 and December 2005. There was also a significant nominal appreciation against the British pound and the Swedish krona during this period, while the appreciation against the rouble was more moderate. This appreciation was probably driven by the increasing interest rate differential between the United States and the euro area as well as the other major industrialized economies, but the purchase of US currency and government bonds by Asian central banks also played a role. Since March 2006, however, the dollar has weakened again, as financial markets appear to have refocused attention on the huge US current account deficit and improving growth prospects in the euro area and Japan (graph 3.1.1).

---

[12] Mr. Dieter Hesse, Senior Economic Affairs Officer, UNECE Environment, Housing and Land Management Division, Palais des Nations, CH-1211 Geneva, Switzerland, tel. +41 22 917 2479, fax +41 22 917 0107, e-mail: Dieter.Hesse@unece.org, www.unece.org.

[13] Dr. Al Schuler, Research Economist, Northeast Forest Experiment Station, USDA Forest Service, 241 Mercer Springs Road, Princeton, West Virginia, 24740, USA, tel. +1 304 431 2727, fax +1 304 431 2772, e-mail: aschuler@fs.fed.us, www.fs.fed.us/ne.

[14] Mr. Craig Adair, Director, Market Research, APA-The Engineered Wood Association, P.O. Box 11700, Tacoma, Washington, 98411-0700, USA, tel. +1 253 565 7265, fax +1 253 565 6600, e-mail: craig.adair@apawood.org, www.apawood.org.

---

[15] These growth rates are GDP-weighted averages using purchasing power parities. World output growth rates for 2005 and 2006 are 3.4% and 3.5%, respectively, when these weights are based on market exchange rates.

GRAPH 3.1.1
Exchange rates of selected currencies vs the US dollar, 2004-2006

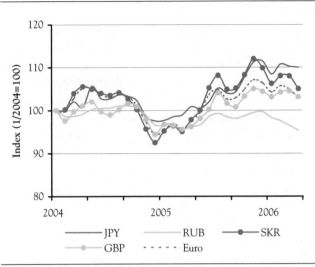

Notes: National currency unit per dollar. JPY is Japanese yen, RUB is Russian ruble, SKR is Swedish krona and GBP is British pound Sterling.

Source: IMF International Financial Statistics, 2006.

3.1.1.2 Western Europe

Recovery in western Europe in 2005 was weaker than expected. Economic growth was dampened by high oil prices, a cautious spending behaviour of private households and a moderate investment propensity in the business sector. Exports were the most dynamic demand factor. For the area as a whole (20 countries), real GDP rose by 1.6% compared to the preceding year. In the euro area, average annual economic growth was only 1.4% in 2005, which is significantly below the estimated growth of potential output, and which is itself moderate at approximately 2%.

Annual GDP growth rates of individual member countries of the euro area continued to diverge significantly in 2005 (table 3.1.1), with below-average growth in Germany (0.9%) and Italy (0.1%) and a somewhat stronger performance in France (1.4%). These variations in growth performance can be traced back to the differential strength of domestic demand and changes in real net exports. In Germany, the recovery continued to be driven by exports, on the back of strengthened international competitiveness. Domestic demand stagnated and changes in real net exports accounted for all of the annual increase in real GDP in 2005. In France and Italy, a deteriorated international competitiveness resulted in net exports making a negative growth contribution, which was, however, more than offset by the rise of domestic demand (which was moderate in Italy). Outside the euro area, in the United Kingdom, annual economic growth slowed down to only 1.8% in 2005, the lowest increase over the past ten years. This reflects a weakening growth of all major components of final domestic demand, notably a softening expansion of private consumption due to the house prices increasing moderately.

TABLE 3.1.1

Annual changes in real GDP in Europe and North America, 2004-2006

(Percentage change over the previous year)

	2004	2005	2006 f
Austria	2.4	1.9	2.3
Belgium	2.4	1.5	2.3
Finland	3.5	2.2	3.2
France	2.1	1.4	1.9
Germany	1.6	0.9	1.7
Greece	4.7	3.7	3.2
Ireland	4.5	4.7	4.7
Italy	0.9	0.1	1.2
Luxembourg	4.5	4.2	4.4
Netherlands	1.7	1.1	2.5
Portugal	1.1	0.3	0.9
Spain	3.1	3.4	3.1
Euro area	1.8	1.4	2.0
Denmark	1.9	3.4	2.7
Sweden	3.6	2.7	3.4
United Kingdom	3.1	1.8	2.2
EU-15	2.3	1.6	2.2
Cyprus	3.8	3.8	3.8
Czech Republic	4.7	6.0	5.1
Estonia	7.8	9.6	7.4
Hungary	4.6	4.1	4.3
Latvia	8.5	10.2	7.7
Lithuania	7.0	7.5	6.5
Malta	1.0	2.5	2.8
Poland	5.3	3.2	4.5
Slovakia	5.5	6.0	6.1
Slovenia	4.2	3.9	3.8
New EU-10	5.3	4.5	5.0
EU-25	2.4	1.6	2.3
Norway	2.9	3.9	3.1
Switzerland	2.1	1.8	2.3
Europe-27	2.4	1.7	2.3
Canada	2.9	2.9	3.0
United States	4.2	3.5	3.3
North America	4.1	3.5	3.3

Note: f = forecasts.

Sources: Eurostat, National statistics; Consensus Economics, *Consensus Forecasts*, 2006.

Against the backdrop of a continued favourable international environment and supportive financial conditions, economic growth in western Europe is expected to accelerate in 2006. For the whole area, real GDP is forecast to increase by 2.3%, half a percentage point more than in 2005. In the euro area, the average annual growth rate of real GDP is forecast to strengthen to 2.0% in 2006, broadly in line with the estimated increase in potential output.

The strengthening economic expansion in the euro area and western Europe at large will be driven largely by a pick-up in fixed investment. Business spending on new equipment is expected to strengthen significantly following surprisingly subdued growth in 2005. Business investment will be supported by strong corporate profitability, favourable financing conditions and continued robust growth of foreign demand. Construction investment is also expected to pick up. But the acceleration of investment activity will be limited by the continued moderate expansion of private consumption, the major domestic expenditure item. This reflects largely the situation in the labour markets, where minor increases in employment and wage restraint entail modest gains in labour incomes and, associated with this, real disposable incomes. Household precautionary savings will, moreover, remain high in the face of lingering labour market risks and ongoing discussions on reforms of pension and health systems. Exports will therefore continue to be the major driver of economic activity in western Europe, supported by the ongoing robust expansion of global demand. Changes in real net exports are, however, expected to make only a small positive growth contribution in 2006.

Among the major economies, annual economic growth is expected to accelerate to 1.7% in Germany in a context of favourable global demand for investment goods, buoyant business confidence and improving consumer confidence. Private household consumption will remain relatively weak in 2006, although some stimulus can be expected from the advancing expenditures in anticipation of the sharp rise in VAT at the beginning of 2007. In France, real GDP is forecast to increase at a stronger rate of 1.9% than in 2005, while in Italy, annual economic growth will be only 1.2%. Outside the euro area, in the United Kingdom, economic growth is expected to pick up to 2.2% in 2006.

Higher energy prices kept headline inflation in the euro area above the European Central Bank's (ECB) target of 2% in 2005, but core inflation (which excludes energy prices) remained subdued in view of weak domestic demand and moderate wage growth. But concerns about the potential inflationary consequences of the ample liquidity supply and possible lagged effects of the sharp rise in energy prices on price and wage setting has led the ECB to raise its key policy rate by 0.25 percentage points in both December 2005 and March 2006 to 2.5%. Financial markets expect further moderate increases in the course of 2006. But the overall stance of monetary policy is still accommodative, and real interest rates have remained at low levels. This is reflected in strong growth of private sector credit, especially

mortgages for house purchases by private households. With the major exception of Germany, low interest rates have spurred housing investment, and house prices in many countries have risen to elevated levels.

In the United Kingdom, the stronger than anticipated economic slowdown in the first half of 2005 led the Bank of England's Monetary Policy Committee to reduce the bank lending rate in August 2005. With inflation forecast to remain close to the central target of 2% and economic growth expected to return to trend in 2006, it can be assumed that interest rates will not be cut further in 2006.

Risks to the outlook in western Europe are tilted mainly to the downside. They are related to the further expected rise in oil prices, a disorderly unwinding of global imbalances and an associated renewed strong appreciation of the euro, and a sharper increase in long-term interest rates in case of a more pessimistic assessment of inflation prospects in financial markets. A potential upside risk could be a stronger-than-expected response of business investment to rising activity levels in the presence of continued favourable financing conditions and strengthened corporate balance sheets. A sharp fall in house prices from their current elevated levels remains another major downside risk in the United Kingdom and some other western European economies (France, Ireland and Spain).

3.1.1.3 The new EU members

Economic activity in most of the new EU members[16] (EU-10) preserved its dynamism in 2005, but the pace of growth was uneven across countries. Aggregate GDP rose by 4.5% in 2005, down from 5.3% in 2004. This average slowdown mainly reflects, however the weakening economic growth in Poland (to 3.2%) (table 3.1.2). The Baltic States remained the fastest growing part of EU-10 with GDP growing by some 7% on average in 2005. Macroeconomic policies have been broadly supportive of growth.

The economic outlook for 2006 is favourable. On average, real GDP growth in the new EU-10 will accelerate to 5%, partly also reflecting the somewhat stronger growth momentum in western Europe. Significant inflows of foreign direct investment (FDI) continue to support domestic economic activity in the new EU Member States from central and eastern Europe. A major downside risk to the short-term outlook is a significant increase in oil prices, apart from a faltering recovery in the euro zone.

---

[16] New EU members in 2004 were Cyprus, Czech Republic, Estonia, Hungary, Latvia, Lithuania, Malta, Poland, Slovakia and Slovenia.

3.1.1.4 Southeast Europe

Economic growth in southeast Europe remained buoyant in 2005, with real GDP increasing on average by some 5%. The EU accession candidates (Bulgaria, Croatia and Romania) benefited from further strong inflows of FDI, continuing restructuring and expansion of export-oriented productive capacity, and improving financial intermediation. In the remaining part of southeast Europe, economic activity was also upward-oriented, continuing the process of economic consolidation, combining successful post-conflict reconstruction and restructuring, and further macroeconomic stabilization. Growth in southeast Europe continued to be mainly driven by domestic demand in 2005. Forecasts are for economic growth to continue at a strong pace in 2006, but the strong reliance on domestic demand as a source of growth and the associated external imbalances are a main risk to the outlook.

3.1.1.5 Eastern Europe, Caucasus and Central Asia (EECCA)[17]

The pace of economic expansion in the EECCA slowed significantly to 6.5% in 2005, when real GDP still rose by more than 8% (table 3.1.2). There was notably a pronounced slowdown in the Ukraine, but growth forces weakened also in some of the other countries, especially Russia, the largest economy in the region. External factors were generally supportive for net energy-exporting countries in 2005, with oil and gas prices reaching new heights. But softer steel prices and sharply lower cotton prices exerted a negative influence on the economies specializing in these products. Domestic demand remained the main driver of economic expansion in the EECCA. A temporary slowdown in the growth of oil production in Russia triggered by production bottlenecks reduced export growth, which contributed to the weaker economic growth.

The pace of economic activity in the EECCA as a whole is set to remain robust in 2006. Real GDP is forecast to increase by 6%. Growth in Russia and other net energy-exporting countries will be supported by continued high global demand for oil and high oil prices. The main long-term challenge faced by the region is to create a more favourable environment for business investment outside the energy and commodity sectors to broaden the base of economic growth.

---

[17] The name "Eastern European, Caucasus and Central Asia" is a new UNECE term introduced this year in place of the Commonwealth of Independent States (CIS). It is comprised of the same 12 countries (see table 3.1.2 for list of countries).

TABLE 3.1.2

Annual changes in real GDP in Eastern Europe, Caucasus and Central Asia subregion, 2004-2006

(Percentage change over the previous year)

	2004	2005	2006[f]
Armenia	10.1	10.0	8.0
Azerbaijan	10.2	26.4	25.7
Belarus	11.4	9.2	6.9
Georgia	6.2	7.7	6.4
Kazakhstan	9.6	9.2	8.5
Kyrgyzstan	7.0	-0.6	5.0
Republic of Moldova	7.3	8.0	6.5
Russian Federation	7.2	6.4	6.2
Tajikistan	10.6	6.7	8.0
Turkmenistan	7.5	17.2	9.6
Ukraine	12.1	2.4	3.1
Uzbekistan	6.0	7.2	6.6
EECCA	8.4	6.5	6.0

Note: f = forecasts.

Sources: *Consensus Forecasts*, IMF, 2006.

3.1.1.6 North America

In the United States, economic activity moderated during 2005. This reflected not only the maturing of the business cycle, but also the devastating effects of two hurricanes in the autumn and the associated upward pressures on energy prices, which dampened consumer spending. Despite these events, real GDP rose by 3.5% in 2005 compared to 2004, when there was an increase by 4.2%. The growth slow down is expected to continue in 2006, albeit at a moderate rate. GDP is forecast to increase by about 3.3% for the year as a whole. Economic activity will continue to be supported by relatively low real interest rates, good corporate profits and the improving labour market. Private consumption, which over the past years has been supported by strong increases in wealth (due to rising real estate and stock markets) and a related sharp fall in savings to low levels, is expected to moderate as house prices are cooling off and interest rates continue moving upward. This will lead households to raise their savings. Weaker growth of consumer demand, in turn, will tend to dampen business investment.

The US Federal Reserve has pursued a policy of steady increases in interest rates since mid-2004. The key policy interest rate was gradually raised from 1% in June 2004 to 5% in May 2006 against the backdrop of strong output growth and persistent concerns about upward risks to inflation. Further, albeit moderate, increases in interest rates are therefore expected in 2006. The overall stance of monetary policy is now judged to be slightly restrictive. Fiscal policy, which was broadly neutral to restrictive in 2005, is expected to be slightly expansionary in 2006, reflecting the increase in government spending for the reconstruction of areas devastated by the hurricanes.

In Canada, economic activity strengthened during 2005, supported by high oil and raw material prices and a relatively accommodative monetary policy stance. (It should be recalled that Canada is a net exporter of oil and will therefore, on balance, benefit from higher oil prices.) Real GDP rose by 2.9% in 2005 and a similar growth rate is forecast for 2006, reflecting robust domestic demand and a favourable international demand for commodities.

3.2 Construction sector developments[18]

3.2.1 North America

3.2.1.1 United States

Residential real estate was the backbone of the US economy once again in 2005 (National Association of Realtors, 2005). Home sales set a record for the fifth consecutive year and home price appreciation in most markets was solid. A good labour market and healthy home price appreciation provided a boost to consumer spending (two-thirds of the economy).

The US housing market reached a 30-year high in 2005 when 2.066 million units were started (graph 3.2.1). Most of the starts, 83%, were single family, which accounted for 1.73 million (figure 3.2.1). Multi-family starts totalled 336,000. These totals do not include factory-manufactured homes, i.e. mobile homes (which are built to a different building code than that used for conventional homes). This development is even more remarkable considering that conventional houses today are nearly 40% larger than in the 1970s. Single-family homes, with an average area of 225 m² (2,400 square feet), now account for 80% or more of all new housing starts (single family and multiple family), compared with 60% in the 1970s. This is good news for producers of building materials. The average single-family home requires about 36 cubic metres (15,000 board feet) of sawnwood and 11 cubic metres (11,000 square feet) of

structural panels (OSB and plywood). The multi-family sector continues to underperform, due largely to the affordability and availability of single-family homes.

GRAPH 3.2.1
United States housing starts, 2003-2006

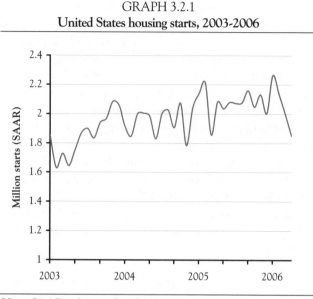

Note: SAAR = Seasonally adjusted annual rate.
Source: US Bureau of the Census, 2006.

FIGURE 3.2.1
US residential construction

Source: APA—The Engineered Wood Association, 2006.

[18] The major source for European construction sector data was Euroconstruct (www.euroconstruct.org), whereas for North America, particularly the United States, the authors had access to more information sources including the US Federal Government's Bureau of Census, and numerous private construction sector organizations such as the National Association of Homebuilders and the National Association of Realtors. The apparent imbalance of the focus of analysis in this chapter on construction markets is due to the relationship between the general economy (GDP) and investments in construction activity, both in Europe and North America. In North America, residential construction consumes most of the solid wood products (plywood, lumber, OSB and even engineered wood products) due to wood frame construction, and the major drivers for these markets are interest and employment rates – both of which are related directly to GDP. Similarly, in Europe, wood product markets are also related to residential activity, although renovation is a key driver in western countries. As in North America, GDP, interest and employment rates are economic drivers for these markets as well.

Strong demographics, including healthy immigration levels, are the primary reason for today's robust residential market. This is being augmented by solid affordability factors such as attractive mortgage rates, which remain low by historical standards although the trend is upward, solid job markets, and rising incomes. However, during the fourth quarter of 2005 and through April 2006, the market was beginning to show signs of cooling, which is actually welcome due to concern that an overheated housing market bubble might burst: existing homes remain on the market longer; the inventory of new homes for sale is the highest it has ever been; home price increases are beginning to moderate and even fall in some

TABLE 3.2.1

US construction starts, 2004-2006

(Billion $)

Type of construction	2004	2005	2006^f	% change 2004-2005	% change 2005-2006
Residential	332	368	366	+10.7%	-0.5%
Single-family	283	3068	302	+8.3%	-1.5%
Multiple-family	50	618	64	+23.9%	+4.2%
Non-residential building	163	169	182	+3.5%	+8.0%
Non-building construction	94	101	107	+6.8%	+6.0%
Total construction	589	637	654	+8.1%	+2.8%

Note: f = forecast.

Source: US Bureau of the Census, *Report C30,* 2005.

areas; mortgage delinquencies are up; lending standards are tightening; and affordability is deteriorating as mortgage rates increase.

Despite the continuing strength in housing, building material prices moderated slightly in 2005 due to a better balance between demand and supply of sawnwood and structural panels. Availability improved due to increased production in North America and increased sawnwood imports from Europe and plywood from South America. The Random Lengths Framing Lumber[19] Composite Price fell by 4% in 2005 after increasing by 30% in 2004. The Random Lengths Structural Panel Composite Price fell by 11% in 2005 after increasing by 26% in 2004.

The value of total construction grew by 8.1% from 2004 to 2005, led by extremely strong residential markets (table 3.2.1). However, non-residential markets were showing strength in 2006, meaning that construction markets are becoming better balanced.

A full reversal in trends is expected in 2006 with residential expenditures expected to fall by 0.5%, while non-residential building expenditures are expected to grow by 8% and non-building construction expenditures by 6%. The key non-residential market is the commercial office sector. Corporate profits have been good in recent years and banks have eased lending standards for commercial real estate. Prospects have improved for commercial office construction for 2006 and 2007 (Bank of Nova Scotia, 2006). Through the first quarter of 2006 compared with the same quarter of 2005, the year-to-date construction contract value from McGraw-Hill shows total construction up 8%, led by non-residential building up 16%, non-building construction up 5%, and residential building up 6%. The more active growth will be in non-residential building markets comprised of office buildings, hotels and motels, other commercial and manufacturing buildings. This turnaround is being driven

in large part by the strength in the manufacturing sector and the overall strength in the economy.

There still are concerns about housing price bubbles (and their collapse) in parts of the country. Both coasts are most susceptible due to the rapid price increase over the past two years. However, price increases have been moderating since the fourth quarter of 2005, so the hope is for a "soft landing" in those regions. The south and midwest did not experience the rapid price increases, so there are no bubble concerns in those regions.

Until recently, the induced rise in the short-term rates of the US Federal Reserve Board was not followed by a similar rise in long-term rates. Historically, long-term rates follow short-term rates, but excess manufacturing capacity throughout the world plus a world savings glut have combined to keep inflation expectations low. As a result, long-term rates have remained low. However, the strengthening economy together with tightening labour markets are beginning to push up long-term rates. Consequently, the 30-year fixed-rate mortgage is expected to continue trending upward, reaching 7% by year end 2006, or about 110 basis points higher than the average rate in 2005. This rate remains attractive by historical standards and is not expected to derail the housing market. The consensus forecast for 2006 is for a pullback in starts of between 5% and 8% with most of the reduction in the single-family sector. The multi-family sector may strengthen.

3.2.1.2 *Canada*

The Canadian housing market had another good year in 2005 even though starts slipped by 3% from a 17-year high in 2004. The strength of the housing market in Alberta and British Columbia offset the weakness in the market in Ontario and Quebec. Higher interest rates and reduced demand point to a gradual cooling in residential markets during 2006 and 2007, mostly in the single-family sector. Housing bubbles are not an issue for most of Canada.

_____

[19] Lumber is used synonymously with sawnwood.

3.2.2   Europe

The value of total construction is expected to increase by 1.3% in 2005, reaching approximately $1,500 billion (graph 3.2.2). This is considerably lower than the 2.2% growth registered in 2004 (Euroconstruct,[20] 2005) and is due to the slowing of the economy in the second half of the year, which adversely affected construction markets. The outlook for the forecast period (2006 to 2008) is for a gradual strengthening of both the economy and construction markets. There are significant differences in projected growth patterns for 2006 to 2008. The fastest growing countries are also the smallest by market volume (e.g., Hungary, Poland, Czech Republic), while the slowest are the larger market-value countries (Germany, Italy, France).

GRAPH 3.2.2
Construction and economic growth for all Euroconstruct countries, 2002-2008

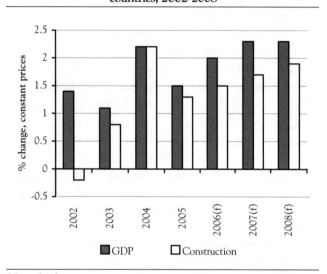

Note: f = forecast.
Source: Euroconstruct, 2005.

The two largest sectors, building renovation (37% of construction value) and new housing construction (24%), are moving in opposite directions. New housing is slowing down in western countries and moving to a period of stagnant growth for 2006 to 2008. This was expected as it follows two years of relatively robust growth during 2003 to 2004. By contrast, building renovation is expected to continue to grow throughout the euro region over the forecast period. Civil engineering, accounting for 21% of

[20] Euroconstruct's 19 countries include 17 EU Member States (Austria, Belgium, Czech Republic, Denmark, Finland, France, Germany, Hungary, Ireland, Italy, the Netherlands, Poland, Portugal, Slovakia, Spain, Sweden and the United Kingdom), together with Norway and Switzerland. Euroconstruct's western European countries are not the EU25, but the first 17 countries listed above. Euroconstruct's analysis of central and eastern European construction is based on Czech Republic, Hungary, Slovakia, and Poland.

the market, is also expected to continue to grow over the forecast period. This sector has shown the most rapid growth over the past several years. Transportation infrastructure, particularly roads, is the key growth driver, although this activity is not a major user of wood. The other market, new non-residential building, was disappointing in 2005, as the long-awaited recovery in this market continues to be postponed.

There was a much greater rate of growth in the central and eastern countries across all markets than in western Europe (table 3.2.2).

TABLE 3.2.2

European construction sector developments, 2004-2007

(% change by volume)

Western countries	2004	2005	2006[f]	2007[f]
New residential	5.3	2.0	-0.5	-0.9
New non-residential	0.9	0	1.5	2.0
Building R&M	1.4	1.0	1.7	2.1
Civil engineering	0.8	1.3	1.3	1.4
Total	2.1	1.1	1.3	1.4
Central and eastern countries	2004	2005	2006[f]	2007[f]
New residential	9.9	0	4.0	9.0
New non-residential	3.2	4.3	6.3	4.1
Building R&M	5.6	4.6	4.1	4.5
Civil engineering	7.3	9.8	11.7	11.5
Total	6.1	5.4	7.3	7.5

Notes: R&M is remodelling and maintenance. f = forecast.
Source: Euroconstruct, 2005.

The renovation market is extremely important in Europe, accounting for over a third of total output. This is in contrast to North America, where homes are younger. As a result, renovation expenditures, though important in North America, are less so than in Europe. Excluding civil engineering, renovation accounts for nearly half of the value of the building market in Europe due largely to the important role of renovation in Germany, France, Italy and the United Kingdom. These are the largest markets by volume in the Euroconstruct region. In the renovation market, total renovations (complete buildings renovated) account for 15 to 20%; partial renovations (functional part of the building is repaired) account for 33%; and smaller renovations, primarily by private individuals, account for the remainder. Long-term prospects are good as 150 million European dwellings are at least 25 years old.

3.3 References

Bank of Nova Scotia. 2006. *Real Estate Trends.* 2 March 2006. Toronto, Canada. Available at: www.scotiabank.com

Consensus Economics. 2006. *Consensus Forecasts.* Available at: www.consensuseconomics.com

Euroconstruct. 2005. Barcelona Conference, November 2005. Available at: www.euroconstruct.org

Eurostat. 2006. Available at: www.epp.eurostat.cec.eu.int

McGraw-Hill Construction, Engineering News Record, 2005. *Forecast 2006: A Rebound in Non-residential Building Markets keeps Growth Going.* By T. Grogan and T. Ichniowski. Available at: www.mcgraw-hill.com

National Association of Realtors (NAR). 2005. *Profile of Real Estate Markets, The United States of America.* Prepared by the Research Division, NAR. December. Available at: www.nar.org

Random Lengths. 2006. *North American Composite Prices.* Random Lengths Publications, Eugene, Oregon, USA. Available at: www.randomlengths.com

Chapter 4
Higher global demand for sawnwood drives timber harvests to new record levels: Wood raw material markets, 2005-2006[21]

Highlights

- For the fifth year in a row, total removals of roundwood in the UNECE region again reached record levels in 2005, primarily as a result of increased consumption of sawnwood in Europe and the United States.

- The UNECE region increased its share of the total global roundwood production and is a particularly important player in the softwood market, with about 82% of global removals.

- Consumption of softwood roundwood in Europe increased by 22% between 2001 and 2005 as sawnwood production continued to increase.

- Almost all of the over 60 million m3 of damaged timber from the storm that hit Sweden in early 2005 has been removed and the timber market is entering conditions similar to those before the storm.

- The Russian Federation has increased timber harvests by 18% over the past five years and exported as much as 34% of the total harvest in 2005.

- Softwood roundwood harvests in the United States increased by 9% in the past three years, largely as a result of an expanding sawmilling sector.

- For the first time in five years, wood fibre consumption fell in the European pulp industry in 2005, primarily as a result of the strike in the Finnish pulp and paper industry when production was down for six weeks.

- Sawlog prices were higher in 2005 than the previous year in North America, Northwest Russia and central Europe due to high demand and increased transport costs.

- Wood fibre costs, including roundwood and residual chips, increased in local currencies for many pulp producers in both North America and Europe during 2005 and early 2006 due to higher fuel prices.

---

[21] By Mr. Håkan Ekström, Wood Resources International.

Secretariat introduction

The secretariat greatly appreciates the close collaboration with Mr. Håkan Ekström,[22] President, Wood Resources International. The *Review* once again benefits from his expertise and global perspective in roundwood, chip and wood energy markets for this analysis of wood raw material markets in the UNECE region. He is the Editor-in-Chief of two publications that follow global wood fibre markets, including prices: *Wood Resource Quarterly* and *North American Wood Fiber Review*.

We also thank his contributors, Ms. Bénédicte Hendrickx, European Panel Federation and co-author of the panels chapter, Mr. Bernard Lombard, Confederation of European Paper Industries and contributing author to the paper and pulp chapter, Mr. Ralf Dümmer, Ernährungswirtschaft, Germany, Dr. Riitta Hänninen and Mr. Yrjö Sevola, both from the Finnish Forest Research Institute. Dr. Nikolai Burdin, Director, OAO NIPIEIlesprom, contributed information on the Russian roundwood markets.

4.1   Introduction

Removals of industrial roundwood in the UNECE region account for approximately 70% of the world's total removals. Despite the expansion of short-rotation plantations in South America and Asia, roundwood production in the UNECE region as a share of the total global roundwood production is higher today than it was ten years ago. This region is a particularly important player in the softwood market, with about 82% of global removals, while hardwood species account for approximately half of the world's total but a large share of the temperate hardwood removals.

The total removals in 2005 were an estimated 1.35 billion m³, or up 3.8% from 2004 and 10.8% higher than in 2000. Almost 1.2 billion m³ was for industrial purposes, of which 76% consisted of softwood species used mainly by the sawmilling sector. The remaining 24% was hardwood species predominantly consumed by the pulp and paper industry.

Consumption of softwood roundwood has been increasing since 2001 in all three subregions of the UNECE region (graph 4.1.1). The highest increases came in the Eastern Europe, Caucasus and Central Asia (EECCA) subregion[23] and Europe where consumption in

[22] By Mr. Håkan Ekström, President and Editor-in-Chief, Wood Resources International, P.O. Box 1891, Bothell, Washington 98041, US, tel: +1 425 402 8809, fax: +1 425 402 0187, website: www.woodprices.com; email: hekstrom@wri-ltd.com.

[23] The name "Eastern Europe, Caucasus and Central Asia" is a new UNECE term introduced this year in place of the

2005 as compared to 2001 was up 25% and 22%, respectively. The total consumption of hardwood roundwood in the UNECE region has been practically unchanged the past five years (graph 4.1.2).

GRAPH 4.1.1

Consumption of softwood roundwood in the UNECE region, 2001-2005

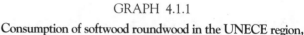
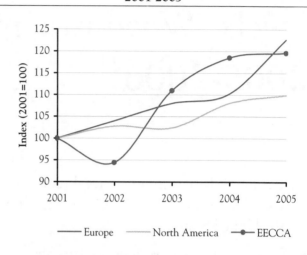

Source: UNECE/FAO TIMBER database, 2006.

GRAPH 4.1.2

Consumption of hardwood roundwood in the UNECE region, 2001-2005

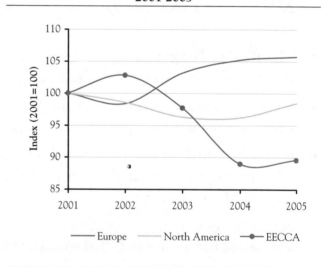

Source: UNECE/FAO TIMBER database, 2006.

Global trade flows are changing with forest products increasingly being shipped to markets further away from the manufacturing locations (graph 4.1.3). The expansion of global trade is not limited to manufactured wood products. Unprocessed logs are also increasingly

Commonwealth of Independent States (CIS). It is comprised of the same 12 countries (see annex for list of countries).

shipped to markets far away from where they were harvested. Worldwide, an estimated 7% of softwood logs are exported to foreign markets, up from 5% in the 1990s. Over the past five years, roundwood exports from the UNECE region have increased by almost 20% and imports by 11%. This has been made possible by the low costs of modern shipping.

FIGURE 4.1.1

Roundwood removals

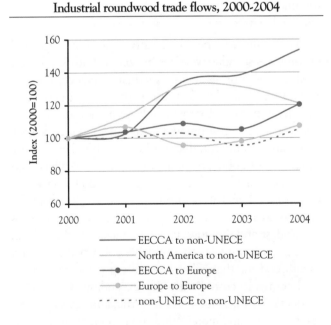

Source: Nordic Timber Council, 2006.

GRAPH 4.1.3

Industrial roundwood trade flows, 2000-2004

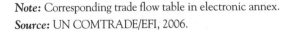

Note: Corresponding trade flow table in electronic annex.
Source: UN COMTRADE/EFI, 2006.

4.2   Europe subregion

The demand for forest products in Europe, including sawnwood, wood-based panels, and pulp and paper was stronger in 2005 than in 2004. Higher operating rates in the forest industry resulted in increased demand for wood raw material for the fifth year in a row, and as a result, industrial roundwood[24] removals reached a record of 403 million m³ in 2005, or 8.3% higher than in 2004 (table 4.2.1). The biggest change came in softwood roundwood, which was 12% higher in 2005 than in 2004 and as much as 38% higher than ten years ago. The biggest increases were in Sweden, Germany, Slovakia and Latvia, while harvest levels in Finland declined by over 5%.

TABLE 4.2.1

Roundwood balance in Europe, 2004 - 2005

(1,000 m³)

	2004	2005	Change %
Removals	435 398	467 994	7.5
Imports	62 394	68 126	9.2
Exports	36 638	38 170	4.2
Net trade	-25 756	-29 957	...
Apparent consumption	461 153	497 951	8.0
of which: EU25			
Removals	371 798	405 603	9.1
Imports	56 632	61 634	8.8
Exports	32 981	34 328	4.1
Net trade	-23 650	-27 305	...
Apparent consumption	395 449	432 908	9.5

Source: UNECE/FAO TIMBER database, 2006.

In 2005, fuelwood removals were estimated at approximately 14% of total removals, or 65 million m³. The accuracy of the fuelwood data, which are based on national statistics, can be questioned since they have not changed much in the past three years. However, it is clear that roundwood consumed for fuel has consistently increased over the past few years.

Despite greater harvesting, the increasing demand for raw material forced many European forest companies to source wood outside Europe, predominantly from the Russian Federation, especially when costs were lower for high quality logs. The log trade deficit increased from 25.7 million m³ in 2004 to 29.7 million m³ in 2005. In addition to 39.2 million m³ imports of softwood logs and 25.7 million m³ of temperate hardwoods, Europe also imported 1.5 million m³ of tropical hardwood logs in 2005. Imports of tropical logs have seen a steady decline in the past six years and are now only at 40% of the peak volume in 1999.

The removals of industrial roundwood in Europe have not only increased in real terms over the past five years, but the region has also grown as a global supplier of

---

[24] Note that roundwood is composed of industrial roundwood and woodfuel, as shown in the annex diagram.

softwood-based forest products. Between 2001 and 2005, softwood harvests in Europe increased from 26.7% of global softwood harvests to an estimated 28.9%. Softwood removals in Europe now exceed that of the United States for the first time since 2000, when a major storm hit southern Germany and temporarily spiked timber removals in central Europe.

As a result of Hurricane Gudrun, which hit Sweden and the Baltic States in early 2005, harvest levels almost doubled in southern Sweden compared with 2004. The increased supply of spruce, in particular, impacted the flow of logs in the Baltic Sea region. As a result of the high availability of logs, including both sawlogs and pulpwood, the need for imports to Sweden declined in 2005 and the log trade deficit declined from 7.9 million m³ in 2004 to an estimated 5.6 million m³ in 2005. Most of the over 60 million m³ of timber damaged by the storm was removed by the end of May 2006. An estimated 11 million m³ is being kept in inventory in lakes and under sprinkler systems, and will be processed over the next three to four years.

FIGURE 4.2.1

Hurricane damage in Sweden, 2005

Source: Swedish Ministry of Industry, Employment and Communications, 2005.

Industrial roundwood removals in Finland were down substantially to 47.1 million m³ in 2005. The reduction was the result of a six-week lockout and strike in the pulp and paper industry in the summer of 2005. The disruption affected production levels in both the paper and wood products sectors throughout the Baltic Sea region. The reduced demand for logs by the forest industry resulted in a 15% decline of harvest levels on non-industrial private land. The decline has continued in 2006 but for a different reason. During the first quarter of the year, roundwood removals on private forests were 42% lower than in the same quarter last year as a result of a new taxation law as of January 2006. Rather than taxing the annual growth of a landowner's forest, the new tax is assessed on the actual timber volumes sold. Initially, the

new system has resulted in reduced interest in logging by small forestland owners who do not necessarily require periodic revenues from their forests. Later this year logging volumes are expected to return to the same levels as last year.

With domestic log prices having almost doubled in three years, many sawmills in Latvia have found it difficult to stay competitive in the European market place and have increasingly imported less expensive logs from Russia, Belarus and Lithuania. However, it is questionable if the sawmill sector can continue to rely on these suppliers in the future as the costs for imported logs are increasing.

For the first time in five years, wood fibre consumption in the pulp industry fell in 2005. The total wood fibre usage was 151 million m³, a decline of 1.6% compared to 2004, but still 11% higher than five years ago. Most of the reduction was the result of the strike in the Finnish pulp and paper industry last summer when production was down, thus reducing wood fibre consumption in the second quarter of 2005 by 35% compared with the previous quarter. General developments in the European pulp industry in the past three years include an increased reliance on imported roundwood, reduced usage of softwood logs, and higher consumption of hardwood logs and softwood chips. In 2005, the industry's furnish of virgin fibre was 74% roundwood and 26% chips, a distribution that has been fairly stable in the past five years.

The composite board industry is a fairly large and growing forest industry sector in Europe, with the largest producing countries being Germany, France, Turkey, Poland and Italy. In 2005, the particle board and MDF industry consumed approximately 46 million m³ of wood fibre, of which an estimated 46% was roundwood, 43% by-products from sawmills, and 11% recovered wood. The biggest shift in fibre procurement in recent years has been that from sawdust and shavings to wood chips and roundwood fibre. Faced with hotter competition from the biomass energy sector, which has resulted in higher prices for sawdust and shavings, panel manufacturers have been forced to increasingly rely on higher cost wood chips and roundwood for their fibre furnish, especially with rising road transport costs. With the expanding wood pellet production in central Europe, particularly in Germany, the trend of using more roundwood and recovered wood is expected to continue in the panel sector.

The European wood panel industry is squeezed between a growing energy sector that is able to pay high prices for sawdust and shavings, and a pulp industry that usually has higher purchasing power to buy roundwood. In addition, sawmills are increasingly getting ready to utilize smaller logs that traditionally only pulpmills and panel mills use. With increased competition for both sawmill by-products and roundwood, wood costs can be expected to continue to rise for particle board and fibreboard manufacturers over the next five to ten years.

FIGURE 4.2.2

Chips and roundwood

Source: Nordic Timber Council, 2006.

The total European chip exports declined for the first time since 1998 by 2% to 16.7 million m³, mainly as the result of reduced exports from Germany, where new pulp capacity was added in 2005. Other countries such as Latvia, Estonia and the Czech Republic, which have a growing sawmill sector and limited or no pulp production, increased wood chip exports slightly in 2005. Total imports of wood chips to Europe were 23.4 million m³ in 2005, or 61% higher than five years ago. The biggest importing countries were Italy, Germany and the Nordic countries.

4.3   EECCA subregion

The EECCA region increased roundwood removals to 209 million m³ in 2005, which was 3.9% higher than in 2004 (table 4.3.1). Of the total removals, softwood industrial roundwood accounted for 55.0%, hardwood industrial roundwood for 17.8%, and the remaining 27.2% was estimated to be fuelwood. Not surprisingly, a clear majority of the logging activities in the region were carried out in the Russian Federation where 140 million m³ of industrial roundwood was harvested. Much of the increase in logging in the Russian Federation over the past few years has been driven by export markets in China and Europe.

The Russian Government now acknowledges that in addition to the official harvests there is another 10% of "undocumented" timber harvested in the country. Studies by both Russian and international organizations, however, have estimated that 15 to 20% of timber harvests may be defined as illegal (Wood Resources

International LLC and Seneca Creek Associates, 2004). Based on these two estimates, the volume of Russian illegal logging therefore ranges from 15 to 30 million m³.

TABLE 4.3.1

Roundwood balance in EECCA, 2004 - 2005

(1,000 m3)

	2004	2005	Change %
Removals	201 301	209 146	3.9
Imports	1 652	1 383	-16.3
Exports	46 341	52 481	13.2
Net trade	44 689	51 099	14.3
Apparent consumption	156 612	158 047	0.9

Source: UNECE/FAO TIMBER database, 2006.

The annual growth in domestic consumption of roundwood in Russia has averaged 3% in the past four years and reached 92 million m³ in 2005. Despite the expanding domestic industry, Russia exports a large share, 34%, of the total removals; few countries in the world export such a high percentage of their available wood supply. Over the next few years the rate of growth of domestic consumption of sawlogs and pulpwood is expected to outstrip the rate of growth of exports. However, this will only be possible if foreign investors find the business climate in Russia more favourable than in other "wood baskets", e.g. Latin America and Asia.

Despite increased prices of both sawlogs and pulplogs in Northwest Russia, roundwood exports to Europe reached a record level of over 20 million m³ in 2005, or 20% higher than in 2004. The major consumers of both pine, spruce and birch logs are the pulp companies in Sweden and Finland. These two countries alone imported 86% of Russia's total shipments to Europe of over 20 million m³ in 2005. Other major importers were sawmills in Estonia and Latvia, which are increasingly dependent on Russia for sawlogs.

It is doubtful that the recent substantial increase in log exports to Europe will continue since the prices of Russian logs have gone up to levels comparable to domestic prices for marginal volumes in most countries in Europe. In addition to already costlier logs, the Russian Government has implemented an export tax on logs as a way of encouraging increased domestic processing. In 2006, this export tax is 6.5% of the log value, or a minimum of €4/m³ ($5/m³). This will be raised to 10% in 2007, with a minimum of €6/m³ ($7.50/m³). If the log exports do not decline and domestic pulp and wood products manufacturing have not increased by 2007, the Government might adjust the export tax upward.

Log trade between Russia and China was also higher in 2005, with official customs statistics showing total log shipments up from 16.3 million m³ in 2004 to 19.2

million m³ in 2005. As well as documented exports, there are also substantial volumes of undocumented logs moving over the Chinese border. The study *Illegal Logging and Global Wood Markets: The Competitive Impacts on the U.S. Wood Products Industry* (Wood Resources International LLC and Seneca Creek Associates, 2004) estimates that approximately 30% of the Russian export volumes are not included in the official trade statistics.

4.4 North America subregion

In the UNECE region, North America is by far the largest consumer of industrial roundwood, accounting for 53% of the total removals. Consumption in 2005 was estimated at 622 million m³, of which 74% was softwood species (table 4.4.1). Although pulp production fell in both the United States and Canada in 2005, demand for roundwood was higher due to higher sawnwood and wood-based panel production. Both production and consumption of logs have increased by approximately 5% in the past three years as a result of strong markets for solid wood and paper products in the US market. The biggest adjustment in harvesting volumes in this subregion has been softwood roundwood removals in the United States, particularly on the west coast, where logging activities have increased in order to support an expanding sawmill sector. Although there were regional differences between developments in the western and eastern provinces, roundwood removals in Canada were practically unchanged in 2005, at just under 200 million m³.

TABLE 4.4.1

Roundwood balance in North America, 2004 - 2005

(1,000 m3)

	2004	2005	Change %
Removals	662 235	671 207	1.4
Imports	8 615	12 997	50.9
Exports	14 576	15 475	6.2
Net trade	5 961	2 479	-58.4
Apparent consumption	656 274	668 729	1.9

Source: UNECE/FAO TIMBER database, 2006.

North America continues to have a sawlog trade surplus with exports of mainly Douglas fir and hemlock to Japan, China and the Republic of Korea. Trade of roundwood between Canada and the United States increased dramatically in 2005 and was over 30% higher than in 2004. Approximately 80% of the trade occurred between the western province of British Columbia (B.C.) and the US Northwest. As a result of the higher exports, there are now demands from the public, political parties, labour unions and environmental groups that the provincial Government should restrict or ban exports of

sawlogs and instead encourage more value-added manufacturing in the province. With the unfavourable investment climate and a strengthening Canadian dollar, many B.C. forest industry companies have increasingly turned to the United States for investments in additional sawnwood capacity. As a consequence, demand for logs on the B.C. coast has declined and forest owners in the region have been exploring lucrative markets on the other side of the border.

In the B.C. interior, the sawmill sector has expanded substantially in the past few years, due to large volumes of beetle-killed timber available to the forest industry. Lumber production in B.C. was 33% higher in the first quarter of 2006 than in the same quarter three years ago. The mountain pine beetle has now affected over 8 million hectares of mature lodgepole pine stands and an estimated 400 million m³ of timber is currently in need of removals before the quality and value as raw material for the forest industry will deteriorate. The annual allowable cut, set by the provincial Government, was recently increased from 13 to 23 million m³ in the worst impacted area in the northeast part of the province.

In August of 2005, Hurricane Katrina hit southeastern United States, affecting one million hectares of timberlands and damaging as much as 50 million m³ of sawtimber and pulpwood, a volume comparable to approximately 80 per cent of the annual harvest in that region. The damaged timber was expected to have a major impact on log flows and log prices, and create major bottlenecks in the procurement system. Initially, most pulpmills and sawmills in the region were without both power and communications. Further, due to the devastation, loss of homes and commuting problems, many workers had difficulties in reporting to their workplace. However, many of the problems were short-lived and the industry adapted to the situation quickly, running at normal hours again in less than two months.

In eastern Canada, consumption of roundwood is diminishing due to a forest industry struggling to stay competitive in the global market place. The industry is in a crisis due to high energy costs, high wood costs and a business climate that is turning investors away from the region. To add to the problems, in 2005 the Provincial Government of Quebec decided to reduce the annual allowable cut by as much as 20% over 2006 to 2008. For the forest companies in eastern Canada, the restructuring is not only a result of a less competitive industry and a diminishing timber supply, but also due to a strengthening Canadian dollar. The provincial Governments of eastern Canada are now considering different options for how to assist the important but struggling forest industry. They have so far promised more than one billion dollars over the next five years in different aid packages. In Ontario, the Government will invest over Can$ 200 million (US$

177 million) to reduce stumpage fees and to improve forest access roads. Over Can$ 250 million (US$ 222 million) has been approved for mill upgrades in New Brunswick and a similar investment package has been promised to the forest industry in Quebec.

4.5 Raw material costs

Wood cost is by far the largest cost component in the production of softwood sawnwood. Wood costs range from 60 to 75% of the total variable cost depending on the region of the world. Sawmills in North America and Europe typically have higher wood costs, both in real terms and as a percentage of the total production cost, than in countries with short-rotation plantations, such as Brazil, Chile and New Zealand.

GRAPH 4.5.1

Delivered softwood sawlog prices in Europe, 2001-2005

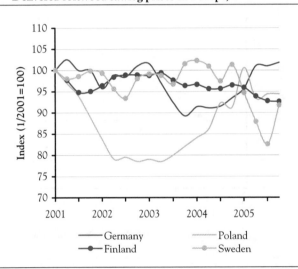

Note: Index is based on delivered log prices in local currency.
Source: *Wood Resource Quarterly*, Wood Resources International, 2006.

Prices for softwood sawlogs have increased in most of North America, Northwest Russia and central Europe in 2005 and 2006, while they have declined in the Nordic countries (graphs 4.5.1 and 4.5.2). The major reasons for these higher costs include higher fuel costs and longer hauling distances thus impacting the transport costs. The biggest increases have been in eastern Europe, where log prices have gone up in the Baltic States, Poland and the Czech Republic because sawmills have run at higher production levels and availability of locally sourced raw material has diminished. Prices for average log grades typically processed into construction and better grade sawnwood are now almost as high in the Baltic States as in the Nordic countries.

GRAPH 4.5.2

Delivered softwood sawlog prices in North America, 2001-2005

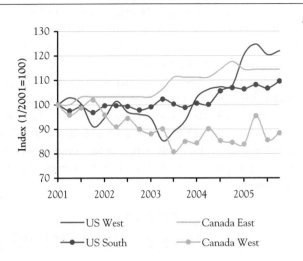

Note: Index is based on delivered log prices in local currency.
Source: *Wood Resource Quarterly*, Wood Resources International, 2006.

GRAPH 4.5.3

Delivered hardwood sawlog prices, 2001-2005

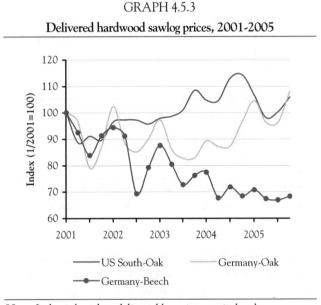

Note: Index is based on delivered log prices per in local currency.
Source: *Wood Resource Quarterly*, Wood Resources International, 2006.

Oak sawlog prices in the US South did decline in 2005 and early 2006 as slowing housing starts, together with rising imports of value-added products, had an impact on the demand for flooring, cabinets and furniture (graph 4.5.3). Average oak prices in the first quarter of 2006 were 12% lower than in early 2004, as well as being the lowest in five years. This is in contrast to prices in one of the major markets in Europe, namely Germany, where prices for oak were increasing due to a growing demand for parquet flooring both domestically and in the export market. Prices in early 2006 were the highest in at least six years.

For the production of chemical wood-based pulp, wood fibre costs account for between 38 to 52% of the total variable production costs. Pulpwood costs have traditionally been higher in North America and Europe than in regions with faster-growing plantations such as Brazil, Chile and Indonesia, but in recent years the cost spread between the northern and southern hemisphere has declined. Wood fibre costs, including roundwood and residual chips, have been increasing in local currencies for many pulp producers in both North America and Europe during 2005 and 2006 (graphs 4.5.4 and 4.5.5). The increase has been the result of higher fuel prices affecting transport costs and increased wood fibre demand by the pulp industry.

and North American hardwood pulp producers currently have only slightly higher wood fibre costs than what Brazilian producers pay for open market pulpwood. The cost for internally sourced wood fibre from pulp company-owned plantations are still some of the lowest cost fibre in the world. Brazil continues to attract foreign investors and the forest sector is expected to expand further. Over the next ten years, it is estimated that over $15 billion will be invested in the pulp and paper sector alone. In addition, there will also be substantial investments in the solid wood sector. With the higher demand for wood fibre and continued tight supply, wood costs will probably continue to increase, but at a slower rate than in the 2003 to 2006 period.

GRAPH 4.5.4

Delivered softwood pulplog prices in Europe, 2001-2005

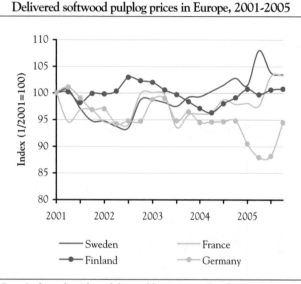

Sweden — France
Finland — Germany

Note: Index is based on delivered log prices in local currency.
Source: *Wood Resource Quarterly*, Wood Resources International, 2006.

GRAPH 4.5.5

Delivered softwood pulplog prices in North America, 2001-2005

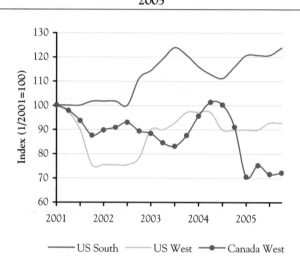

US South — US West — Canada West

Note: Index is based on delivered log prices in local currency.
Source: *Wood Resource Quarterly*, Wood Resources International, 2006.

Since the dollar has been strengthening against many currencies around the world in the past year, pulp manufacturers in Europe have become slightly more competitive in 2006 than in 2004 and 2005. Wood fibre costs for most markets in Europe were substantially higher than the first quarter of 2006: the Global Average Wood Fiber Price was $87.17/oven-dry metric ton (odmt) (delivered) for softwood fibre and $85.63/odmt for hardwood fibre.

The biggest change in the past two years has been the dramatically increased costs for hardwood fibre (eucalyptus) in Brazil. As a result of major investments in pulp production capacity in the past five years, supply of wood fibre in Brazil has tightened substantially and prices for roundwood traded in the open market have increased dramatically. Eucalyptus log prices have increased by 125% in terms of the Brazilian real, and as much as 300% in terms of the dollar in the past three years. European

4.6   References

Confederation of European Paper Industries. 2006. Available at: www.cepi.org

European Panel Federation. 2006. Available at: www.europanels.org

Timber Mart-South. 2006. Available at: www.tmart-south.com

UNECE/FAO TIMBER Database. 2006. Available at: www.unece.org/trade/timber

Wood Resources International, LLC. 2006a. North American Wood Fiber Review. Available at: www.woodprices.com

Wood Resources International, LLC. 2006b. Wood Resource Quarterly. Available at: www.wood prices.com

Wood Resources International LLC and Seneca Creek Associates. 2004. Illegal Logging and Global Wood Markets: The Competitive Impacts on the U.S. Wood Products Industry. Study conducted for the American Forest & Paper Association. Washington D.C. Available at: www.afandpa.org

Zentrale Markt- und Preisberichtstelle für Erzeugnisse der Land-, Forst- und Ernährungswirtschaft. 2006. Bonn, Germany. Available at: www.zmp.de

Additional statistical tables for this chapter may be found in the electronic annex on the UNECE Timber Committee and FAO European Forestry Commission website at: www.unece.org/trade/timber/mis/fpama.htm

Tables for this chapter include:

- Roundwood apparent consumption, 2001-2005
- Removals of roundwood, 2001-2005
- Exports and imports of roundwood (volume), 2001-2005
- Exports and imports of wood residues chips and particles, 2001-2005
- Exports and imports of roundwood (value), 2001-2005
- Roundwood balance in UNECE, 2001-2005
- Major industrial roundwood trade flows, by major countries, 2003-2004

Full statistics used in the *Forest Products Annual Market Review, 2005-2006* may be found in the UNECE/FAO TIMBER database at:

www.unece.org/trade/timber/mis/fp-stats.htm#Statistics

Chapter 5
North America peaking, Europe and Russia climbing:
Sawn softwood markets, 2005-2006[25]

Highlights

- 2005 was a stellar year for sawn softwood producers and exporters in the UNECE region, but may be the high-water mark as markets look more challenging in 2006 and beyond.

- Opposing developments, both growth and contraction, occurred among the leading western European producer countries in 2005.

- Western Europe remained a net exporter in 2005, but offshore export markets in both the United States and Japan became variable and competitive because of a strong euro.

- In 2005 Europe strengthened its market share in its largest overseas market, the United States, but this rapidly weakened by mid-2006.

- Membership of the Baltic States in the EU has caused log market prices to converge quickly with European prices, reducing profitability for sawnwood producers.

- Russia continued to expand its sawnwood output (up 5.3%) and exports (up 19.5%) in 2005, gaining market share in many export markets at the expense of traditional suppliers.

- The long-awaited Russian Forest Code has not yet been adopted; combined with rising log export taxes, this Code could be a catalyst for expanding sawnwood output.

- United States' demand and prices for sawnwood reached new highs again in 2005 as a result of low interest rates and a soaring housing market.

- The long-running United States' housing market finally peaked late in 2005 and new housing construction is forecast to decline by a total of 13% through 2007; this will directly affect domestic producers and European exporters.

- Similarly to the effects of the Swedish windstorm in early 2005, expanding timber harvests in British Columbia, Canada, due to the mountain pine beetle epidemic, and conversely, government-imposed harvest reductions in Ontario and Quebec, will affect sawmills' raw material availability and their sawnwood production over the next few years.

- The long-running dispute on sawn softwood between Canada and the United States was getting closer to a new seven-year agreement in mid-2006 following four years of litigation, as well as countervailing and anti-dumping duties on Canadian sawnwood.

---

[25] By Dr. Nikolai Burdin, OAO NIPIEIlesprom, Mr. Arvydas Lebedys, FAO Forestry Department, Mr. Jarno Seppälä, Pöyry Forest Industry Consulting, and Mr. Russell E. Taylor, International WOOD MARKETS Group Inc.

Secretariat introduction

We are pleased to welcome some new and returning analysts to the production of the sawn softwood chapter. We wish to thank the authors of this chapter (in alphabetical order):

Dr. Nikolai Burdin,[26] Director, OAO NIPIEIlesprom, Moscow, is our statistical correspondent for Russia and wrote the analysis for the Russian Federation as in previous years. Dr. Burdin was formerly Chairman of the UNECE Timber Committee and the FAO/UNECE Working Party on Forest Economics and Statistics. He is a member of the UNECE/FAO Team of Specialists on Forest Products Markets and Marketing.

Mr. Arvydas Lebedys,[27] Forestry Officer – Statistics, FAO, as in previous years contributed information about central and eastern European markets, with a focus on the Baltic countries.

Mr. Jarno Seppälä,[28] Consultant, Pöyry Forest Industry Consulting, wrote the western Europe subregion analysis. In April 2006 he presented strategic market planning at our marketing capacity building workshop in Serbia. His work in the solid wood products business area has been in international trade, market development and strategies. Formerly he worked on the *Review* as a student assistant while attending the University of Helsinki. He is scheduled to present this chapter at the 2006 Timber Committee Market Discussions.

Mr. Russell E. Taylor,[29] President, International WOOD MARKETS Group Inc., acted as coordinator of this year's sawn softwood chapter and also analysed the North American markets. He is a member of the UNECE/FAO Team of Specialists on Forest Products Markets and Marketing, and presented forest products market and policy developments at the 2004 Timber Committee Market Discussions. He is scheduled to present this chapter at the 2006 Discussions.

[26] Dr. Nikolai Burdin, Director, OAO NIPIEIlesprom, Klinskaya ul. 8, Moscow, Russian Federation, RU-125889, tel: +7 095 456 1303, fax +7 095 456 5390, e-mail: nipi@dialup.ptt.ru

[27] Mr. Arvydas Lebedys, Forestry Officer – Statistics, Forestry Department, FAO, Viale delle Terme di Caracalla, I-00100 Rome, Italy, tel: +3906 5705 3641, fax +3906 5705 5137, e-mail: Arvydas.Lebedys@fao.org, website: www.fao.org

[28] Mr. Jarno Seppälä, Consultant, Pöyry Forest Industry Consulting, P.O. Box 4, Jaakonkatu 3, FIN-01621Vantaa, Finland, tel: +358 989 472 640, fax +358 987 82 881, e-mail: Jarno.Seppala@poyry.com, website: www.forestindustry.poyry.com

[29] Mr. Russell E. Taylor, President, International WOOD MARKETS Group Inc., Forest Industry Strategic Services, Ste. 501, 570 Granville Street, V6C 3P1 Vancouver, British Columbia, Canada, tel: +1 604 801 5996, fax +1 604-801-5997, e-mail: retaylor@woodmarkets.com and website: www.wood markets.com

5.1 Europe subregion

In 2005, overall consumption of sawn softwood in the UNECE region increased by almost 2% to 235.7 million m³ (graph 5.1.1). There were great differences in the trends, however, with stronger consumption in Europe (and North America) offsetting a continued decline in the Eastern Europe, Caucasus and Central Asia (EECCA) subregion.[30]

GRAPH 5.1.1

Consumption of sawn softwood in the UNECE region, 2001-2005

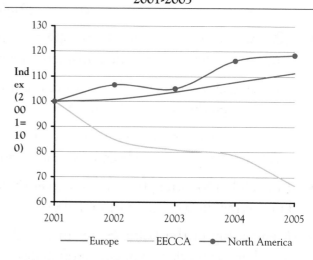

Source: UNECE/FAO TIMBER database, 2006.

In 2005, production in the UNECE region posted another substantial gain of 7.3 million m³ over 2004 to reach 257.7 million m³, while EU25 sawn softwood production greatly increased by 4.2 million m³, or 4.7% (table 5.1.1). The year was notably characterized by a contradictory development in Germany and Sweden, where production increased, compared with Finland. In Germany, the largest European sawnwood producer since 2004, local sawmills combined with new mill construction showed another strong year, with production increasing by almost 2.6 million m³ (14%) to 21.0 million m³.

As a response to the effects of the storm in January 2005, the Swedish sawmilling industry increased its output by 1.1 million m³, a significant 6.6% increase, to reach 17.8 million m³, posting an all-time production record. Fortunately, market demand for sawnwood was at its highest level ever in 2005, and Swedish sawmillers were able to sell their production due to competitive pricing and the exchange-rate advantage of the Swedish krona. Reduced production from another major producer,

Finland, also contributed to Sweden's increase in market share. Forest damage caused by storms in Europe is becoming more frequent, or at least the extent of the damage is better known today. The market disruptions affect not only regular trade by other producer countries, but also the fledgling exports of countries developing their log and sawnwood exports.

TABLE 5.1.1

Sawn softwood balance in Europe, 2004-2005

(1,000 m³)

	2004	2005	Change %
Production	102 090	106 400	4.2
Imports	39 470	38 797	-1.7
Exports	46 004	46 408	0.9
Net trade	6 534	7 611	16.5
Apparent consumption	95 556	98 789	3.4
of which: EU25			
Production	90 829	95 064	4.7
Imports	36 863	35 946	-2.5
Exports	42 371	43 229	2.0
Net trade	5 508	7 283	32.2
Apparent consumption	85 321	87 781	2.9

Source: UNECE/FAO TIMBER database, 2006.

In the summer of 2005, Finnish pulp and paper mills were stopped for seven weeks due to a labour dispute that also directly affected the sawmill industry. As a result, production in Finland decreased by a massive 1.3 million m³, down by 9.4%, to 12.2 million m³ – the lowest level since 1997.

In 2005, western Europe remained a net exporter. Out of the traditional major exporters, Finland (down 559,920 m³ or by 6.8% in volume and by 8.5% in value) in particular, but also Austria (down 135,000 m³) faced a decline compared with 2004. Western Europe's leading exporter, Sweden, increased its export volume by almost 650,000 m³ (5.7%). In addition to Sweden, the only other western European countries that were able to increase their exports significantly in 2005 were Germany and France – by 206,000 m³ and 104,000 m³, respectively.

In Japan, imports from western Europe decreased for the first time in eight years (graph 5.1.2). Russia and the Czech Republic, as well as some other central and eastern European suppliers, gained a foothold over their western counterparts. Sweden was able to maintain its volumes, whereas Finland and especially Austria lost market share.

China's sawnwood imports from western Europe, including, in order of volume, Finland, Sweden, Germany and Austria remained at their 2004 levels near 120,000

m³. Although China is Canada's third largest market by country, its imports slowed in the second half of 2006.

GRAPH 5.1.2

European and Russian sawn softwood exports to Japan, 2000-2005

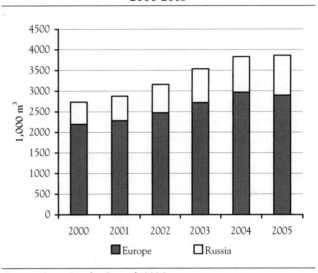

Source: Japan Lumber Journal, 2006.

The United States increased its position in 2005 as the largest overseas market for western European countries (graph 5.1.3). Sweden, however, using its incremental timber due to the windstorm, overtook Austria as the second biggest exporter with an additional volume of almost 200,000 m³, approximately two thirds of overall western European growth. Germany remained the main exporter. However, a United States market slowdown in 2006 will offer a competitive market for European exporters.

GRAPH 5.1.3

Sawn softwood exports between North America and Europe, 1992-2005

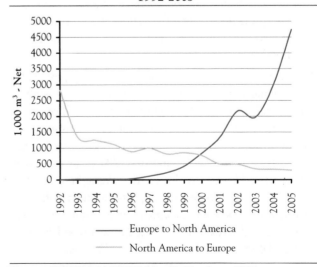

Source: WOOD MARKETS Monthly Newsletter, 2006.

In North Africa, leading European suppliers Finland and Sweden were able to increase their combined export volume by approximately 220,000 m³ for the second consecutive year after a decreasing trend since the late 1990s. However, Russia is now by far the main supplier, reaching the record levels of Finland and Sweden in the late 1990s.

Among the main western European import countries, only France (up 4.4%) and Italy (up 1.3%) increased their import volumes. Unexpectedly, Finland also increased its imports from neighbouring countries by over 100,000 m³ (up 31.3%) in 2005. In contrast, Germany faced a massive decrease (down 19.9%, or almost 900,000 m³) in overall imports, down to approximately 3.6 million m³, the lowest level in several decades. Part of the imports has been offset by further production increases.

In 2006, some developments that occurred in 2005 are expected to continue. Finnish sawmills have started to experience some problems in log cost and supply due to the higher tax basis for harvests affecting private forestland owners; in particular, record high stumpage prices and reduced imports from Russia. Estimates of decrease in supply compared with 2004 range between 4 to 5 million m³. In the first quarter, sawn softwood production was 7% less than the equivalent figure for last year.

Sweden and Germany are expected to continue on a growth path. A great majority of the logs felled by the storm have been cleared and stored for later processing in Sweden (as mentioned in chapter 4), and consequently, sawn softwood production was up 5% in the first quarter. Exports were about 15% higher in comparison to 2005 due to good performance in North Africa and the United States.

In the Baltic States, the log market has quickly matured, as no additional domestic supply is forecast for the next few years. Log prices have quickly converged with European prices since the Baltic States entered the EU in 2004. They are now fully comparable to Scandinavian prices.

Sawlog exports from the Baltic States have practically ceased while imports from Russia have been constantly increasing. Estonia and Latvia imported two million m³ in 2005 from Russia, or about 20% of total log consumption. During the first four months of 2006, softwood log imports to Latvia grew by another 12% (year over year basis). In addition to logs, the Baltic region has consistently been increasing imports of sawn softwood (mainly from Russia and Belarus), much of it for domestic processing and re-exporting. In 2005, sawnwood imports by the Baltic countries increased by 7%, reaching 1.7 million m³. In 2001, only 500,000 m³ were imported.

During the last two to three years, no new sawmill capacity came on stream in the Baltic States. However, existing sawmills continue to make investments into various technologies such as new kilns, planing lines and boilers, among others. Many smaller producers have shifted to further processed products such as joinery goods and prefabricated houses, and have found niche markets in both external markets and in local markets growing in line with the economy.

In 2005, Latvia and the Czech Republic were Europe's fifth and sixth largest sawn softwood exporters, with 2.3 million m³ and 1.7 million m³, respectively.

During the first quarter of 2006, sawn softwood exports declined in Latvia and Lithuania by 6% and 10%, respectively. This was caused by a dramatic drop in shipments to the United Kingdom. Baltic sawmills are losing some traditional European markets (United Kingdom, Germany) to sawnwood from Russia.

5.2   EECCA subregion

In the EECCA subregion, sawn softwood markets grew faster than in the other subregions, but in smaller volumes (table 5.2.1). In Russia, sawnwood production represents 11% of the total product output of the forest and forest industry sector. The total number of sawmilling enterprises in Russia is approximately 10,000, but only around 400 would be classified as medium or large. In recent years, there has been that significant growth in the number of small sawmills and all sawmilling enterprises are privately owned.

TABLE 5.2.1

Sawn softwood balance in EECCA, 2004-2005

(1,000 m³)

	2004	2005	Change %
Production	22 757	23 612	3.8
Imports	1 004	1 006	0.2
Exports	14 564	16 810	15.4
Net trade	13 560	15 803	16.5
Apparent consumption	9 197	7 809	-15.1

Source: UNECE/FAO TIMBER database, 2006.

In the period 2000 to 2005, sawn softwood production in the Russian Federation increased by 13.1% (graph 5.2.1). Exports doubled between 2000 and 2005, and the rise of 15.4% from 2004 to 2005 dominates sawnwood trade flows (graph 5.2.2). The major volumes of sawnwood production are concentrated in Northwest and Siberian regions.

GRAPH 5.2.1

Russian sawn softwood consumption, exports and production, 2000-2006

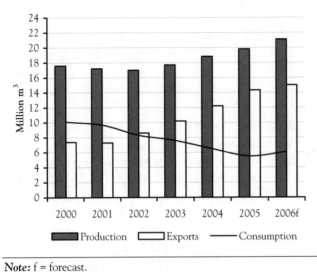

Note: f = forecast.

Sources: UNECE/FAO TIMBER database and OAO NIPIEIlesprom, 2006.

According to official statistics, however, domestic consumption of sawnwood in the Russian Federation continues to decline. For example, between 2003 and 2005, consumption dropped by nearly one third, but in 2006 is forecast to rise by 11%. However, reporting errors can occur when small to medium-sized mills produce for local use, such as in the construction of houses and dachas.

GRAPH 5.2.2

Sawn softwood trade flows, 2000-2004

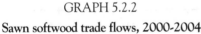

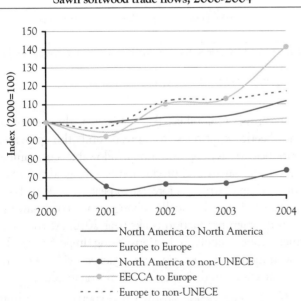

Note: Corresponding trade flow table in the electronic annex.
Source: UN COMTRADE/EFI, 2006.

Russian sawn softwood production and exports increased constantly between 2003 and 2005. In 2006, sawn softwood production is forecast to increase further to over 21 million m³, and exports to 15 million m³.

Sawn softwood is exported from Russia to the countries of Europe, Asia and Africa (graph 5.2.3).

GRAPH 5.2.3

Russian sawn softwood leading export destinations, 2005

Note: * = Islamic Republic of Iran.
Source: OAO NIPIEIlesprom, 2006.

To date, increased export duties in Russia have not negatively affected sawnwood or roundwood exports to any considerable degree. Sawn softwood customs export duties account for 3% of customs value but not less than 2.50 euros/m³ (approximately $3/m³). At present, the Russian Government is considering increasing unprocessed roundwood export duties further to encourage greater log processing in Russia and to provide domestic mills with improved supplies of roundwood.

The Russian Forest Code has been under discussion by the Government and industry over the last few years, but has not yet been adopted. The current draft version contains no special proposals for stimulating production of sawnwood. Originally, the strategic long-term development plan for the Russian Federation forest sector envisaged a tripling of sawnwood output by 2015.

The large sawmilling enterprises are expected to be constructed in the regions of the Northwest, the Urals, Eastern Siberia and the Far East, and will feature modern equipment that will improve the quality of sawnwood and allow for increased exports. Large sawmilling enterprises provide better situations for producing certified sawnwood and it would generally be more difficult for these firms to purchase illegally logged timber. The smaller sawmills are considered the main culprits for using illegally logged timber and their share of production is expected to fall.

North America subregion

North American sawn softwood consumption reached another all-time high in 2005 at 129.1 million m³, or an increase of 2.5 million m³ (up 2.0%) (table 5.3.1). The United States accounts for 85% of all North American sawn softwood consumption. Its demand is driven primarily by new residential construction – as determined by housing starts and interest rates – as well as repair and remodelling activity.

TABLE 5.3.1

Sawn softwood balance in North America, 2004-2005

(1,000 m³)

	2004	2005	Change %
Production	125 563	127 656	1.7
Imports	42 133	42 805	1.6
Exports	41 127	41 361	0.6
Net trade	-1 006	-1 444	…
Apparent consumption	126 569	129 101	2.0

Source: UNECE/FAO TIMBER database, 2006.

United States' housing starts have increased each year since 2000, from 1.57 million units in 2000 to 2.07 million units in 2005, a 500,000 unit increase (up 5% per year) (graph 5.3.1).

GRAPH 5.3.1

Housing starts in North America and Europe, 1999-2006

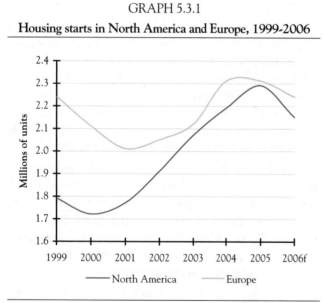

Note: f = forecast.

Source: Canadian Mortgage & Housing, National Association of Home Builders, Euroconstruct, 2006.

Demand levels for sawnwood were strong again in 2005, but the housing cycle peaked late in the year and new housing construction is forecast to decline in 2006 to below 1.95 million and to under 1.8 million units through 2007. Sawnwood consumption will be negatively impacted in 2006 and 2007, a significant concern for

producers in North America as well as exporters in Europe and from around the world. As a result, the boom years for sawnwood demand and prices since mid-2003 in North America appear to be over and prices have already quickly eroded, starting in the second quarter of 2006. The United States has only had two minor housing corrections since 1991, and although the current one is simply a timing issue, the potential impact of this downturn is possibly greater than anything experienced since the 1980s.

Record sawnwood prices were achieved in 2004 and the second highest average price levels were also recorded in 2005, a culmination of surging demand factors from low interest rates and GDP (graph 5.3.2). After mid-2006, North American markets are expected to be oversupplied with the prospect of falling prices.

GRAPH 5.3.2

Sawn softwood price trends in Canada, Europe and Japan, 2003-2006

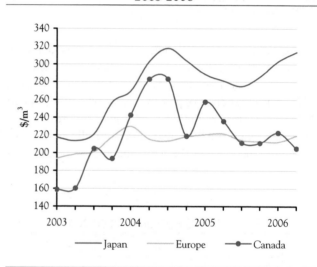

Note: Canadian prices for US market with same trends as US prices.

Source: WOOD MARKETS *Monthly Newsletter*, 2006.

In British Columbia (B.C.), Canada, the mountain pine beetle continues to spread and the province continues to step up its annual allowable cut, timber harvest and sawnwood production to salvage the timber. This epidemic, which is forecast to peak in 2008 in B.C., is expected to drastically change the B.C. sawmill industry when production peaks near 2010. At the same time, timber supply reductions being imposed by the Governments of Ontario and Quebec will have the opposite effects in those provinces starting in 2006.

North American sawnwood exports to offshore markets have remained at steady levels since 2000, unlike offshore imports. The key sawnwood exporters to the United States in 2005 were Canada and Europe. Canada remains the major sawn softwood supplier, providing about 31% of US consumption (34.2 million m³ in 2005), with an import sawnwood share of 86.5%. In 2005 European sawnwood imports into the United States rose to 5.4 million m³, including 0.7 million m³ of sawn hardwood. The bulk of European shipments were structurally graded dimension sawnwood and studs for use in home construction and repair and renovation applications. Other products include appearance grade knotty boards, industrial sawnwood and some glulam stock.

After reaching new highs in 2005, Europeans exporting sawnwood to the United States have become challenged by negative currency exchange rates against the dollar and are facing much higher domestic log costs.

Canada and the United States were close to negotiating a new seven-year deal in mid-2006 following four years of litigation as well as countervailing and anti-dumping duties on Canadian lumber. Canadian producers aimed at the following results from the negotiations:

- Certainty of seven years of US market access;
- Return of 80% on the duties paid to date (about US$ 4 billion); another 10% would go to the US Government and 10% to the US sawmilling industry;
- Acceptance of export taxes based on a sliding scale tied to average lumber price thresholds and/or quotas;
- Protection from decreased market share due to other countries' exports, e.g. from European countries;
- Freedom for B.C. to manage its timber pricing system to take into account the mountain pine beetle epidemic.

Despite an increasingly poor showing in North American Free Trade Agreement (NAFTA) and World Trade Organization (WTO) judgements, the new agreement would give the US industry significant protection from Canadian lumber exports in weak market conditions and also pay out $500 million in cash. Canadian producers in each region (i.e. the B.C. interior, the B.C. coast, and in each of the other nine provinces east of B.C have two options to choose from:

- Option "A" – a variable export tax (between 0% and 15%) based on the Random Lengths Framing Composite Lumber Price;
- Option "B" – a lower variable export charge (between 0% and 5%) plus a volume restraint, where both the rate and volume restraint (varying between a 30% to 34% Canadian import market share) vary according to the market price.

US producers hoped to achieve market stability, including maintenance of domestic market share and stable, presumably higher, prices.

Due to the many intricacies and stakeholder interests, this agreement was given approximately a 50/50 chance of being implemented following the second draft agreement completed on 1 July 2006.

The outlook from mid-2006 to mid-2007 is for declining North American sawnwood consumption as a result of lower housing starts, rising interest rates and inflationary fears. This net result will be reduced domestic sawnwood output and lower prices yielding a decline in offshore imports as a consequence of an oversupplied market.

5.3 References

British Columbia Ministry of Forests. 2006. Mountain Pine Beetle Action Plan Update, 2006. Available at: www.for.gov.bc.ca

EUWID No. 12 March 22 2006; No. 15 April 12 2006; No. 19 May 10 2006; No. 21 May 24 2006.

International WOOD MARKETS Group – Global Database. Available at: www.woodmarkets.com

Japan Lumber Reports, No. 433, April 28, 2006.

Ministry of Agriculture of Latvia, Department of Forest Resources. Latvian Forest Sector Trade Statistics. Available at: www.zm.gov.lv

OAO NIPIEIlesprom. 2006. Joint Stock Company Research and Design Institute on Economics, Production Management and Information of Forestry, Pulp & Paper and Woodworking Industry, Moscow.

Pöyry Forest Industry Consulting databases. Homepage: www.poyry.com

Timber Trade Journal, 15/22 April 2006.

Wood Focus. March 2006; May 2006.

WOOD MARKETS Monthly Report, August 2005a. B.C. Interior's "New" Future – Pine Beetle Creates Opportunities & Challenges. Available at: www.woodmarkets.com

WOOD MARKETS Monthly Report, August 2005b. European Lumber Capacity Soars. Available at: www.woodmarkets.com.

WOOD MARKETS Monthly Report, September 2005. US Softwood Lumber Imports. Available at: www.woodmarkets.com

WOOD MARKETS Monthly Report, November 2005. US Market Outlook 2006 – Prices Vulnerable to Oversupply. Available at: www.woodmarkets.com

WOOD MARKETS Monthly Report, December 2005a. Global Lumber Benchmarking 2004. Available at: www.woodmarkets.com.

WOOD MARKETS Monthly Report, December 2005b. Global Lumber Outlook, 2006. Available at: www.woodmarkets.com

WOOD MARKETS Monthly Report, February 2006. Global Competitiveness. Available at: www.woodmarkets.com

WOOD MARKETS Monthly Report, March 2006. Canada & US Lumber Statistics – 2004 vs. 2003. Available at: www.woodmarkets.com

WOOD MARKETS Monthly Report, April 2006. The Billion Board Foot Club: 2005 – 22 Companies = 25% of Global Lumber. Available at: www.woodmarkets.com

WOOD MARKETS Monthly Report, May 2006a. Global Housing Trends, 2006. Available at: www.woodmarkets.com

WOOD MARKETS Monthly Report, May 2006b. Global Outlook 2006/2007. Available at: www.woodmarkets.com

WOOD MARKETS Monthly Report, May 2006c. US Imported Wood Products Soar. Available at: www.woodmarkets.com

WOOD MARKETS Monthly Report, June 2006. US & Canadian Exports Decline in 2005. Available at: www.woodmarkets.com

WOOD MARKETS Monthly Report, June 2006a. Low U.S. Dollar Hits Home - Effects of Strong U.S. Market Also Waning. Available at: www.woodmarkets.com

WOOD MARKETS Monthly Report, June 2006b. Lumber Outlook for 2006/07 - Lower Demand + High Capacity = Weak Prices. Available at: www.woodmarkets.com

Additional statistical tables for this chapter may be found in the electronic annex on the UNECE Timber Committee and FAO European Forestry Commission website at: www.unece.org/trade/timber/mis/fpama.htm

Tables for this chapter include:

Sawn softwood apparent consumption, 2001-2005

Production of sawn softwood, 2001-2005

Exports and imports of sawn softwood, 2001-2005

Sawn softwood balance in UNECE, 2001-2005

Exports and imports of sawn softwood, 2001-2005

Major sawn softwood trade flows in UNECE region 2003-2004

Full statistics used in the *Forest Products Annual Market Review, 2005-2006* may be found in the UNECE/FAO TIMBER database at:

www.unece.org/trade/timber/mis/fp-stats.htm#Statistics

Chapter 6

Increasing prices and raw material shortages amidst the rising influence of China: Sawn hardwood markets, 2005-2006[31]

Highlights

- Consumption of sawn hardwood in the UNECE region decreased by 1.5% in 2005, mainly due to the continuing decline of furniture manufacturing in Europe and North America.

- Total UNECE region sawn hardwood production fell by 0.7% to 47.8 million m³ in 2005, despite a marginal increase in the Russian Federation, partly due to increased competition for raw materials from China.

- Overall European production was down last year, partly the result of a fall in demand for wood processing in the region, but also due to lower production in Romania following severe flooding.

- Governments in the United Kingdom, France, the Netherlands, Denmark, Germany, Belgium and Japan have made commitments to source "legal and sustainable" timber, including hardwood, in new public procurement policies, with other countries likely to follow.

- Hardwood flooring production and consumption in Europe increased considerably last year and marked a continuing trend in this sector, despite the ever-increasing threat of competitive imports from Asia.

- Oak continues to dominate hardwood consumption, with increasing demand across Europe and Asia; European and American white oak now represents over 50% of all European hardwood flooring production.

- Sawn hardwood production in North America decreased by 1.1% last year due to restructuring of several hardwood production and sales organizations, numerous sawmill closures, and increased importing of components and finished goods by domestic end-users, as well as rising log prices amidst competition for raw material from China.

- China's influence in all aspects of the global hardwood market is likely to develop further in 2006, putting pressure on roundwood supplies and raising sawn hardwood prices.

- Despite the slow development of the hardwood processing sector in Russia, exports of sawn hardwood increased significantly in 2005 and were mainly destined for China.

---

[31] By Rupert Oliver and Rod Wiles, both at Forest Industries Intelligence Ltd.

Secretariat introduction

The secretariat of the UNECE Timber Committee and the FAO European Forestry Commission is grateful to have Messrs. Roderick Wiles[32] and Rupert Oliver[33], both of Forest Industries Intelligence Limited as co-authors in this chapter of the *Forest Products Annual Market Review*. They have previously been authors and contributors, and have spoken at the Timber Committee Market Discussions. They are also members of the UNECE/FAO Team of Specialists on Forest Products Markets and Marketing.

This chapter is possible thanks to the support of Mr. David Venables, European Director, American Hardwood Export Council (AHEC), London, UK. The continuing collaboration between AHEC and the secretariat are mutually rewarding, as shown by, *inter alia*, this chapter's analysis, which is also useful for AHEC. Mr. Venables was also a contributor and reviewer of the chapter, and a member of the Team of Specialists and of the UNECE/FAO Forest Communicators Network. He has also spoken at the Timber Committee Market Discussions.

6.1   Introduction

As with the previous year, 2005 saw increased globalization in the hardwood industry together with the increasing influence of China in all aspects of the global trade in hardwood products, neither of which is expected to change through 2006. In addition, higher fuel, transport and energy costs throughout the world have contributed to rising prices for all wood products. While hardwood secondary processors have continued to chase cheap labour around the world, and investment and trading in the sector have become increasingly geographically flexible, the impact of Chinese capacity building has been felt even more widely.

Furthermore, exports from China and neighbouring countries, such as Vietnam have begun to include significant quantities of hardwood products other than furniture, which is putting pressure on all industry subsectors across the UNECE region. This has had an even greater impact on the consumption of sawn hardwoods, or at least secondary processing, which has continued to shift towards the East and away from the former EU-15 region, and from North America to Asia.

In addition, the shift in consumption has begun to lead to a shift in production in the region as a whole, which has also moved towards the East, reflecting to decreases in production in all subregions, except in the eastern Europe, Caucasus and Central Asia (EECCA) subregion[34], where it grew by 2.3% to 3.7 million m³.

The UNECE region's hardwood resource is increasingly important to the world's marketplace, with temperate hardwood species in high demand through last year and the first half of 2006 in the region. The emphasis is still on oak (European and American white), which remains fashion throughout the region. However, American red oak continues to face weak demand in the US domestic market; dramatic price falls were seen well into last year and remain low in 2006. As a direct reflection of the importance of oak, just over 50% of all European hardwood flooring is manufactured with oak (European and American white oak), while the use of beech – Europe's main hardwood species – has dwindled further (graph 6.1.1).

GRAPH 6.1.1

European hardwood flooring species, 2005

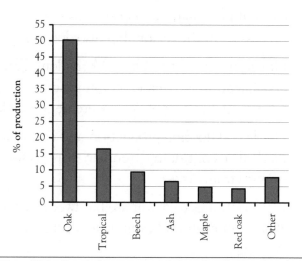

Note: "Other" includes species with less than 3% market share: cherry, birch, eucalyptus, acacia, pine and chestnut.
Source: European Federation of the Parquet Industry, 2006.

Consumption of sawn hardwood fell in the UNECE region in 2005, mainly due to a 3.0% drop in North America (graph 6.1.2). Despite the year-on-year increase in hardwood flooring production in Europe, the subregion's furniture industries have been hit hard by competitive imports from Asia, leading to further rationalization within the sector and offshore manufacturing. In North America, the housing boom has

[32] Mr. Roderick Wiles, Emerging Markets Office, Forest Industries Intelligence Limited, Milehouse Cottage, Chittlehampton, Umberleigh, Devon, EX37 9RD, UK, tel. and fax: +44 1769 540 092, e-mail: rod@sustainablewood.com, www.sustainablewood.com

[33] Mr. Rupert Oliver, Head Office, Forest Industries Intelligence Limited, 19 Raikeswood Drive, Skipton, North Yorkshire, BD23 1NA, UK, tel. and fax: +44 1756 796 992, e-mail: Rupert@sustainablewood.com, www.sustainablewood.com

[34] The name "Eastern European, Caucasus and Central Asia" is a new UNECE term introduced this year in place of the Commonwealth of Independent States (CIS). It is comprised of the same 12 countries (see annex for list of countries).

now all but ended, and both sawn hardwood production and imports have begun to slow. However, sawn hardwood usage in the building sector has taken up a certain amount of the slack in production, and architects and other specifiers are turning towards hardwood as a fashionable and sustainable building and interior finishing material. With this in mind, numerous promotional campaigns across the UNECE region, such as the American Hardwood Export Council, have shifted their focus towards the specifying sector and have already achieved quantifiable results.

6.2   Europe subregion

European sawn hardwood production fell 0.8% last year, partly because of lower output by the main EU producers, France and Germany, but also a drop in production in Romania due to poor harvesting conditions explained below (table 6.2.1). Turkey, Europe's largest sawn hardwood producer, increased production to just under 2.7 million m³. While this volume is significant, much of the sawn hardwood produced in Turkey is from low-grade domestic forests, as well as small-dimension poplar plantation logs. Almost all of the sawnwood is consumed domestically, with the small volume exported, having little impact on overall trade in the UNECE region.

Compared with 2004, German production decreased marginally in 2005, partly the result of a lack of sawlogs for the domestic sawmilling industry as logs were diverted to Asian markets, as well as issues on forest management and the quality of logs. Germany's sawmilling industry has seen much rationalization in recent years, but this may be changing as new mills open to supply the rising demand for sawn beech (especially steamed) in the US and Middle East markets. In France, the excess log supply after the December 1999 storms is no longer an issue, and supply and demand for sawn hardwood are beginning to even out. Nevertheless, due to the storms, the French industry is suffering from a lack of good quality raw material and French sawmillers rely heavily on domestic demand for sawnwood from furniture manufacturers, which has been steadily declining. After a number of years of steady decline, the changes in Germany and France helped European beech prices to level off towards the end of 2005 and even to rise in the first quarter of 2006 (graph 6.2.1).

GRAPH 6.1.2

Consumption of sawn hardwood in the UNECE region, 2001-2005

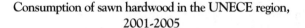
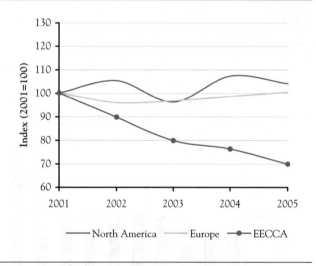

Source: UNECE/FAO TIMBER database, 2006.

TABLE 6.2.1

Production of sawn hardwood in Europe, 2001-2005

(1,000 m³)

	2001	2002	2003	2004	2005	Change 2004 to 2005 Volume	%
Europe	15 602	15 173	15 351	16 068	15 940	-129	-0.8
of which:							
Turkey	2 645	2 564	2 629	2 590	2 658	68	2.6
France	2 804	2 329	2 099	2 057	2 000	-57	-2.8
Romania	1 254	1 432	1 550	1 780	1 737	-43	-2.4
Germany	1 242	1 140	1 071	1 089	1 083	-6	-0.6
Latvia	645	848	868	1 108	1 002	-106	-9.6
Spain	1 055	843	920	1 000	1 000	0	0.0
EU-25	10 291	9 815	9 737	9 858	9 701	-158	-1.6

Source: UNECE/FAO TIMBER database, 2006.

GRAPH 6.2.1

German and French beech sawnwood prices, 2002-2006

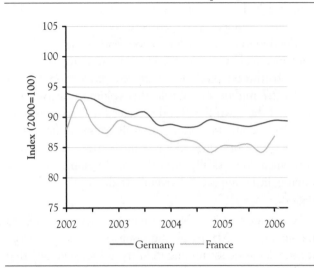

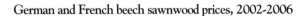

Sources: Statistischen Bundesamt Preise, Germany, 2006 and Centre de l´Économie du Bois, France, 2006.

TABLE 6.2.2

Sawn hardwood balance in Europe, 2004-2005

(1,000 m³)

	2004	2005	Change %
Production	16 068	15 940	-0.8
Imports	8 308	8 242	-0.8
Exports	5 700	5 165	-9.4
Net trade	-2 608	-3 077	...
Apparent consumption	18 677	19 017	1.8
of which: EU25			
Production	9 858	9 701	-1.6
Imports	7 825	7 774	-0.7
Exports	3 756	3 443	-8.3
Net trade	-4 069	-4 331	...
Apparent consumption	13 927	14 031	0.7

Source: UNECE/FAO TIMBER database, 2006.

Exports of rough sawn hardwood from the Europe subregion fell by 1.5% last year, although by only 0.1% in the EU-25 (table 6.2.2). A significant reduction in the production and shipments of sawn hardwood from Romania was the main cause, which followed severe flooding in parts of the country during the third and fourth quarters of 2005. Access to forests was limited during that time and, in some cases, less than half the annual allowable cut was harvested.

In contrast to Romania, German exports rose significantly in 2005, partly due to the rising interest in beech in international markets and to higher demand for beech and oak in neighbouring Poland. Croatia's exports of sawn hardwood in 2005 also rose, spurred on by the ever-increasing global demand for oak.

Total apparent consumption of sawn hardwood in all of Europe has remained reasonably steady since 2001 and rose marginally in 2005. However, in the EU-25, there has been a gradually falling trend (albeit rising in 2005) due to the transfer of processing eastwards. At the same time, imports of semi-finished and component products into the EU have increased. One of the key market drivers in Europe has been hardwood flooring production, which grew substantially in 2005 and was partly responsible for reversing the decline in consumption (graph 6.2.2). Another has been the relative strength of the European housing sector despite overall poor economic performance. Coupled with a rising interest in specifying hardwood as a building and interior finishing material, these developments have offset some of the decline in the need for hardwood by the shrinking furniture sector.

GRAPH 6.2.2

European hardwood flooring production, 1996-2005

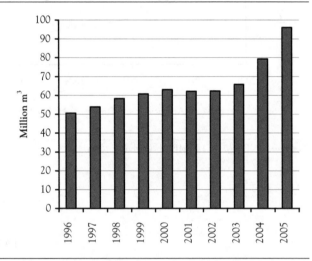

Source: European Federation of the Parquet Industry, 2006

6.3 North America subregion

The US accounts for 55% of UNECE region production. Since its peak of 31 million m³ in 2000, total North American sawn hardwood production has oscillated between 29.5 million m³ and 26.7 million m³. In 2005, production dropped by 1.1% overall from 2004 levels, and since Canadian production only accounted for 6.1% of the total, much of which is based on logs and green or unsorted sawnwood from the US, the main fall in production occurred in the US (table 6.3.1). Significant restructuring of several hardwood production and sales organizations, numerous sawmill closures, and increased importing of components and finished goods by domestic end-users were among the reasons for lower domestic production. In addition, higher stumpage prices and lower availability of hardwood logs for the domestic sawmilling industry, caused by increased raw material demand from China, have been major influencing factors.

TABLE 6.3.1

Sawn hardwood balance in North America, 2004-2005
(1,000 m³)

	2004	2005	Change %
Production	28 456	28 149	-1.1
Imports	4 853	4 387	-9.6
Exports	4 758	4 833	1.6
Net trade	-95	445	…
Apparent consumption	28 551	27 704	-3.0

Source: UNECE/FAO TIMBER database, 2006.

Sawn hardwood exports from the United States rose by 10.3% in 2004 to 3.4 million m³, mainly stimulated by heavy demand in China (much of which is for the manufacturing of products for the US market). In 2005, US exports remained near this record level, as a slight drop in demand from European (and Middle Eastern) buyers, was balanced by growing exports to China, Southeast Asia and Mexico. While sawnwood exports were steady 2005, domestic sawnwood production was dropped, hence the relative importance of export markets increased. Roughly 12.3% of US sawn hardwood produced in 2005 was sold into export markets, up from an estimated 7.5% in 1998.

Despite widespread concerns about China reducing its purchases in 2005, exports of nearly every species to China were at or above 2004 levels, including a 17% jump in shipments of red oak, the species that has been generating the most concern. The combined increase in shipments to China and Mexico (65,000 m3) easily offset reduced exports to Canada (-49,500 m³). In addition to China and Mexico, Viet Nam and the UK were the only markets to increase purchases of American sawn hardwood by more than 10,000 m³, while at the opposite end of the spectrum, shipments to Taiwan Province of China (PoC), Italy, Japan, Spain and Thailand all fell by more than 10,000 m³, with shipments to Taiwan PoC down by nearly 50%.

The enormous growth in the Chinese market, while providing a much needed boost for US hardwood exports, has caused a diversion away from traditional end-user markets. With the European furniture sector under pressure from imports from China, as well as Viet Nam and other Southeast Asian producers, demand for US sawn hardwood in the subregion has begun to show signs of weakening. Despite this, the EU still remains as the United States' highest value export destination, taking

32% of the value of US sawn hardwood exports in 2005, compared to 17.7% to China, Hong Kong S.A.R. and Taiwan PoC. The difference in the value of these two major markets for US sawn hardwood can be explained by the difference in how the wood is being used. While the emphasis in the EU is on the higher value interior joinery sector, moving away from furniture, the emphasis in China is still very much on furniture, flooring and components. This situation is also changing, however, as the Chinese domestic market for wood products is also developing and the higher value interiors sector is gaining in importance.

FIGURE 6.3.1

Alder bedroom furniture

Source: American Hardwood Export Council, 2006.

At the same time as production of sawn hardwoods in North America fell in 2005, imports also dropped by 10%, having risen significantly in 2004. However, this fall was entirely accounted for by Canada, while US imports rose by 8%. Imports of tropical sawn hardwood, principally South American, and beech from Germany have played an increasingly significant role in the US in recent years, benefiting from the housing boom, as well as developing fashions for darker species. Last year, the US imported 778,000 m³ of sawn hardwood, excluding those from Canada, a rise of 16.0% against 2004. The principal supplier was Brazil, with imports also rising from other Latin American and Asian suppliers.

6.4 EECCA subregion

In 2005, sawn hardwood production in the EECCA region was 3.7 million m³, an increase of 2.3% on 2004, or 7.8% of production in the UNECE region as a whole (table 6.4.1). The increase probably occurred entirely in the Russian Federation, despite inadequacies in the data available for the other major hardwood producers, Belarus and Ukraine.

TABLE 6.4.1

Sawn hardwood balance in EECCA, 2004-2005

(1,000 m³)

	2004	2005	Change %
Production	3 638	3 721	2.3
Imports	140	113	-19.2
Exports	986	1 279	29.8
Net trade	846	1 166	37.9
Apparent consumption	2 793	2 555	-8.5

Source: UNECE/FAO TIMBER database, 2006.

In the past few years, against the background of the huge timber resources in Russia, prospective investors have announced many projects in sawn timber production, but few have been realized. To date, there have been only a few projects, mainly in northwest Russia and eastern Siberia, with comparatively small production capacities and focused mainly on softwood. Efforts have been made to boost wood processing in Russia, and President Putin has personally asked for far-reaching measures to improve the sector. In 2005, for example, tax cuts were granted for imports of woodworking machinery. In addition to the modernization of the forest and timber industry, structural improvements, the introduction of international standards and the creation of improved conditions for investors, the rapid introduction of the new Forestry Act will be of decisive importance for the development of this branch. The industry lags well behind the rest of the UNECE region in terms of wood processing capacity, and with increasing Chinese demand for logs just across the border, the incentives for increased sawn hardwood processing are not yet that significant. The introduction of an export tariff on logs in 2005 does seem to have had an impact. Value-added exports and exports of sawn hardwood did rise in 2005 to just under 1.3 million m³, which marks an increase of 30%, most of which was exported to the Chinese market.

Imports of sawn hardwoods into the EECCA subregion remained low in 2005, at only 113,000 m³. Further Russian and overall EECCA demand for imported hardwoods lacks consistency due to limited secondary processing capacity and a lack of organization in end-user sectors.

6.5 The 2006 sawn hardwood market

The market for sawn hardwood in the UNECE region in the latter stages of 2005 gives a clear indication of what has been happening in 2006. For example, China's role in the global sawn hardwood market is becoming even more significant, with rising domestic consumption and re-export production producing a significant demand for hardwood logs and sawnwood. It is estimated that 80% of wood products produced in China are consumed domestically and, while furniture is the main product, the interiors and flooring sectors are now beginning to take off in earnest. Together with production for re-export, the need for wood in the Chinese market has forced up sawn hardwood prices across the globe, as supplies have been put under increased pressure. This is particularly relevant for European and American white oak, which has seen 3 to 5% annual price increases for the past three years or so and is likely to increase by as much as 10% through 2006 (graph 6.5.1). This has given a much-needed boost to European and American sawn hardwood producers, but has also created a vacuum in oak log supply to European and American sawmills, as well as traditional oak-consuming markets. Together with rising demand, rising fuel prices, and therefore, production and shipping costs, have also contributed to the overall price increases seen in sawn hardwoods. The situation for red oak, however, remains uncertain through 2006, although the status of supply and demand may now be showing signs of levelling out.

FIGURE 6.5.1

Soft maple kitchen panelling

Source: American Hardwood Export Council, 2006.

Other significant factors in the UNECE sawn hardwood markets in 2006 include the status of the US housing market. Through 2004 and much of last year, demand for sawn hardwood, both domestically produced and imported, rose considerably, driven by unprecedented growth in the housing and general construction sectors. With 95% of new homes in the US constructed from wood, any change in this sector will have a profound impact on overall demand for wood products. In 2006, however, US housing starts have levelled-off or even fallen, while interest rates have begun to rise. The US housing boom is now at an end, which will mean that US sawn hardwood suppliers will be forced to rely more heavily on export markets.

GRAPH 6.5.1

United States sawn hardwood prices, 2002-2006

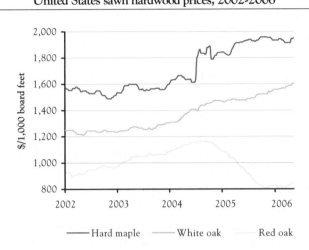

Note: 1,000 board feet equal 4.5 m³.
Source: *Hardwood Review,* 2006.

GRAPH 6.5.2

Sawn hardwood trade flows, 2000-2004

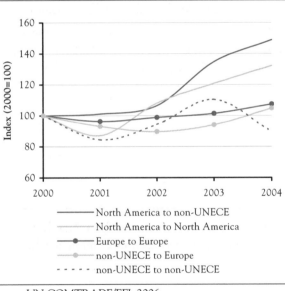

Sources: UN COMTRADE/EFI, 2006.

Data for sawn hardwood trade flows in the UNECE region are not yet available for 2005 when this chapter was written, but some of the trends shown below are expected to have continued (graph 6.5.2). The most positive trend was in non-UNECE to non-UNECE markets, which is dominated by tropical sawn hardwood suppliers shipping to markets such as China. It is possible, however, that in 2005 this curve began to level off, as tropical hardwood supplies became increasingly limited and as China started to import far greater volumes of sawn hardwood from Russia. In Europe, demand from both European suppliers and non-UNECE suppliers has been steadily increasing. This trend may have slowed marginally in 2005, but has been supported mainly by the

fashion for oak and also the increasing trend towards dark, tropical species in products such as flooring.

Forest certification and environmental procurement policies are two other factors becoming more important for the marketing of temperate sawn hardwoods during 2006 (see also policy chapter 2). Until recently, the direct impact of these issues was fairly limited for temperate sawn hardwoods. Consumers' environmental concerns have tended to focus on tropical rather than on temperate hardwoods. With little interest from final consumers and the lack of any price premium, the incentive for temperate hardwood producers to adopt certification has generally been limited. Furthermore, the barriers to entry into the certified wood products markets tend to be high for temperate hardwoods because a significant proportion derives from smaller non-industrial forest owners in North America and Europe. The chain of custody is relatively complex and the unit costs of certification tend to be higher than for large industrial and state forest owners (see also certified forest products chapter 9).

However, the market situation has changed in the last 18 months for two reasons. First, the significant increase in the area of FSC certified state forests in eastern Europe and of PEFC-certified forests in France and Germany in the last five years has finally begun to filter through into the sawn hardwood market. As availability of certified logs has increased, European hardwood trading companies have been pursuing chain of custody certification and have begun to actively market certified wood products to their customers. Many suppliers of European sawn hardwood are now able to offer these products as standard without requiring a price premium, which is encouraging greater market interest.

FIGURE 6.5.2

Aspen used in sauna

Source: American Hardwood Export Council, 2006.

Second, international concern about illegal logging is now encouraging wider uptake of public sector procurement policies (see also policy chapter 2). Far-reaching commitments to sourcing "legal and sustainable" timber in the public sector have been made by Governments in the UK, France, the Netherlands, Denmark, Germany, Belgium and Japan. These Governments are now developing technical standards and applying procedures to ensure more effective implementation; other countries are likely to follow. As these procedures have yet to be fully implemented in most countries, their real market impact is still unsure. It seems certain, nevertheless, that temperate hardwood suppliers will come under increasing pressure to provide reliable assurances of sustainable management.

6.6   References

American Forest & Paper Association, www.afandpa.org

American Hardwood Export Council, www.ahec-europe.org

Centre de l'Économie du Bois. 2006. Paris, France.

Eurostat, europa.eu.int/comm/eurostat

Euwid, euwid-wood-products.com

Federation of the European Parquet Industry, www.parquet.net

Fédération Nationale du Bois, www.fnbois.com

Forest Industries Intelligence Limited, www.sustainablewood.com

French Timber, www.frenchtimber.com

Gesamtverband Deutscher Holzhandel, www.holzhandel.de

Hardwood Review Export, www.hardwoodreview.com

Statistisches Bundesamt Preise. 2006. Germany. Available at: www.destatis.de

Sustainable Forestry Initiative, www.afandpa.org/Content/NavigationMenu/Environment_and_Recycling/SFI/SFI.htm

UNECE. 2006. Forest and timber sector expresses concern for economic viability, illegal logging, and the public image of wood: Markets for forest products continue at record levels. Note for the Press, 4 October. Available at: www.unece.org/trade/timber/press.htm

UNECE/FAO TIMBER database, www.unece.org/trade/timber/mis/fp-stats.htm

UNECE Timber Committee market forecasts, www.unece.org/trade/timber/mis/forecasts.htm

United States Bureau of the Census, www.census.gov

United States Department of Agriculture, Foreign Agriculture Service, www.fas.usda.gov

---

Additional statistical tables for this chapter may be found in the electronic annex on the UNECE Timber Committee and FAO European Forestry Commission website at: www.unece.org/trade/timber/mis/fpama.htm

Tables for this chapter include:

Sawn hardwood apparent consumption, 2001-2005

Production of sawn hardwood, 2001-2005

Exports and imports of sawn hardwood (volume), 2001-2005

Sawn hardwood balance in UNECE, 2001-2005

Exports and imports of sawn hardwood (value), 2001-2005

Major sawn softwood trade flows in UNECE region 2003-2004

Full statistics used in the *Forest Products Annual Market Review, 2005-2006* may be found in the UNECE/FAO TIMBER database at:

www.unece.org/trade/timber/mis/fp-stats.htm#Statistics

Chapter 7
Panel industry squeezed by energy costs, fibre supply and globalization: Wood-based panels markets, 2005-2006[35]

Highlights

- Favourable developments in the main demand markets in residential construction and associated demand for cabinetry and furniture had a positive effect on the wood-based panel industry in 2005 throughout the UNECE region.

- Although production and consumption are increasing, producers express mitigated optimism due to soaring production costs.

- The European panel industry is becoming increasingly export oriented, whereas the increase in Russian panel production was used domestically in 2005.

- The European panel industry, confronted with wood supply problems due to increasing competition with the biomass energy sector, is responding through a Renewable Energy Sources Working Group that provided their input to the EU Biomass Action Plan in 2005.

- North American production of particle board declined as a result of plant closings attributed to increased competition for wood supplies.

- Record housing starts in the United States drove the demand for structural panels to new highs.

- North American OSB production is expected to increase by 16% between 2006 and 2008, but a forecasted demand downturn could weaken prices and profits.

- In 2006, declining housing starts in North America have structural panel manufacturers looking to expand demand in the non-residential and industrial market segments.

- High United States furniture imports, especially from China, have undermined demand for particle board and MDF within the domestic furniture industry, and panel manufacturers are reducing production.

- The US applied an 8% import tariff on Brazilian plywood imports in mid-2005; however, Brazil exported increasing volumes of plywood and other panel products to the United States and Europe.

- China, the world's largest plywood exporter, does not yet have the required grade stamp to allow North American structural applications; however, imports are used for other purposes.

---

[35] By Dr. Ivan Eastin, University of Washington, Ms. Bénédicte Hendrickx, European Panel Federation, and Dr. Nikolai Burdin, OAO NIPIEIlesprom.

Secretariat introduction

This chapter benefits from close cooperation with three regional experts in the panel sector and their contributors. We sincerely appreciate the continued collaboration for the second year of Dr. Ivan Eastin,[36] Director, Center for International Trade in Forest Products, University of Washington, who coordinated the production of this chapter, and produced the North American analysis.

Ms. Bénédicte Hendrickx,[37] Economic Advisor, European Panel Federation (EPF), contributed the European analysis. She is a new member of the UNECE/FAO Team of Specialists on Forest Products Markets (EPF) and we look forward to working together. Her analysis is based on the recently published EPF *Annual Report 2006*.

We once again appreciate the analysis by Dr. Nikolai Burdin,[38] Director, OAO NIPIEIlesprom, Moscow, who wrote the section on Russian panel markets. Dr. Burdin is former Chairman of both the Timber Committee and the FAO/UNECE Working Party on Forest Economics and Statistics, a member of the Team of Specialists and a frequent participant in the annual Timber Committee Market Discussions. He is also the statistical correspondent for Russia. We look forward to continued cooperative efforts with all of these authors and their institutions.

7.1 Introduction

Consumption rose in each subregion of the UNECE region in 2005 for wood-based panels, particle board, medium density fibreboard (MDF), plywood and oriented strand board (OSB) (graph 7.1.1). Demand for panels continued rising upwards in the Eastern Europe, Caucasus and Central Asia subregion[39] (EECCA), and although total panel consumption jumped by over 17%, to reach 10.5 million m³, this was lower than consumption in Europe and North America, which was over 68 million

m³ in each subregion. Nevertheless, each subregion posted record high consumption in 2005.

GRAPH 7.1.1

Apparent consumption of wood-based panels in UNECE region, 2001-2005

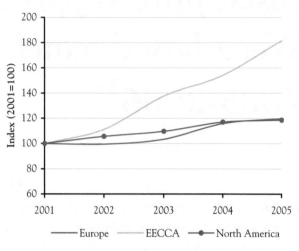

Source: UNECE/FAO TIMBER database, 2006.

GRAPH 7.1.2

Wood-based panels trade flows, 2000-2004

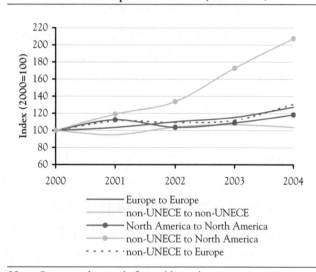

Note: Corresponding trade flow table in electronic annex.
Source: UN COMTRADE/EFI, 2006.

Panels trade was active in the UNECE region, with imports continuing to exceed exports. Panels are the only primary product for which the UNECE region is a net importer. North America, and particularly the United States, is rapidly increasing offshore imports from South America (e.g. Brazil), Asia (e.g. China) and other non-UNECE region countries (graph 7.1.2). European exports, including trade within the subregion, were at record levels in 2005 of 31.1 million m³. In North America, Canada posted new highs in panel exports,

---

[36] Dr. Ivan Eastin, Professor and Director, Center for International Trade in Forest Products, University of Washington, US, tel: +1 306 543 1918, fax +1 206 685 3091, e-mail: eastin@u.washington.edu, www.cintrafor.org.

[37] Ms. Bénédicte Hendrickx, Economic Adviser, European Panel Federation, Allée Hof-ter-Vleest 5, Box 5, B-1070 Brussels, Belgium, tel: +32 2 556 25 89, fax +32 2 556 25 94, e-mail: benedicte.hendrickx@europanels.org, www.europanels.org.

[38] Dr. Nikolai Burdin, Director, OAO NIPIEIlesprom, Klinskaya ul. 8, RU-125889 Moscow, Russian Federation, tel: +7 095 456 1303, fax +7 095 456 5390, e-mail: nipi@dialup.ptt.ru.

[39] The name "Eastern Europe, Caucasus and Central Asia" is a new UNECE term introduced this year in place of the Commonwealth of Independent States (CIS). It is comprised of the same 12 countries (see annex for list of countries).

predominantly to feed the US residential construction demand, while US exports have declined from their peak in 1992, a trend similar to other US primary product exports.

7.2 Europe subregion

The production of wood-based panels continued to grow in 2005, albeit at a slightly lower pace than in 2004 (table 7.2.1). Demand from the main outlet markets was temporarily lower during the first half of the year but picked up during the third quarter. The production of kitchen furniture accelerated in the course of 2005 in some countries, such as Portugal, Spain and some newer EU Member States. Production of office and shop furniture, which has been down for a long time, also picked up in the second half of 2005. The European construction industry flourished in 2005. Residential construction, including associated demand for furniture, mouldings, flooring and cabinetry, continued to be the main source of panel demand, although the strongest growth rates were recorded for civil engineering projects. These favourable developments in the main demand markets had a positive effect on wood-based panel consumption.

TABLE 7.2.1

Wood-based panels balance in Europe, 2004-2005

(1,000 m³)

	2004	2005	Change %
Production	66 955	69 411	3.7
Imports	29 686	29 701	0.1
Exports	30 856	31 100	0.8
Net trade	1 170	1 399	19.5
Apparent consumption	65 785	68 012	3.4
of which: EU25			
Production	59 757	61 119	2.3
Imports	26 242	25 686	-2.1
Exports	28 184	28 345	0.6
Net trade	1 942	2 659	36.9
Apparent consumption	57 816	58 460	1.1

Source: UNECE/FAO TIMBER database, 2006.

Although production and consumption of wood-based panels in Europe has been improving, soaring production costs mitigate optimism. The woodworking industries are directly affected by the oil price hike, which raised energy costs, as well as resin and transport costs. Moreover, higher oil prices have been stimulating biomass energy use (see chapter 9). Consequently, competition for wood as a raw material has been strong. Wood prices increased strongly and some countries' panel manufacturers were even affected by wood availability problems and associated continued increases in raw material costs (graph 7.2.1).

GRAPH 7.2.1

European panel manufacturers wood costs, 2002-2006

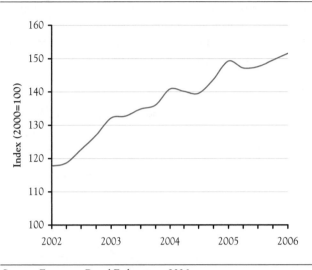

Source: European Panel Federation, 2006.

Despite a subdued second quarter, panel production in Europe attained a new record of 69.4 million m³. Particle board consumption gained momentum again due to improved demand from both the construction and the furniture sector. Three of Europe's largest particle board consuming countries registered a remarkable increase in demand, which pushed up overall European consumption. During the last months of 2005, a downward stock movement was observed. Furthermore, particle board trade increased sharply, especially within the EU and neighbouring countries. For 2006 and 2007 some new capacity expansions are under way to allow the European panel industry to meet increasing demand within the subregion. On the other hand, it remains a question whether wood availability will continue to cause supply problems. During 2005, the market did not accept price increases (graph 7.2.2); however, the manufacturers are concerned about continuous strong cost increases.

2005 was a good year for the MDF industry in Europe: production grew at a high pace to 13.3 million m³, beating the previous record by 7%. Profitability decreased, however, with higher energy and raw material costs as well as price instability. European demand for MDF accelerated further in 2005. In Europe, total consumption of MDF reached 12 million m³, an increase of 7.6%. Exports to North America and Asia decreased due to the unfavourable euro-to-dollar exchange rate.

During 2005, OSB production attained the level of 3 million m³. Compared to 2004, production growth reached 8%. In Europe, commercial production has been growing strongly since it began in 1994 (graph 7.2.3); exports in particular gained momentum. More than 75%

of the total European OSB production is traded mainly within Europe. Demand comes first from western European countries, absorbing 64% of total exports, whereas 13% of total European OSB exports were purchased by eastern European countries. OSB is used in diverse construction applications, residential and non-residential, as well as in civil engineering projects. Due to the improving domestic and foreign consumption, demand pulled down the stock levels by 5%.

GRAPH 7.2.2

European OSB, MDF and particle board prices, 2002-2006

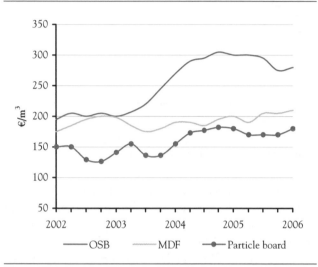

Notes: OSB/3 18mm, MDF standard 16-19mm, particle board V100 PF 19mm.
Source: EUWID Wood Products and Panels, 2006.

GRAPH 7.2.3

European OSB production and exports, 1995-2005

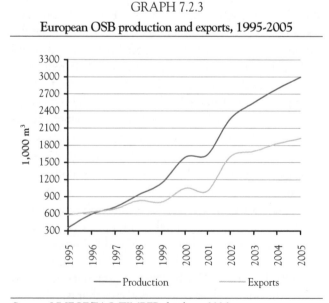

Source: UNECE/FAO TIMBER database, 2006.

Plywood production stagnated in 2005 due to increased activity in the EECCA subregion and increasing European imports. Production slow-downs were greatest in western European countries as the market for tropical plywood continued to shrink. Considerably more hardwood plywood was put on the market. Here the strong performance of the Baltic States was significant. A marked fall-back is projected for 2006. Plywood consumption also stagnated. European production was heterogeneous: some larger western producers such as Finland cut production and some eastern producers such as Poland slightly increased their production.

FIGURE 7.2.1

Plywood in residential construction

Source: European Federation of the Plywood Industry, 2006.

The main countries of origin of extra-EU plywood imports were Brazil, Russia, China, Indonesia, Malaysia and Chile. The European plywood manufacturers were therefore facing strong competitive pressure. In particular, Chinese imports were increasing most aggressively, registering a growth rate of more than 100%. Approximately 10% of EU consumption of 6.9 million m³ was supplied by China in 2005 (634,000 m³). Since the European Commission imposed anti-dumping measures for Chinese okoumé plywood in November 2004, many other tropical species as well as Chinese broadleaved plywood have been entering the EU.

7.3 EECCA subregion (focussing on Russia)

Wood-based panels, including plywood, particle board and fibreboard occupy an important place in the forest sector of EECCA. Over recent years the growth rates of panel products have been higher than other primary wood products (table 7.3.1).

TABLE 7.3.1

Wood-based panels balance in EECCA, 2004-2005

(1,000 m³)

	2004	2005	Change %
Production	9 426	10 483	11.2
Imports	3 234	3 385	4.7
Exports	3 304	2 882	-12.8
Net trade	70	-502	...
Apparent consumption	9 356	10 986	17.4

Source: UNECE/FAO TIMBER database, 2006.

From 2000 to 2005 in the Russian Federation, production of plywood increased by 71.9%, particle board by 73.3% and fibreboard by 42.7%. In 2006, plywood production is expected to grow by 7% against 2005, particle board by 11.0%, and fibreboard by 26%.

In 2005 the production increases in Russia were consumed domestically. Panels are mainly used for construction and furniture production. In recent years new capacities for production of wood-based panels have been commissioned in different regions of the country. For example, the largest in Russia forest industry complex is being constructed in the town of Sharia in the Kostroma Region, for production of particle board, MDF and OSB. Its combined capacity is planned for 1.2 million m³ per year.

In Russia plywood ranks first among all types of wood-based panels in export volumes, which accounted for 1.5 million m³ in 2005, or 60% of the total plywood output. In 2005, the main export destinations for plywood were the United States (388,200 m³), Egypt (129,400 m³) and Germany (112,400 m³). Imports of plywood are insignificant at only 42,000 m³.

In contrast to plywood, particle board imports at 580,000 m³ were greater than exports at 241,000 m³. Particle board is exported mainly to other EECCA countries, Kazakhstan and Uzbekistan, and imported from Germany, Poland and Austria.

Fibreboard was also exported mainly to EECCA countries, with an export share of 24% of production. In 2005, Russian imports of fibreboard totalled 493,000 m³ from Germany, Poland, China and Ireland.

7.4 North America subregion

Wood-based panel markets stagnated in 2005 with production declining slightly for the first time in five years and imports increasing by almost 5% (table 7.4.1). As a result, panel consumption increased slightly from 67.5 to 68.5 million m³. Most of the production decline can be attributed to declines in the production of plywood and particle board. Particle board prices, which began dropping in mid-2004, continued dropping through the

first half of 2005 before rallying slightly during the second half of 2005. US particle board production decreased from 7.6 to 6.5 million m³ between 2004 and 2005, while Canadian particle board production declined from 2.9 to 2.7 million m³ over the same period. The closure of two particle board mills in the United States and another three mills in Canada sent prices spiralling higher in the beginning of 2006 (graph 7.4.1). As a result of these mill closures, North American particle board production declined by 12.4% to 9.2 million m³. In addition, concerns about future raw material shortages (particularly given the strong competition with biomass energy generation in Canada) and the strengthening Canadian dollar further fuelled the price surge during the first half of 2006.

TABLE 7.4.1

Wood-based panels balance in North America, 2004-2005

(1,000 m³)

	2004	2005	Change %
Production	61 131	61 014	-0.2
Imports	22 688	23 724	4.6
Exports	16 323	16 290	-0.2
Net trade	-6 366	-7 434	...
Apparent consumption	67 497	68 448	1.4

Source: UNECE/FAO TIMBER database, 2006.

Particle board imports into North America decreased by 5.0% in 2005, to a level of 1.6 million m³. While US imports from Canada remained relatively stable, the Canadian share of the US market dropped from 98% in 2001 to just under 91% in 2005. US imports of particle board from Germany, France and Brazil have increased rapidly, with their aggregate market share increasing from 0.6% to 5.0% between 2001 and 2005.

GRAPH 7.4.1

US particle board prices, 2000-2006

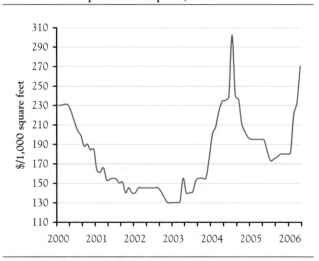

Source: Random Lengths Yardstick, 2006.

MDF prices in North America weakened slightly throughout 2005, with eastern MDF prices dropping about 4% while western MDF prices fell almost 12%. However, concern about particle board shortages in early 2006 led some buyers to substitute MDF in some specialty applications and helped restore MDF prices to their early 2005 price levels. Between 2004 and 2005, North American production of MDF increased from 5.1 to 5.3 million m³ with approximately 70% of North American MDF production in the US. US production of MDF increased slightly from 3.6 to 3.7 million m³, while Canadian production increased from 1.5 to 1.6 million m³. Increasing imports of furniture from China and Viet Nam have undermined the demand for domestically produced MDF within the furniture industry.

North American imports of MDF totalled 1.7 million m³ in 2005, approximately one-third of the volume of domestic MDF production. MDF imports into North America were down by 10.5% in 2005, with almost all of the decline in US imports. The biggest suppliers of MDF into the North American market are South America (Chile, Argentina, Brazil and Venezuela) and Oceania (Australia and New Zealand).

OSB prices were on a roller coaster throughout most of 2005, rising in response to high housing starts at the beginning of the year and again following the devastation of Hurricane Katrina (graph 7.4.2).

GRAPH 7.4.2

US OSB prices, 2001-2006

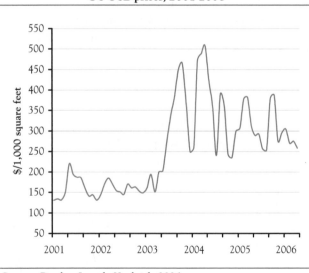

Source: Random Lengths Yardstick, 2006.

Neither price rise could be sustained, however, as increased production and higher imports worked to lower prices. OSB production in the United States increased from 14.3 million m³ in 2004 to 15.0 million m³ in 2005, while Canadian OSB production increased from 8.3 to 8.8 million m³. US housing starts, which totalled 2.1 million in 2005, are expected to decline slightly over the

period 2006-2008, when they should bottom out at approximately 2 million. However, the decline in housing starts will have serious implications for the structural panel industry, particularly the OSB industry, especially since North America production capacity is planned to increase from 23.4 million m³ in 2004 to 29.9 million m³ in 2008.

FIGURE 7.4.1

OSB in North American residential construction

Source: APA – The Engineered Wood Association, 2006.

While North American OSB production capacity is scheduled to increase by 16% by 2008, demand for structural panels in North America could decline slightly from 40.1 million m³ in 2005 to 39.5 million m³ by 2008. As a result, capacity utilization rates in the North American OSB industry are expected to drop from 99% in 2005 to 80% by 2008. In addition, imports of OSB, which totalled 9.5 million m³ in 2005, are expected to remain steady in 2006 and 2007. As a result of increased supply, lower capacity utilization rates and decreased demand, OSB prices should soften substantially over the next two years.

Almost three-quarters of OSB production (73%) was used in the residential construction market in 2005. With the large increase in production capacity scheduled to come on-line by 2008, there has been a concerted effort by the industry to expand the use of OSB in the remodelling, industrial and non-residential markets. As a result, it is expected that demand in these markets will increase from 6.3 million m³ in 2005 to 7.2 million m³ in 2008 while demand in the residential market is expected to decline slightly from 17.3 million m³ to 17.2 million m³ over the same time period.

Of particular concern is that imports of OSB from outside North America jumped by 123% to a record 657,000 m³ in 2005. Imports from Europe, primarily Germany and France, increased from 177,000 m³ in 2004 to 487,000 m³ in 2005. Similarly, OSB imports from Brazil almost doubled, increasing from 88,000 m³ in 2004 to 152,000 m³ in 2005. Finally, Chinese OSB has begun to show up in the United States, with exports increasing from 212 m³ in 2004 to 1,550 m³ in 2005. However, since no Chinese panel mills, neither OSB nor softwood plywood, have been certified to produce structural panels, all softwood plywood and OSB imports from China will continue to be used in non-structural applications, e.g. cabinets and furniture.

Demand for structural softwood plywood, which had been increasing in recent years, is expected to resume its slow decline as housing starts begin dropping. North American softwood plywood production, which decreased from 15.0 million m³ in 2004 to 14.7 million m³ in 2005, is expected to drop further to 14.4 million m³ in 2006. As a result, capacity utilization in the North American softwood plywood industry will drop from 99% in 2005 to 95% in 2006. A higher capacity utilization rate has been maintained by shutting down mills that are less efficient, both technically and economically.

Softwood plywood production in the United States dropped from 13 million m³ in 2004 to 12.7 million m³ in 2005, while Canadian softwood plywood production was relatively stable at 2.0 million m³. US softwood plywood production fell across the southern (by 2.2%), western (by 1.8%) and inland regions, i.e. east of the Rocky Mountains (by 3.8%).

North American softwood plywood imports, which increased from 1.9 million m³ in 2004 to 2.3 million m³ in 2005, are expected to level off in 2006. Despite that an 8% import tariff was applied to Brazilian softwood plywood imports in mid-2005, softwood plywood imports from Brazil increased from 1.1 million m³ in 2004 to 1.4 million m³ in 2005. Imports of Brazilian plywood during the first four months of 2006 declined slightly, falling by 4.3% in volume terms and 0.1% in value terms. However, US softwood plywood imports increased by 18.2% over the same period, and as a result, Brazil's market share declined from 65.4% in 2005 to 47.5% in the first four months of 2006. This suggests that the import tariff has been effective in moderating Brazilian exports of softwood plywood to the US. Imports of softwood plywood from China remained stable in 2005 at 38,000 m³. To date, no Chinese softwood plywood mills have received grade stamp certification for the production of structural softwood plywood and US industry association sources suggest that this will also be the case in 2006.

7.5 References

APA – The Engineered Wood Association. 2006a. Regional Production and Market Outlook, 2006-2011. Available at: www.apawood.org

APA – The Engineered Wood Association. 2006b. Personal Communication. 28 June, 2006.

Composite Panel Association. 2006. Personal Communication. 28 June, 2006.

European Federation of the Plywood Industry (FEIC). 2006. Annual Report 2005/2006. Available at: www.europlywood.com

European Panel Federation. 2006. Annual Report 2005/2006. Available at: www.europanels.org

EUWID. 2006. Wood Products and Panels (various issues). Available at: www.euwid-wood-products.com

Ganguly, I. & Eastin, I. 2006. Material Substitution in the US Residential Construction Industry, 1995-2005. CINTRAFOR News, Winter 2006. Available at: www.cintrafor.org

OAO NIPIEIlesprom. 2006. Joint Stock Company Research and Design Institute on Economics, Production Management and Information of Forestry, Pulp & Paper and Woodworking Industry, Moscow.

Random Lengths, 2006. Forest Product Market Prices and Statistics, 2005 Yearbook, Available at: www.randomlengths.com

Random Lengths. 2005. Panel Supplies Show no Sign of Lagging. Random Lengths Yardstick. V(15)N(4). Available at: www.randomlengths.com

Random Lengths. 2005. Hurricane Katrina Sparks Historically Strong Rally. Random Lengths Yardstick. V(15)N(8). Available at: www.randomlengths.com

Random Lengths. 2005. Most Lumber, Panel Prices Falter From 2004 to 2005. Random Lengths Yardstick. V(15)N(12). Available at: www.randomlengths.com

Random Lengths 2006. Non-residential Construction May Ease Housing Sting. Random Lengths Yardstick. V(16)N(4). Available at: www.randomlengths.com

United States Department of Agriculture (USDA), Foreign Agricultural Service. 2006. Online Trade Database. Available at: www.fas.usda.gov/ustrade /USTExBICO.asp?QI=

Wood Market Reports, 2006. OSB Capacity Growth. February 2006. Available at: www.woodmarkets.com

Additional statistical tables for this chapter may be found in the electronic annex on the website of the UNECE Timber Committee and FAO European Forestry Commission at: www.unece.org/trade/timber/mis/fpama.htm

Tables for this chapter include:

- Wood-based panels apparent consumption, 2001-2005
- Particle board apparent consumption, 2001-2005
- Plywood apparent consumption, 2001-2005
- Fibreboard apparent consumption, 2001-2005
- Production of plywood, 2001-2005
- Exports and imports of plywood (volume), 2001-2005
- Plywood balance in UNECE, 2001-2005
- Exports and imports of plywood (value), 2001-2005
- Production of particle board (excluding OSB), 2001-2005
- Exports and imports of particle board (volume) (excluding OSB), 2001-2005
- Particle board (excluding OSB) balance in UNECE, 2001-2005
- Exports and imports of particle board (value) (excluding OSB), 2001-2005
- Production of OSB, 2001-2005
- Exports and imports of OSB (volume), 2001-2005
- OSB balance in UNECE, 2001-2005
- Exports and imports of OSB (value), 2001-2005
- Production of MDF, 2001-2005
- Exports and imports of MDF (volume), 2001-2005
- MDF balance in UNECE, 2001-2005
- Exports and imports of MDF (value), 2001-2005
- Wood-based panels balance in UNECE, 2001-2005
- Wood-based panels trade flows in the UNECE region 2003-2004

Full statistics used in the *Forest Products Annual Market Review, 2005-2006* may be found in the UNECE/FAO TIMBER database at:

www.unece.org/trade/timber/mis/fp-stats.htm#Statistics

Chapter 8

Pulp & paper markets cope with high energy prices and growth in Asia: Markets for paper, paperboard and woodpulp, 2005-2006[40]

Highlights

- Pulp and paper markets in the UNECE region were influenced by higher energy prices and demand growth in Asia in 2005 and 2006.

- Important developments in Europe included the launching of the EU Emissions Trading Scheme, which was followed by substantial increases in electrical energy prices.

- High global energy prices pushed up costs of production and prices for pulp, paper and paperboard, with price increases absorbed by relatively strong global market demands.

- China continues to be a growing source of global demand for wood fibre, including recovered paper, which China imports in large volumes from the UNECE region.

- The European pulp and paper industry is deeply involved with the implementation of the Lisbon Agenda to improve the competitiveness of European industry, for instance, through the drafting of a Strategic Research Agenda.

- European producers of paper and paperboard set a new record for output, at 104 million m.t. in 2005, growing slowly by 0.4% from 2004.

- In 2005 in North America, output of paper and paperboard decreased by 1.5% to 101.1 million m.t. from 2004, although prices continued to increase in 2005 and the first half of 2006.

- In June of 2006, the International Council of Forest and Paper Associations announced the signing of an agreement by its global member companies on sustainability.

- Continued expressions of interest in sustainable forest management by forest and paper associations (and by customers of paper and paperboard products) suggest that related public procurement policies for paper and paperboard might become more common in the future.

- Production and consumption of pulp and paper declined in both the United States and Canada in 2005, but the production decline was much greater for Canada (-4.5%) than the United States (-0.8%).

_____

[40] By Dr. Peter J. Ince, USDA Forest Service, Prof. Eduard Akim, PhD, the St. Petersburg State Technological University of Plant Polymers and the All-Russian Research Institute of Pulp and Paper Industry, Mr. Bernard Lombard, Confederation of European Paper Industries, and Mr. Tomás Parik, Wood and Paper, A.S.

Secretariat introduction

The UNECE/FAO Timber Section expresses its appreciation to Dr. Peter Ince,[41] Research Forester, USDA Forest Service, for once again leading the production of this chapter with his co-authors. Professor Eduard Akim, PhD,[42] The Saint Petersburg State Technological University of Plant Polymers and The All-Russian Research Institute of Pulp and Paper Industry analysed the Russian pulp and paper sector. Mr. Bernard Lombard,[43] Trade and Competitiveness Director, Confederation of European Paper Industries (CEPI), described trends in CEPI member countries in Europe. Mr. Tomás Parik[44], Director, Wood and Paper, A.S., analysed developments in central and eastern Europe.

Mr. Eric Kilby, CEPI Statistics Manager, produced again this year the European data from CEPI member associations, which is the basis for the European analysis. Since there are some discrepancies between CEPI and UNECE/FAO definitions, the figures may vary slightly, but the trends remain the same. Thanks to these regular contributors, the *Review* has an overview of paper, paperboard and woodpulp market and policy developments across the UNECE region

8.1 Global trends

Global markets for pulp, paper and paperboard remained mostly firm in 2005 and in the first half of 2006, with limited expansion of production capacity in the UNECE region (and a slight decline of capacity in North America). Markets were characterized by generally higher prices (in US dollars) for most pulp, paper and paperboard products, continuing the general upward price trend observed since 2003. Higher prices and robust demand were stimulated by favourable global economic conditions, continued global expansion of industrial production, and continued growth in consumption of paper and paperboard in Europe and Asia (and China in particular). It can be noted, however, that 2006 prices for some commodities in Asia are lower

[41] Dr. Peter J. Ince, Research Forester, USDA Forest Service, Forest Products Laboratory, One Gifford Pinchot Drive, Madison, Wisconsin, US, 53726-2398, tel: +1 608 231 9364, fax: +1 608 231 9592, e-mail: pince@fs.fed.us, www.fpl.fs.fed.us

[42] Prof. Eduard Akim, PhD, The Saint Petersburg State Technological University of Plant Polymers, The All-Russian Research Institute of Pulp and Paper Industry, 4, Ivana Chernykh Str., Saint Petersburg, RF-198095 Russia, tel: +7812 247 3558, fax: +7812 534 8138, e-mail: akim@Ed.spb.su

[43] Mr. Bernard Lombard, Confederation of European Paper Industries, 250 avenue Louise, B-1050 Brussels, Belgium, tel: +32 2 627 49 11, fax: +32 2 646 81 37, e-mail: b.lombard@cepi.org, www.cepi.org

[44] Mr. Tomás Parik, Director, Wood & Paper a.s., Hlina 18, CZ-66491 Ivancice, Czech Republic, tel: +420 546 41 82 11, fax: +420-546 41 82 14, e-mail: t.parik@wood-paper.cz, www.wood-paper.cz

than those in the UNECE region, such as those for newsprint in China, which were reportedly as much as 20% lower than in the United States, a phenomenon attributed to ongoing capacity expansion in China (PaperAge, 2006). Also, in the UNECE region in 2005, prices for some products appeared to occasionally waver, and subsequent price increases stemmed in part from higher global energy prices as higher energy costs were passed along from producers of pulp, paper and paperboard to consumers.

FIGURE 8.1.1

Paper Production

Source: Stora Enso, 2006.

Within the UNECE region, effects of higher energy prices were readily apparent in regional trends for paper and paperboard. Higher global energy prices boosted exchange values of currencies for countries that exported large volumes of oil and gas, notably Canada and Russia, two countries that also produce large quantities of pulp, paper and paperboard. The higher exchange values of the Canadian dollar and Russian ruble (versus the euro and the US dollar) contributed to comparatively less robust market conditions for pulp, paper and paperboard producers in Canada and Russia. Canadian output of paper and paperboard declined in 2005, with a decline in the value of net exports, significantly lower capacity utilization rates, and lower profitability. The Russian trade balance in paper and paperboard (value of exports minus imports) also remained negative and continued to deteriorate in 2005, which was partly due to the effect on competitiveness of an increasing exchange value of the Russian ruble and high global oil prices.

In 2005, rates of growth in apparent consumption of paper and paperboard increased slightly in Europe and decreased slightly in the Eastern Europe, Caucasus and Central Asia (EECCA) subregion[45], while consumption

[45] The name "Eastern Europe, Caucasus and Central Asia" is a new UNECE term introduced this year in place of the Commonwealth of Independent States (CIS). It is comprised of the same 12 countries (see map in annex for list of countries).

declined again in North America (graph 8.1.1). In recent years, aggregate growth in paper and paperboard consumption has been relatively low but fairly steady in Europe, while apparent consumption in North America has varied, declining in 2003, increasing in 2004, and declining again in 2005. In both Europe and North America the growth trends for certain products are notably divergent from aggregate trends, with declining consumption of newsprint, for example, but increasing consumption of packaging paper and paperboard products. Meanwhile, apparent consumption of paper and paperboard continued to increase in Russia and the EECCA subregion, but at a slower rate of growth. Despite a slower growth rate relative to the previous year, the growth rate of consumption in the EECCA subregion in 2005 (including Russia) remained well above other UNECE regions.

GRAPH 8.1.1

Consumption growth rates for paper and paperboard in the UNECE region, 2002-2005

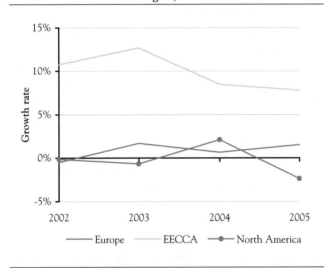

Source: UNECE/FAO TIMBER database, 2006.

For many decades until recently, North American paper and paperboard production exceeded European production. European production, however, has expanded more rapidly since 1990 while North American production peaked and levelled off after 1999. Consequently, European production reached equivalency in total tonnage with North American production several years ago (graph 8.1.2), and in 2005, European production exceeded North American production for a third consecutive year. Production dropped in the EECCA subregion during the early 1990s but has been steadily climbing since then.

GRAPH 8.1.2

Production of paper and paperboard in the UNECE region, 1991-2005

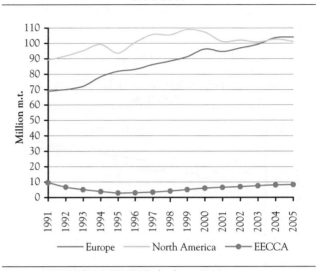

Source: UNECE/FAO TIMBER database, 2006.

Trends in major paper and paperboard trade flows of the UNECE region reveal that shipments from Europe to non-UNECE regions (mainly to Asia) have experienced the largest relative increase in recent years (graph 8.1.3).

GRAPH 8.1.3

Major paper and paperboard trade flows in the UNECE region, 2000-2004

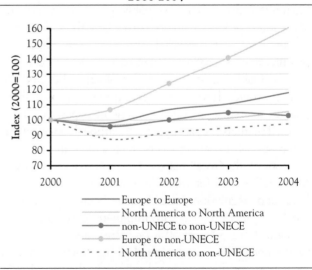

Note: Corresponding trade flow table in electronic annex.
Source: UN COMTRADE/EFI, 2006.

Other major trade flows have experienced adjustments that fall within a narrow band, and there was much less of an increase in trade flow from North America to non-UNECE regions, when compared to the increase for Europe to non-UNECE. The trends appear to indicate that Europe is participating much more than North America in meeting the growing demands of Asia for paper and paperboard products.

In the case of woodpulp trade flows, shipments from countries in Europe to other countries in Europe, and shipments from non-UNECE regions to other non-UNECE regions experienced the largest increases (graph 8.1.4).

GRAPH 8.1.4

Major woodpulp trade flows in the UNECE region, 2000-2004

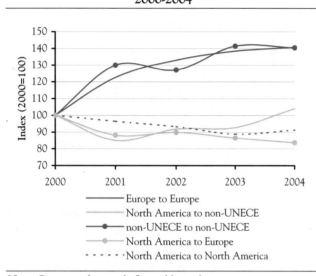

Note: Corresponding trade flow table in electronic annex.
Source: UN COMTRADE/EFI, 2006.

A question being considered by the UNECE Timber Committee this year is how public procurement policies affect forest product markets, particularly those favouring procurement of recycled products or favouring procurement of products obtained from forests certified for sustainable forest management. Within the UNECE region, there have been government procurement policies related to recycled content in paper that have affected markets for paper products, although government purchases of paper products represent only a small fraction of the total market for most paper products. Many US states, for example, have paper procurement laws and regulations that require state agencies to purchase paper products with minimum recycled content (ranging from 30% to 50% or more), and the Federal Government has similar regulations. Such laws and regulations for the most part date back to the early 1990s, and thus markets have largely already absorbed their impact. Procurement policies related to certification for sustainable forest management are not common in the United States insofar as paper products are concerned. However, continued expressions of interest in sustainable forest management by forest and paper associations (and by customers of paper and paperboard products) suggest that related public procurement policies for paper and paperboard might become more common in the future.

In June 2006, the International Council of Forest and Paper Associations (ICFPA) signed an agreement on sustainability. Through this statement, ICFPA members made a commitment to sustainable development and to working with other stakeholders to ensure that environmental, social and economic benefits of natural resources are available to current and future generations. The global forest products industry committed to continuously improve its sustainability performance through action in the following core areas: promoting sustainable forest management worldwide, combating illegal logging, supporting and encouraging the recovery of pre-and post-consumer paper and wood products, ensuring respect for the environment, maintaining and improving the resources on which the industry depends, creating solutions to global climate change and energy supply objectives, and investing in workers and communities.

8.2 Europe subregion

8.2.1 Market developments

Despite higher energy prices and high currency exchange values in 2005, European producers of paper and paperboard set a new record, at 104.0 million m.t. in 2005, up from 103.6 million m.t. in 2004 (table 8.2.1). The Confederation of European Paper Industries (CEPI) reported also that paper and paperboard production in Europe reached a new record level during the first quarter of 2006. Production of paper and paperboard among CEPI member countries[46] during the first quarter of 2006 was the highest ever recorded in a single quarter: 2.4% higher than the first quarter of 2005 and 2.1% higher than the last quarter of 2005.

In terms of product sectors, European output increased in the first quarter of 2006 for graphic papers, packaging grades, and for sanitary and household paper products, while output declined for other paper and paperboard products. Among graphic paper products, newsprint production declined, but production of uncoated mechanical paper, uncoated woodfree paper, and coated woodfree paper all increased. Among the packaging grades, production of case materials, carton board, other paper and board for packaging, and wrapping paper all increased.

_____

[46] CEPI member countries include: Austria, Belgium, the Czech Republic, Finland, France, Germany, Hungary, Italy, Norway, Poland, Portugal, the Slovak Republic, Spain, Sweden, Switzerland, the Netherlands and the UK.

TABLE 8.2.1

Pulp, paper and paperboard balance in Europe, 2004-2005

(1,000 m.t.)

	2004	2005	Change %
Woodpulp			
Production	43 028	41 884	-2.7
Imports	18 894	19 250	1.9
Exports	11 740	11 598	-1.2
Net trade	-7 154	-7 652	...
Apparent consumption	50 182	49 537	-1.3
of which: EU25			
Production	39 500	38 542	-2.4
Imports	17 768	18 136	2.1
Exports	10 825	10 696	-1.2
Net trade	-6 944	-7 440	...
Apparent consumption	46 443	45 983	-1.0
Paper and paperboard			
Production	103 605	104 039	0.4
Imports	52 637	51 382	-2.4
Exports	65 343	63 158	-3.3
Net trade	12 706	11 776	-7.3
Apparent consumption	90 898	92 263	1.5
of which: EU25			
Production	96 363	96 775	0.4
Imports	48 477	46 909	-3.2
Exports	61 218	59 260	-3.2
Net trade	12 741	12 351	-3.1
Apparent consumption	83 622	84 424	1.0

Source: UNECE/FAO TIMBER database, 2006.

Although the paper industry in CEPI countries saw increased production (+0.3%) and consumption (+0.8%) of paper and paperboard during 2005 compared to the previous year, the results for the year were unquestionably distorted by the industrial dispute in Finland during the second quarter.

Production of paper and paperboard by CEPI countries increased by 0.3% in 2005 compared with the previous year to reach 99.3 million tons. With paper and paperboard production capacity standing at 109.9 million tons, the calculated operating rate (capacity utilization rate) for 2005 was therefore 90.4%.

Production of packaging grades outstripped that of graphics paper. The production of graphic grades in 2005 was adversely affected by an industrial dispute in Finland during May and June. Overall output of graphic grades among CEPI countries fell by 1.5%. Production of coated mechanicals showed the only increase in the graphics

sector at 1.0%. For the packaging sector, production increased by 1.9%. Most of this increase was in case material grades, where production rose by 3.8%. The output of carton board and wrappings slightly decreased. Hygienic paper manufacturers increased their output by 3.9%. Production of industrial and speciality grades rose by 1.7%.

Output of pulp fell by 2.6%, in part due to the drop in Finnish production and in part due to the strong euro, which made imports financially attractive. Total output of both integrated and market pulp reached 41.6 million tons. Market pulp production for 2005 decreased 0.4% over 2004. Pulp production capacity increased to 47.3 million tons.

Overall consumption of paper and paperboard in CEPI member countries in 2005 rose by 0.8% compared to 2004. Consumption totalled 88.2 million tons. This increase in consumption is below the 1.5% growth in GDP (Eurostat – EU15, 2006). Overall consumption of graphic grades increased 0.5%. Deliveries within CEPI increased 0.3% whereas imports from outside CEPI countries rose by 3.6% and exports fell by 8.5%. Exports represented over 17.7% of deliveries in graphic grades.

Overall demand for packaging grades increased by 1.4% compared to the 2004 total. Imports from outside CEPI rose by 4% and exports by 0.9%. Internal deliveries within CEPI countries increased by 1.3%. Exports represent 13.5% of deliveries of all packaging materials and imports represent 5.4% of demand.

Demand for sanitary and household grades grew by 1.6%. Internal deliveries rose by 1.3%. Imports from outside CEPI countries increased 15.8% and exports increased by 16.2%. Internal deliveries account for 97.7% of apparent consumption in CEPI countries.

Overall consumption of pulp fell by 0.7%. Consumption of mechanical and semi-chemical pulp decreased by 2.4% while consumption of chemical pulp increased by 0.2%.

Paper deliveries by CEPI countries fell by 4.5% compared to 2004. Exports to non-CEPI countries accounted for 14.9% of total deliveries by CEPI countries but declined by 4.5%, reaching 14.8 million tons. Shipments to Asian markets accounted for 30% of exports but fell by 13.6%. Exports to non-CEPI Europe rose by 6.9% whereas deliveries to North America fell by 11.9%.

Imports into the CEPI countries contributed 4.8% of total European paper consumption in 2005 and increased by 3.9%, again due in part to favourable exchange rates and a higher demand. Imports from North America increased by 14.7% and imports from the rest of Europe rose by 3.6%. Imports from Latin America continue to rise. Producers such as Aruaco (Chile) and Aracruz

(Brazil) are growing fast and aggressively (PaperAge, March/April 2006). However, CEPI countries had an overall positive trade balance in paper of 10.5 million tons in 2005.

Utilisation of recovered paper increases by 2.6% over 2004 at 47.3 million tons. Collection increased by 6.0%. Exports of recovered paper to countries outside CEPI reached 7.4 million tons with 94.9% of this being sent to Asian markets. Woodpulp and recovered paper represent both 42% of the fibre used in papermaking in CEPI countries. The European paper industry nearly met its ambitious target to push the paper recycling rate above 56% in 2005. The actual paper recycling rate stood at 55.4%. An extra 9 million tons were recycled compared to 1998, but this does not take into account the volumes of recovered paper exported for recycling. A new target will be launched in the coming months to reach even higher rate in 2010.

8.2.2 Policy developments

In the area of policy development, the European Commission clearly stated its goal of building a sustainable and competitive future for Europe in accordance with the *Lisbon Agenda*, 2000 and the *Growth and Jobs Strategy*, 2005 in partnership with the EU Member States. The European Commission is looking to industry to support this objective and contribute to the Better Regulation initiative, which aims to simplify legislation and better assess its impact on businesses. Sustained efforts in the areas of environmental protection and R&D are required. The European Commission launched a new industrial policy to create better framework conditions for manufacturing industries, and at the end of 2005 created a High Level Group on Competitiveness, Energy and the Environment, in which CEPI and the European pulp and paper industry are deeply involved.

On 15 February 2005, the European forest-based sector launched Vision 2030 as part of its Technology Platform initiative. The aim is to drive the industry toward the continued sustainable development and innovation needed to nurture growth in the sector over the next 25 years. The Forest-Based Sector Technology Platform (FTP) represents a bold step forward. For the first time, all major European stakeholders have joined forces to establish a vision for the future. With clear strategic objectives, the stakeholders have taken on the task of defining a Strategic Research Agenda (SRA) and ensuring its implementation. Stakeholders from all areas including industry, forest owners, researchers and public bodies have taken an active part in this process, with the European Commission observers.

In 2005, the European paper industry continued to face challenges from many corners, most notably the

significant increase in energy prices. Rising logistics costs were another significant contributor.

The introduction of the Emissions Trading Directive in January 2005 was intended to bring a new incentive for industry to reduce the consumption of fossil fuels. It certainly caused anxiety that power prices in Europe would increase as a result of the new system. The expected increase materialized and was dramatic, placing the European paper industry at a competitive disadvantage in relation to most of its global competitors. However, some adjustments to the carbon emissions quotas allotted to the countries and specific industries are expected to better match the latest developments.

The new EU Renewable Energy Policy in 2005 is a source of concern for the European pulp and paper industry. CEPI believes the policy and countries' subsidies to the wood energy sector create unfair competition for the paper industry's main raw material, and are concerned about fibre availability at affordable prices. CEPI is responding through a Renewable Energy Sources Working Group, which provided their input to the EU Biomass Action Plan in 2005.

FIGURE 8.2.1

Paper Production

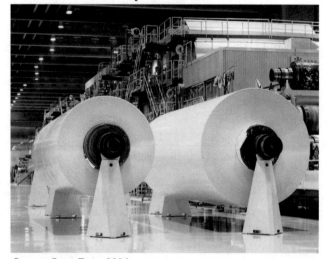

Source: Stora Enso, 2006.

One of the biggest recent changes in legislation affecting production is the new chemicals policy, REACH (Registration, Evaluation, Authorisation of Chemicals), which has been developed with the main objective of ensuring safe use of man-made products from the chemical industry. While in general the impact of REACH on industry will undoubtedly be considerable, the paper industry's main raw materials – cellulose pulp and recovered paper – are now exempt from registration and excluded from the current proposal.

Stepping up its fight against illegal logging, the European paper industry launched its own new code of conduct at the Ministerial Conference on the same topic in St. Petersburg, Russia. The code strongly condemns the illegal logging of wood and trading in illicit logs. It sets out several principles for paper companies to adhere to in a coordinated effort to ensure that industry plays a full role in helping to combat illegal logging. This corresponds to the EU's Forest Law Enforcement, Governance and Trade for private sector initiatives. Reporting on implementation and compliance is expected at both national and European levels.

The economies of other countries in central Europe have continued to experience significant positive development, as many industries are finding new opportunities for investments in these countries. New members of EU are also experiencing significant growth in many areas, including pulp and paper production and consumption. Positive economic development is attracting capital and having some influence on exchange rates of currencies in the region. The strengthening of currencies in general is putting further pressure on productivity, and influencing profitability of the industry in general.

Consumption of paper products has been increasing steadily in central Europe. Growth was not as strong in 2005 as in previous years but still significantly high with good potential, while per capita consumption in this region is lower than in some other regions. Two main policy and economic development areas can be identified as having the most significant influence on development in central Europe.

One area of concern is infrastructure and transport policy, which have a big influence on market conditions. Strong needs for infrastructure development is one of the key issues in all of the new and candidate EU countries, and one of the first conditions for further development in all areas. General public pressure on safer transportation, oil prices, environmental concerns are main driving forces influencing competitiveness of the industry in the region. A good logistics infrastructure and a reliable and affordable energy supply are crucial to the pulp and paper industry.

The environment is the second area of policies that has significant influence on pulp and paper industries. Most production sites already implement high standards of environmental protection policies including environmental certification. More effort should be focused in general on public perceptions of the pulp and paper industry, where its sustainable profile must be better promoted in order to increase general competitiveness of pulp and paper industry. Many wood consumers in central Europe are demanding wood from forest management certified forests. In addition, questions of illegal logging are now taken seriously, and various efforts following the general European development are ongoing.

Central Europe can be seen as having interesting potential in consumption. There are some new projects for production expansion foreseen in the subregion. Some big challenges to be tackled in order to secure sustainability of pulp and paper industry in the subregion – mainly related to raw material availability, especially with increased wood energy production.

8.3 EECCA subregion

In 2005 and the first half of 2006, the subregion of the EECCA continued to experience robust economic growth, reflected by continued but slower growth in Russian pulp and paper output (table 8.3.1). The growth in Russia's paper and paperboard output was 2.8% in 2005 (versus 7.1% in 2004), including a 4.2% increase in output of paperboard.

TABLE 8.3.1

Pulp, paper and paperboard balance in EECCA, 2004-2005

(1,000 m.t.)

	2004	2005	Change %
Woodpulp			
Production	7 059	7 099	0.6
Imports	160	159	-0.4
Exports	1 868	1 951	4.5
Net trade	1 708	1 792	4.9
Apparent consumption	5 351	5 306	-0.8
Paper and paperboard			
Production	8 043	8 274	2.9
Imports	1 880	2 223	18.2
Exports	2 959	2 992	1.1
Net trade	1 079	768	-28.8
Apparent consumption	6 964	7 506	7.8

Source: UNECE/FAO TIMBER database, 2006.

Both demand and output of pulp and paper products increased in Russia through 2005 and into the first half of 2006. Owing to relative economic and political stability established in the country since the major currency revaluation of 1998 and more expansionary macroeconomic policy under President Putin since 1999, there has been a continuous increase in total output of pulp, paper and paperboard in Russia, more than doubling since 1996, although output has yet to reach previous record levels of 1988-1989 pre-transition periods in the late Soviet era (graphs 8.3.1 and 8.3.2).

GRAPH 8.3.1

Russian production and exports of market pulp, 1995-2005

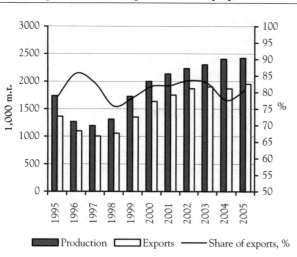

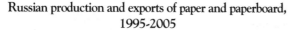

Sources: Goscomstat of the Russian Federation, PPB-Express (Moscow) and author's data interpretation, 2006.

GRAPH 8.3.2

Russian production and exports of paper and paperboard, 1995-2005

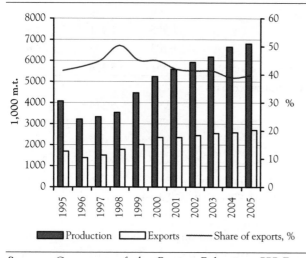

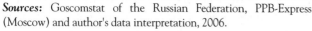

Sources: Goscomstat of the Russian Federation, PPB-Express (Moscow) and author's data interpretation, 2006.

In 2005, the Russian pulp and paper sector continued to expand production of pulp, paper and paperboard, particularly the output of paperboard for packaging. During 2005, Russia's total output of pulp (both pulp for paper and paperboard and market pulp) increased by 0.2% and the output of market pulp increased by 0.4%.

Exports of pulp and paper products hold a dominant position in the total Russian exports of forest-based products, but the overall structure of forest product exports still has a pronounced raw material character. In terms of roundwood equivalents, roundwood timber exports and sawn wood exports accounted for 79% of

Russia's exports in 2003, while pulp and paper accounted for only 21% of exports.

In 2005, exports of pulp and paper products continued to increase. Exports of pulp, paper and paperboard were progressively increasing since 1990 and reached a peak level in 2005. However, Russian exports as a percentage of production have remained largely unchanged since 1996, with exports comprising about 80% of output for market pulp, and around 40% for paper and paperboard. Major export destinations for these Russian products are China (market pulp, kraft linerboard), Ireland (market pulp, kraft linerboard), India (newsprint), and Turkey (newsprint).

Although the tonnage of Russian paper and paperboard exports greatly exceeds the tonnage of imports, the trade balance in value has continued to deteriorate, as Russia has expanded imports of higher value paper products. The annual trade deficit in paper and paperboard has been negative since 2001, and in 2005 it was more than $870 million (graph 8.3.3).

GRAPH 8.3.3

Russian exports and imports of paper and paperboard, 2000-2005

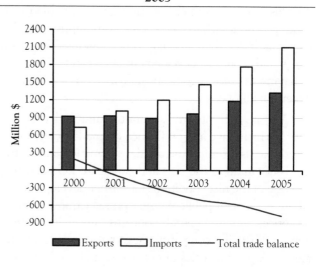

Sources: State Customs Committee, *Pulp. Paper. Board* Magazine, PPB-express, PPB Exports, PPB Imports and author's data interpretation, 2006.

The higher value of imports of paper and paperboard compared to their exports is mainly due to the fact that Russia is importing expensive products such as high quality materials for container and packaging, coated paper, and tissue, whereas less expensive commodity products such as newsprint and kraft linerboard are being exported.

Reconstruction and restructuring of the Russian pulp and paper industry is continuing, with some progress being made towards higher value products with better processing of wood raw material.

It can be noted that future development of Russia's pulp and paper sector is linked to expanded production of more technologically advanced products (such as coated printing and writing paper rather than newsprint for example), and also more integrated utilization of forest resources.

Implementation of important environmental projects provides examples of steps being taken towards applying the new Russian environmental laws adopted in late 2002 (based on comparison of environmental indices of individual mills and those of "best available technology", or BAT). Furthermore, in connection with ratification of the Kyoto Protocol, a number of mills initiated work on inventorying of greenhouse gas emissions. Such accounting for carbon and greenhouse gas emissions is being done to prepare for limits on emissions and perhaps trading in carbon emissions.

"Forest wars" (a journalistic term for legal disputes among managers and owners of forest enterprises) went on in 2004-2005. In past years such disputes involved occupation of plants by armed guards (hence the term "forest wars"), but more civil and legal proceedings now characterize the settlement of such disputes.

8.4 North America subregion

In North America, output of paper and paperboard decreased by 1.5% in 2005 to 101.1 million m.t., while apparent consumption of paper and paperboard decreased by 2.4% to 96.4 million m.t. (table 8.4.1). Production and consumption declined in both the United States and Canada, but the decline was more pronounced for Canada. Producers in both countries experienced higher energy prices, but Canadian producers also had to cope with a much stronger Canadian dollar, which has impacted competitiveness of Canadian producers in global markets.

Looking at monthly data it is apparent that growth in US paper and paperboard purchases has continued to follow a secular upward trend in line with the recovery of US industrial output since 2002 (graph 8.4.1). There was a steady increase since 2002 in the monthly US industrial production index along with monthly year-to-date totals of US paper and paperboard purchases. The year-to-date purchases show some cyclical variability since 2002, but the long-term trend in purchases has continued to spiral upward along with the upward trend in industrial production.

TABLE 8.4.1

Pulp, paper and paperboard balance in North America, 2004-2005

(1,000 m.t.)

	2004	2005	Change %
Woodpulp			
Production	80 895	79 889	-1.2
Imports	6 388	6 452	1.0
Exports	17 141	16 439	-4.1
Net trade	10 753	9 987	-7.1
Apparent consumption	70 142	69 902	-0.3
Paper and paperboard			
Production	102 683	101 110	-1.5
Imports	21 222	20 621	-2.8
Exports	25 155	25 341	0.7
Net trade	3 933	4 720	20.0
Apparent consumption	98 751	96 390	-2.4

Source: UNECE/FAO TIMBER database, 2006.

GRAPH 8.4.1

US industrial production index and year-to-date purchases of paper and paperboard, 1998-2006

Notes: Monthly data. Purchases on a year-to-date annual basis.
Sources: US Federal Reserve and American Forest & Paper Association, 2006.

The upward trends since 2002 directly coincide with a period during which the trade-weighted exchange value of the US dollar declined from its recent historical peak (in early 2002) to the vicinity of its long-term historical average (where the dollar value was hovering in 2005 and in the first half of 2006). The decline in dollar value to its long-term average value has boosted competitiveness for US manufacturers, and coincides with increased industrial output and a secular upward trend in purchases of paper and paperboard since 2002. By May 2006, year-to-date US purchases of paper and paperboard stood at about 4% above their recent historical low point (in mid-

2002), but purchases still remained about 5% below their historical peak (of 1999). Although overall US industrial production has more than fully recovered from the recession of 2001-2002, US paper and paperboard production has yet to fully recover. In fact, the question is, "Will paper production ever recover its previous strong correlation with industrial production, or is it in secular decline?"

FIGURE 8.2.1

Paper reeling

Source: Stora Enso, 2006.

Cyclicality in domestic paper and paperboard purchases and mill operating rates, along with variability in currency exchange rates, have contributed to some variability in US pulp, paper and paperboard prices, but secular trends in prices have been generally upward (in US dollars) since around 2002-2003. The secular upturn in purchases and prices in recent years along with depreciation in exchange value of the US dollar generally boosted profits for the US pulp and paper industry from 2002 to 2005. However, industry profits began to decline toward the end of 2005 and into 2006, despite relatively high prices for pulp, paper and paperboard commodities. The weakness in profits appears to stem in part from higher energy costs. Higher energy costs have also been cited as a reason for higher pulp, paper and paperboard commodity prices.

Canada experienced a decline in pulp, paper and paperboard output in 2005 as the value of the Canadian dollar rose in tandem with higher crude oil prices in recent years. Canada is the leading source of US crude oil imports. From 2002 to 2006, global crude oil prices more than doubled and the Canadian dollar appreciated in that period by more than 40% in value relative to the US dollar. Since early 2004, the Canadian dollar also appreciated by nearly 20% relative to the euro. Rising energy prices negatively impacted profits and growth for both the Canadian and US pulp and paper industries, but

the strong Canadian dollar contributed to weaker market conditions for Canada than the United States in recent years.

For example, at the end of 2004 Canada's annual production of paper and paperboard increased by just 2.4% over the previous year, compared with an increase of 1.7% in US paper and paperboard production. By the end of 2005, Canada's annual production of paper and paperboard dropped by 4.5%, compared to a more modest decline of just 0.8% for the United States.

Divergent market conditions for Canada and the United States were reflected also in a divergence of capital spending trends. According to a recent survey by *Pulp & Paper Week* (2006), the US pulp and paper industry is expected to increase capital spending by 5% in 2006 to the highest level in five years, while capital spending by the Canadian pulp and paper industry is expected to drop by 7%. However, even in the United States, capital spending levels remain well below the historical peak levels of the 1990s, and many firms continue to maintain capital spending at levels well below depreciation and amortization.

Prices for some fibre inputs have continued to show signs of recovery in North America since 2002, particularly recovered paper prices that are driven in part by booming exports of recovered paper to China. For example, the nationwide average US price indexes for recovered paper in general and for old corrugated containers in particular remained elevated in 2005 and 2006 (graph 8.4.2).

GRAPH 8.4.2

US monthly price indexes for recovered paper (all categories) and for old corrugated containers, 2000-2006

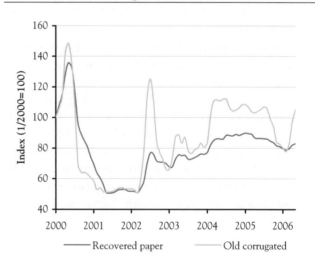

Source: US Department of Labor, Bureau of Labor Statistics, Producer Price Indexes, 2006.

Recent increases in recovered paper prices reflect substantial increases in export demand for recovered paper, particularly demand from China. The United States exported a total of 14.5 million m.t. of recovered paper in 2005, 7.5 million m.t. of which was imported by China. Total Chinese imports of recovered paper reached nearly 17 million m.t. in 2005, up by nearly 40% in just one year (according to Bureau of International Recycling (BIR, 2006). During the first quarter of 2006, at least 75% of China's recovered paper imports were obtained from the UNECE region (48% from the United States and 27% from Europe, according to BIR).

8.5 References

American Forest & Paper Association (AF&PA). 2005. 2005 Annual Statistical Summary - Recovered Paper Utilization. AF&PA, Washington DC. 92 p. Available at: www.afandpa.org/Template.cfm?Section=Browse_by_Category&Template=/Ecommerce/ProductDisplay.cfm&ProductID=106

American Forest & Paper Association (AF&PA). 2006. Paper, Paperboard & Wood Pulp, Monthly Statistical Summary. Volume 84, No. 6. June 2006, and other issues. Available at: www.afandpa.org/Template.cfm?Section=Browse_by_Category&Template=/Ecommerce/ProductDisplay.cfm&ProductID=87

Confederation of European Paper Industries (CEPI). 2006. Available at: www.cepi.org

Pulp & Paper Week. RISI, Vol. 28, No. 20 (and other issues). 2006. Available at: www.risiinfo.com/risi-store/do/product/detail?id=8625&pcId=21&parentId=&rootId=12

Pulp & Paper Products Council of Canada. 2005. Canadian Pulp and Paper Industry Key Statistics. Available at: www.pppc.org/en/1_0/index.html

Stora Enso. 2006. Available at: www.storaenso.com

The Paper Stock Report. McEntee Media Corp. Vol. 17, No. 7. (June 10, 2006). Available via: www.recycle.cc/psrpage.htm

Additional statistical tables for this chapter may be found in the electronic annex on the UNECE Timber Committee and FAO European Forestry Commission website at: www.unece.org/trade/timber/mis/fpama.htm

Tables for this chapter include:
- Chemical woodpulp apparent consumption, 2001-2005
- Paper and paperboard apparent consumption, 2001-2005
- Graphic papers apparent consumption, 2001-2005
- Sanitary and household papers apparent consumption, 2001-2005
- Packaging materials apparent consumption, 2001-2005
- Production of chemical woodpulp, 2001-2005
- Exports and imports of chemical woodpulp (volume), 2001-2005
- Chemical woodpulp balance in UNECE, 2001-2005
- Exports and imports of chemical woodpulp (value), 2001-2005
- Production of mechanical woodpulp, 2001-2005
- Exports and imports of mechanical woodpulp (volume), 2001-2005
- Mechanical woodpulp balance in UNECE, 2001-2005
- Exports and imports of mechanical woodpulp (value), 2001-2005
- Production of graphic paper, 2001-2005
- Exports and imports of graphic paper (volume), 2001-2005
- Graphic paper balance in UNECE, 2001-2005
- Exports and imports of graphic paper (value), 2001-2005
- Production of packaging paper, 2001-2005
- Exports and imports of packaging paper (volume), 2001-2005
- Packaging paper balance in UNECE, 2001-2005
- Exports and imports of packaging paper (value), 2001-2005
- Wood pulp balance in UNECE, 2001-2005
- Paper and paperboard balance in UNECE, 2001-2005
- Major paper trade flows in the UNECE region 2003-2004
- Major woodpulp trade flows in UNECE region 2003-2004

Full statistics used in the *Forest Products Annual Market Review, 2005-2006* may be found in the UNECE/FAO TIMBER database at:

Chapter 9
Soaring fossil fuel prices give wood energy a major boost:
Wood energy markets 2005-2006[47]

Highlights

- Insecurity about future fossil fuel supplies and corresponding escalating prices boosts development of alternative energies, among which woodfuels are the most promising in the short term for medium- and large-scale heat and electricity production; woodfuels also have long term potential for transportation fuel.

- In Sweden, Finland and Austria, combinations of large domestic wood supply and policy measures have led to woodfuels now making up substantial shares of energy supply with national markets having become relatively mature.

- Woodfuel energy is increasing rapidly in response to EU policies to significantly raise bioenergy consumption, albeit from low starting levels in countries such as Belgium, Germany, the Netherlands and the UK.

- The EU Biomass Action Plan (2006) promotes the use of biomass fuels based on forest resources with the aim to increase the renewable share of electricity production in Europe from 14% in 1997 to 21% in 2010.

- In Sweden, the large growth of woodfuel energy use since the 1980s has in many ways been a result of policy measures such as carbon dioxide (CO_2) taxes and government funding for conversion from fossil fuels to woodfuels.

- Increased use of woodfuels in countries with limited forest resources is creating new trade, which will continue in coming years.

- Increased European demand for woodfuels will lead to integration of national markets for woodfuels with favourable logistic properties, such as pellets.

- Trade in woodfuels depends on the economic viability of low transport costs; ship transport will therefore be the dominant means of transport in an integrated pan-European woodfuels markets.

- Dependence on low transport costs will probably limit the European trade in woodfuels to mainly coastal areas for large-scale energy production.

_____

[47] By Dr. Bengt Hillring and Mr. Olle Olsson, both at the Swedish University of Agricultural Sciences.

Secretariat introduction

Driven by rising energy prices and subsequent policy decisions to use more biofuels, wood energy markets have expanded rapidly in the UNECE region over the past years, and are forecast to accelerate as new and existing policy measures take effect. Wood is both one of the oldest energy sources and the newest; with today's technologies it can be harvested, processed and burned efficiently. It not only generates heat and electricity, but also creates employment and economic development, especially in rural forested areas. It also generates competition for wood residues and small diameter roundwood from traditional wood and paper products producers, specifically panel and pulp manufacturers.

The UNECE Timber Committee follows wood energy markets and it took action to improve data reliability. A draft questionnaire on wood energy underlined the importance of wood energy for both the timber and the energy sector. An additional regional wood energy overview compared existing data from UNECE/FAO forestry statistics with energy statistics from the International Energy Agency (IEA), revealing discrepancies of not less than 200 million m³ for Northern America and 58 million m³ for Europe (table 9.0.1).[48] Despite these differences, it confirmed that enormous amounts of wood are already used today for energy production (sawmill residues, recovered wood, wood waste, black liquor, etc.). Together with the IEA it was agreed that close cross-sectoral cooperation would improve data reliability and coverage. Results of a new task force established will provide the 2007 chapter with more comprehensive information on the consumption sector and more complete data by country. The 2006 chapter draws primarily on experience and developments in Sweden, one of the forerunners in wood energy policies and markets.

The secretariat of the UNECE/FAO Timber Section greatly appreciates the analysis in this chapter by Dr. Bengt Hillring[49] and Mr. Olle Olsson[50], both at the Department of Bioenergy, Swedish University of Agricultural Studies. Dr. Hillring addressed the Timber Committee Market Discussions in 2000 on wood energy and was the Leader of the Team of Specialists on

Recycling, Energy and Market Interactions in 1997 and 1998. The authors are experts on the European wood energy markets and have focused on case examples when wider statistical information is unavailable.

TABLE 9.0.1

Wood energy consumption in North America and Europe, 2004

(1,000 m³)

	2004
EU-25 / EFTA	
Total consumption of industrial roundwood	640 000
Total wood energy consumption in roundwood equivalent	298 000
Wood energy consumption / industrial roundwood consumption (%)	46.5%
North America	
Total consumption of industrial roundwood	542 000
Total wood energy consumption in roundwood equivalent	182 000
Wood energy consumption / industrial roundwood consumption (%)	34%

Source: UNECE/FAO, Steierer, F. & Clark, D., *Regional Wood Overview*, 2006.

9.1 Introduction

Uncertainties about fossil fuel supply, combined with growing concerns that burning fossil fuels contributes to global warming, have led to rapidly increased interest in finding alternative, preferably, renewable energy sources. Recently, the importance of this subject was highlighted by the Secretary General, who stated in a speech on 10 May 2006, "We need to scale up investment in mature renewables" (UN News Centre, 15 May 2006).

The increasing use of renewables is likely to lead to the establishment of new energy markets. As regards woodfuels, which are among the more mature and established renewable energy sources, such markets are already in effect and rapid development. In countries such as Sweden, Finland and Austria, woodfuels are not only an integral part of the energy system, but are continuing to grow apace. With increased interest in woodfuels in other parts of Europe, new trade patterns are being established. This chapter will examine the future possibilities for the development of international woodfuels markets. Moreover, it attempts to put this development into the wider context of energy markets in general. It is hoped that using examples from the electricity and oil markets will not only aid understanding of the woodfuels market, but will also provide insight on

---

[48] www.unece.org/trade/timber/docs/stats-sessions/stats-28/stats-28.htm.

[49] Dr. Bengt Hillring, Associated Professor, Department of Bioenergy, Swedish University of Agricultural Sciences (SLU), P.O. Box 7061, SE-75007 Uppsala, Sweden, tel: +46 1867 3548, fax: +46 1867 3800, e-mail: Bengt.Hillring@bioenergi.slu.se, www2.bioenergi.slu.se

[50] Mr. Olle Olsson, M.Sc., Department of Bioenergy, Swedish University of Agricultural Studies (SLU), P.O. Box 7061, SE-75007 Uppsala, Sweden, tel: +46 1867 3548, fax: +46 1867 3800, e-mail: Olle.Olsson@bioenergi.slu.se, www2.bioenergi.slu.se

what lies ahead in terms of possible integration of European woodfuels markets.

9.2 Policy instruments for promotion of wood energy

In the European context, wood is an attractive source of energy for two major reasons: it decreases the EU's dependency on energy imports, and it contributes to efforts to reduce greenhouse gas emissions, particularly CO_2.[51] In addition, sustainable forest management in the UNECE region has resulted in a surplus of growth over harvests, part of which could go towards wood energy – wood is a renewable energy source.

The 1997 Kyoto Protocol is the policy basis for the reduction of greenhouse gas emissions. The main instrument of European policy measures to mitigate CO_2 emissions is the establishment of the emissions trading scheme. The scheme commenced in January 2005 and attempts to use market-based incentives to motivate companies to reduce emissions. Since large parts of European electricity generation take place in fossil-fuelled power plants, the emissions trading scheme has had and will continue to have a profound effect on the European energy sector. One example of this is *co-firing*, where coal is fired with a small proportion of woodfuel, thereby reducing the net release of CO_2 into the atmosphere.

Some suggestions for the shaping of future European energy policy are presented in the EU green paper, *A European Strategy for Sustainable, Competitive and Secure Energy*, issued in March 2006. The green paper acknowledges that price vulnerability, supply uncertainties and environmental issues call for European countries to develop a common strategy for coping with energy issues. Although woodfuels are not mentioned explicitly in the paper, it emphasizes the importance in Europe of promoting "climate-friendly diversification of energy supplies".

The EU *Biomass Action Plan* to promote the use of biomass as fuel is the most important policy measure focused strictly on woodfuels. Fuels based on forest resources (woodfuels) are the most available biofuel in most European countries. It is estimated that the plan will play a major part in the effort to increase the renewable share of electricity production in Europe from 14% in 1997 to the target of 21% in 2010 (EU *Biomass Action Plan*, 2006).

While the EU policy measures will play an important part in the energy policies of individual countries, it is also important to look at some of the national policy measures that have been used to promote woodfuels. For example, in Sweden, the large growth in the use of woodfuels for energy since the 1980s has been an effect of policy measures such as CO_2 taxes and government funding for conversion from fossil fuels to woodfuels. Another important factor was the introduction of the electricity certificate system in 2003, a market-based system intended to make renewable electricity more competitive by forcing electricity consumers to use a proportion of renewable electricity (Swedish Energy Agency [STEM], 2005).

9.3 Energy markets

This section explores energy markets in general, and the process of price formation in particular for its relevance to the outlook for wood energy. The examples are mostly from Sweden, a country with an advanced and efficient wood energy market.

9.3.1 The oil market

Energy prices reflect not only the economic relationship between supply and demand, but also politics and policies. Changes in energy prices not only affect conventional fossil fuels, but also wood energy production, consumption and trade. Price changes also have effects throughout economies, as explained in chapter 3. For example, current and previous political turmoil in the oil-producing countries has had a drastic effect on oil production capacity, such as the oil crises of the 1970s, 1991 and the mid-2000s (graph 9.3.1)

GRAPH 9.3.1

US oil import prices, 1980-2006

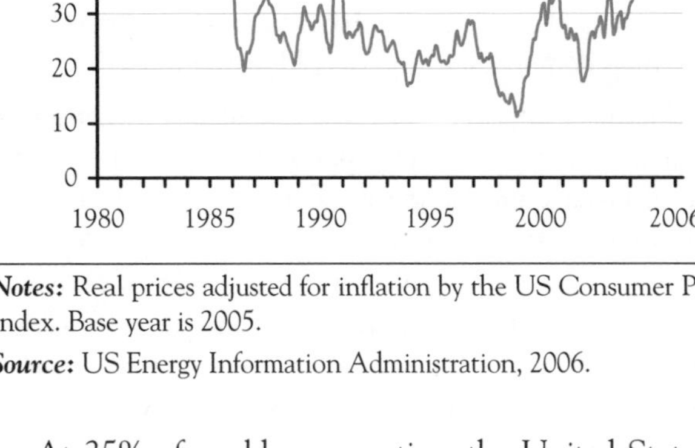

Notes: Real prices adjusted for inflation by the US Consumer Price Index. Base year is 2005.

Source: US Energy Information Administration, 2006.

At 25% of world consumption, the United States is the largest consumer of oil products; Western Europe is second and China is catching up. Production is mostly in

---

[51] Wood energy is CO_2-neutral since the amount of carbon dioxide released, for example, through the burning of a tree is equal to the amount absorbed by the tree in its lifetime.

the Middle East (30%), followed by Russia, west Africa and South America (figure 9.3.1).

FIGURE 9.3.1

Oil trade flows, 2005

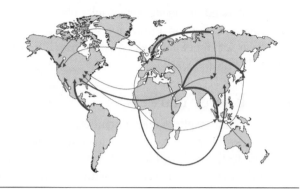

Source: World Coal Institute, based on figures from British Petroleum, 2005.

9.3.2   The electricity market

Unlike other forms of energy, electricity's main characteristic is that it cannot be stored, but rather, must be consumed and produced simultaneously. This naturally affects all aspects of the electricity market. For example, water reservoirs are filled during spring and summer to generate electricity in the coming autumn and winter (STEM, 2006).

9.3.2.1   Price formation

Since the deregulation of the Swedish electricity market in the early 1990s and the ensuing process of creating a common Nordic electricity market, the price of electricity has depended on supply and demand. More precisely, the price formation is set by production costs according to the principle known as marginal cost pricing. In economic terms, the price of a product is set to cover the marginal cost, i.e. "the increase in total cost resulting from a unit increase in output" (Parkin and King, 1995). For the electricity market, this means that the market price is based on the costs of the expensive marginal production that is brought in during periods of extra high demand, e.g. during cold winter days.

The most important factor is the effect of weather on the available supply of electricity at any point in time. The electricity production capacity of both wind power and, more importantly, hydropower, is dependent on weather. During a normal year, roughly half of Sweden's electricity is produced from hydropower. If there is a "dry" year with little electricity being produced in hydro plants, this supply deficit has to be made up by electricity produced in expensive fossil-fuelled power plants. For example, low precipitation in 2003 resulted in the lowest annual hydropower production in 30 years and led to a

spike in prices (graph 9.3.2). Electricity produced in fossil-fuelled power plants has become increasingly costly in recent years with high prices for oil and natural gas, and the introduction of an emissions trading system in the EU. In general, however, Nordic electricity prices are still about half the German prices (STEM, 2006).

GRAPH 9.3.2

Average Swedish electricity prices, 2000-2006

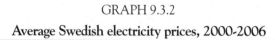

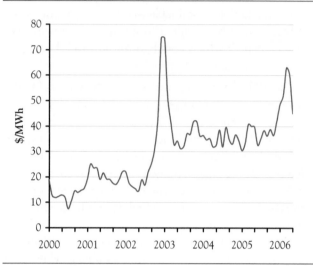

Source: Nordpool (The Nordic Power Exchange), 2006.

The present construction of a nuclear power plant in Finland can easily be seen in the context of the price formation mechanisms of the Nordic electricity market. The plant is largely the initiative of the pulp and paper industry, which consumes vast amounts of electricity. The reasoning behind it, is that the availability of relatively inexpensive nuclear power will reduce the need for expensive fossil-fuelled power, in turn lowering the market price of electricity.

9.4   Characteristics of the Swedish woodfuels market[52]

9.4.1   Prices

Price formation on woodfuels varies with the different types of fuels and the origin of the fuel in question. Prices of fuels made from sawmill by-products generally depend on supply and demand. On the other hand, the price of chips made from tops and branches from fellings is generally set by the cost of extracting the fuel.

Real prices for Swedish woodfuels have fallen continuously since 1970, which is remarkable considering the rapid expansion of the bioenergy sector, particularly,

---

[52] This section will describe some key concepts necessary for understanding woodfuel trade. The data is based on research in the context of Swedish woodfuel trade, but are nonetheless viable for comprehension of woodfuel trade in general.

the district heating sector, in the last 20 years. This development has been explained as an effect of essentially two factors. First, the vast supply of woodfuels in Sweden in the form of residues from the forest industry has enabled supply to meet the increasing demand. The second factor is the low-cost imported woodfuels that started to appear in Sweden in larger amounts at the beginning of the 1990s. These imported fuels have helped keep prices for woodfuels, in general, at a lower level than would otherwise have been the case (Hillring, 1999). In the last five years, however, this development seems to have changed; Swedish woodfuels' prices increased 25% between 2001 and 2004 (graph 9.4.1).

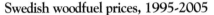

GRAPH 9.4.1

Swedish woodfuel prices, 1995-2005

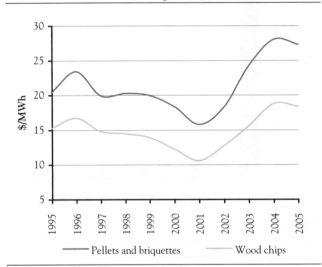

Note: Nominal prices.

Source: Swedish Energy Agency, 2006.

9.4.2 Competition with other wood products

It is important to see the development of wood energy in the context of other forest products, which is particularly true for woodfuels made from roundwood. In simple terms, during and after felling, roundwood is sorted into three categories: sawlogs and veneer logs, pulpwood, and fuelwood. Wood of the highest quality and price is used for veneer and sawnwood. The smaller diameter wood along with wood of lower quality is used for less valuable pulpwood. Traditionally, roundwood that does not meet the standard for pulpwood ends up as woodfuel. Recently, this distinction has begun to change. Woodfuel prices increased 25% between 2000 and 2004. The combination of rising woodfuel prices and falling pulpwood prices has resulted in broadly similar price levels. In some cases, a forest owner may actually be paid more for selling the wood as fuel than as pulpwood.

Sawmill residues (co-products) are another important source of woodfuels. Both refined pellets and briquettes and unrefined biofuels derive partly from sawmill co-

products. Unrefined woodfuels from sawmill co-products include bark and chips whereas refined biofuels, such as pellets and briquettes, are most often made from sawdust. The high demand for woodfuels and the ensuing price rise for refined woodfuels, resulted in a doubling of sawdust prices between 2002 and 2004. In 2004, Swedish sawdust prices were twice as high as Finnish prices and seven times sawdust prices in Poland. This development caused a crisis in the Swedish particle board industry, traditionally the largest buyer of sawmill co-products. According to one study, the high raw material prices have brought many particle board companies to the verge of bankruptcy (Brege and Pihlqvist, 2004).

9.4.3 Transportation and logistics

A major issue when discussing trade in woodfuels is the logistics of transport. This is especially true for the bulky unrefined woodfuels (e.g. tops and branches and fuelwood) that make up a major part of the woodfuels traded in Sweden. Transport accounts for almost 40% of the cost of woodfuel from tops and branches, (STEM, 2003). For this reason, it can be difficult to make woodfuel transport economically viable – 150 km seems to be the upper limit for road transport of woodfuels (STEM, 2003). This is the main reason that woodfuels have traditionally been consumed in the same area where they are produced, e.g. a sawmill in a certain area delivers its co-products to the local district heating plant.

Transport by ship or train is economically viable over longer distances, which explains the increasing import of woodfuels to Sweden from across the Baltic Sea (table 9.4.1). On the other hand, transport by ship and train is a great deal less flexible than by road and feasible only when large amounts are delivered to one destination.

TABLE 9.4.1

Comparison of woodfuel transportation costs

Cost examples of transporting 1 ton of woodfuel 1,000 kilometres	
Highway	€ 100 / ton
Railway	€ 33 / ton
Sea	€ 2 / ton

Source: *Modified from Hektor and Lundberg, 2006.*

9.4.4 Regional distribution of supply and demand

Presently, most woodfuels are used close to where they are produced. Clearly, it makes sense to use resources that are available in large quantities in the same region. Therefore, the largest users of bioenergy in Europe tend to be countries with a lot of forest, a wood burning culture and favourable policies, such as Sweden, Finland and Austria. With the more widespread adoption of bioenergy, this situation is almost certain to change as countries with smaller forest resources increase their use of bioenergy to reduce greenhouse gas emissions and fossil fuel dependency.

9.5   Examples of woodfuels markets

9.5.1   *Intercontinental woodfuel trade patterns – wood chips and particles*

Based on statistics from the European Forest Institute, a survey published in *Biomass and Bioenergy*, of international woodfuel trade, focused on charcoal, wood chips and wood particles, fuelwood, and wood residues (Hillring, 2006). One problem with these statistics is that while fuelwood is likely to be used for energy purposes, wood chips, particles and other co-products can be used for energy and other purposes (figure 9.5.1)

FIGURE 9.5.1

Wood chips

Source: Stora Enso, 2006.

FIGURE 9.5.2

Trade patterns for wood chips and particles

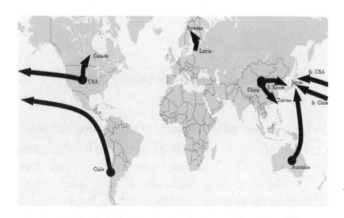

Source: Biomass and Bioenergy, Hillring, 2006.

Wood chips, whose import is dominated by Japan, are used extensively as raw material in the pulp industry (graph 9.5.1 and figure 9.5.2). Japan is by far the world's largest importer of wood chips and particles, importing ten times more than Canada, the second largest importer (graph 9.5.1). Most of Japan's imports, however, are raw material for the pulp industry, one of the world's largest, and which is almost completely dependent on imports. Japan's imports come from North and South America, Oceania, Europe and even China (graph 9.5.2).

GRAPH 9.5.1

Largest wood chip and particle importers, 2000-2001

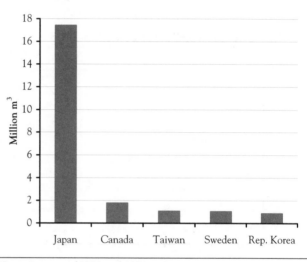

Note: Average of 2000 and 2001.
Source: Biomass and Bioenergy, Hillring, 2006.

GRAPH 9.5.2

Largest wood chip and particle exporters, 2000-2001

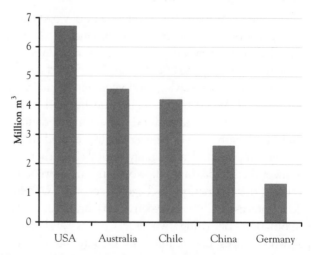

Note: Average of 2000 and 2001.
Source: Biomass and Bioenergy, Hillring, 2006.

9.5.2   European woodfuels trade patterns – fuelwood

The trade flow of wood chips and particles is intercontinental in nature, whereas solid fuelwood (firewood) trade patterns tend to be more restricted regionally. Europe, for example, produces and uses fuelwood and, while there is some trade within Europe, the amounts traded between Europe and the rest of the world are negligible (figure 9.5.3, graph 9.5.3 and 9.5.4).

FIGURE 9.5.3

European fuelwood trade patterns

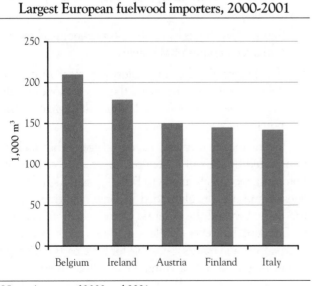

Note: Trade flows above 20,000 m³ per annum.
Source: Biomass and Bioenergy, Hillring, 2006.

GRAPH 9.5.3

Largest European fuelwood importers, 2000-2001

Note: Average of 2000 and 2001.
Source: Biomass and Bioenergy, Hillring, 2006.

GRAPH 9.5.4

Largest European fuelwood exporters, 2000-2001

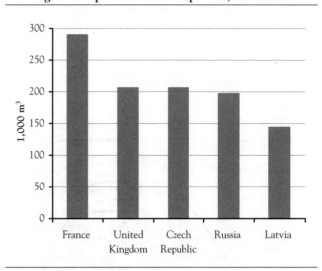

Note: Average of 2000 and 2001.
Source: Biomass and Bioenergy, Hillring, 2006.

9.5.3   Swedish woodfuels imports

In Sweden, woodfuels use has grown steadily since the end of the 1970s: bioenergy accounted for about 17% of Sweden's energy supply in 2004 (STEM, 2005). Bioenergy is used mainly for industrial purposes and for heating residential and commercial premises. A study of the Swedish foreign woodfuels trade in 2003 clarifies the amounts and sources of Swedish woodfuel imports (figure 9.5.4, tables 9.5.1 and 9.5.2)(Olsson, 2006). Traditionally, the Swedish woodfuels market has been predominantly a domestic one in that the majority of woodfuels used in the country have been Swedish in origin. Residues from felling and co-products from forest-related industries formed the major source of woodfuels in the 1980s and early 1990s, and these were vital for the rapid growth of Swedish bioenergy during these years. However, as the demand for woodfuels grew, importing them became economically feasible for large users such as district heating plants.

Tougher European waste legislation, the low cost of sea transport and a partial restructuring and privatization of the district heating sector were some of the driving forces behind the development of Swedish imports of woodfuels. Sweden's woodfuels imports in 2003 were slightly more than 25 PJ (equivalent to 8 to 12 million m³ of wood chips) (Olsson, 2006). A closer look at the data provides insight into what biofuels are imported, from where and how much. Sweden imports from three major regions: mainland Europe, North America and countries across the Baltic Sea, especially Latvia, Estonia and Belarus. Fuel from mainland Europe is exclusively waste products such as recovered wood and fuel from municipal waste steams, whereas North America is a big provider of pellets and tall oil (a pulping by-product used as fuel and as a raw material in the chemical industry). Pellets are also shipped in large quantities across the Baltic Sea, along with large amounts of peat and wood chips.

FIGURE 9.5.4

Swedish biofuel imports in 2003

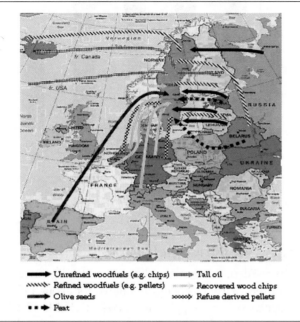

➡ Unrefined woodfuels (e.g. chips) ⟹ Tall oil
〰 Refined woodfuels (e.g. pellets) ⋯ Recovered wood chips
➡ Olive seeds ⋙ Refuse derived pellets
∙∙∙➡ Peat

Source: Olsson, 2006.

TABLE 9.5.1

Main Swedish biofuel import sources, 2003

Country	Volume GWh
Latvia	1,200
Canada	460
Belarus	410
Holland	390
Estonia	325
Spain	115
Norway	48
Finland	39
Total	7,032

Note: 1 GWh = 385 m³ of pellets or 1,282-1,818 m³ of wood chips.
Source: Olsson, 2006.

TABLE 9.5.2

Main Swedish biofuel imports by type, 2003

Biofuel	Volume GWh
Refined woodfuels (e.g. pellets)	1,200-2,100
Tall oil	1,270
Peat	1,260
Unrefined woodfuels (e.g. chips)	1,010
Recovered wood chips	412
Refuse derived pellets	220
Olive seeds	115

Note: 1 GWh = 385 m³ of pellets or 1,282-1,818 m³ of wood chips.
Source: Olsson, 2006.

9.6 Conclusion

9.6.1 Future woodfuels market development

Currently, Sweden and Denmark are the largest consumers of pellets in Europe. Countries with greater populations such as Belgium, Germany, the Netherlands, and the UK are rapidly increasing their pellet consumption, and the general rise in European pellet demand and pellet trade is expected to continue (graph 9.6.1).

GRAPH 9.6.1

Wood pellet consumption, 2001-2004

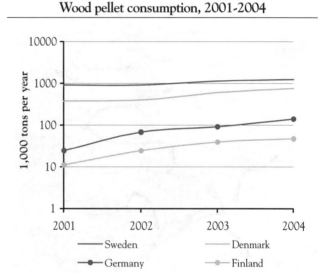

Note: Scale is logarithmic.
Source: Pellets for Europe, 2005.

This section presents available knowledge about woodfuels trade and attempts to predict developments in international trade generally, and for Europe in particular. Two factors seem likely to shape the potential developments:

• Transport by ship is by far the most economical means for larger amounts of woodfuels.

• The higher the heating value per mass unit (the calorific value of the fuel), the more economically viable the transport and thus the greater the potential for long-distance trade.

Taken together, these factors suggest that pellets transported by sea will make up a larger share of a future European woodfuels market. Pellets have high energy density and are already traded in large quantities across the Baltic Sea and the Atlantic Ocean, e.g. from Canada to Sweden. However, while sea transport of pellets is inexpensive and makes it possible for large parts of Europe to be integrated into a common woodfuels market, the transport economies will determine which regions will be integrated.

One plausible theory is that the large cost advantage of sea transport over land transport will limit the pan-European large-scale[53] woodfuels market to coastal regions. It is commonly acknowledged that road transport of woodfuels is not economically viable beyond 150 km. This limits the presumed woodfuels trade zone to coastal strips stretching at most 150 km inland. It should be added, however, that this is subject to change with petrol and diesel prices.

9.6.2 Future price development

While it may be difficult to predict price developments for an integrated European pellet market, it is certain that an integrated European woodfuels market will have a profound effect on current price levels in different countries.

A look at the current prices shows large differences between countries (graph 9.6.2). German prices, for example, are 50% higher than Swedish and Danish prices. Integration of these different national markets is likely to cause price fluctuations, leading ultimately to a common price level for the European woodfuels trade zone, as previously described.

GRAPH 9.6.2

European pellet consumption and prices, 2005

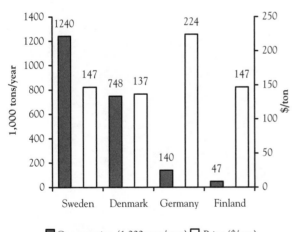

■ Consumption (1,000 tons/year) □ Price ($/ton)

Source: Pellets for Europe, 2005.

9.7 References

British Petroleum. 2005. *Statistical review of world energy 2005.* London.

Brege, S. & Pihlqvist, B. 2004. *Svensk planmöbelindustris beroende av en inhemsk spånskiveindustri samt förutsättningarna för en fortsatt tillväxt.* Swedish

Governmental Agency for Innovation Systems (Vinnova).Stockholm (in Swedish).

EU *Biomass action plan.* 2006. Available at: www.ec.europa.eu/energy/res/biomass_action_plan/ind ex_en.htm

Hektor, B. & Lundberg, H. 2006. *Biobränslen som handelsvara.* Presentation at *Sveriges Energiting 2006.* Available at: www.stem.se/WEB%5CSTEMFe01e.nsf/ V_Media00/C12570D10037720FC1257133004ED72 7/$file/Bo%20Hektor%20och%20Henrik%20Lundbe rg,%20Talloil.pdf (in Swedish).

Hillring, B. 1999. The Swedish Wood Fuel Market. *Renewable Energy* 16.

Hillring, B. 2006. World Trade in Forest Products and Woodfuel. *Biomass and Bioenergy* (in process).

Nordpool. 2006. *Elspot monthly prices.* Available at: www.nordpool.com/elspot/EUR.htm

Olsson, O. 2006. *The Swedish Biofuel Market – Studies of Swedish Biofuel Import and of the Effects of Hurricane Gudrun.* (Master's thesis).Swedish University of Agricultural Sciences.

Parkin, M. & King, D. 1995. *Economics.* Second edition. Addison–Wesley. Boston, Massachusetts, US.

Pellets for Europe. 2005. *Opportunities for Pellet Trade.* Available at: www.dk-teknik.dk/dk-teknik_docs/ showdoc.asp?id=050606173050&type=doc&fname= WIP_D20_Trade_20050517.PDF

Steierer, F. & Clark, D. 2006. *Regional Wood Overview.* A background study paper for the FAO/UNECE Working Party on Forest Economics and Statistics, 3 May. Available at: www.unece.org/trade/ timber/docs/stats-sessions/stats-28/english/regional_ wood_energy_overview.pdf

Stora Enso, 2006. Available at: www.storaenso.com

Swedish Energy Agency (STEM). 2003. *Växande Energi.* Eskilstuna, Sweden. Available at: www.stem.se

Swedish Energy Agency (STEM). 2005. *Energy in Sweden 2005.* Eskilstuna, Sweden. Available at: www.stem.se

Swedish Energy Agency (STEM). 2006. *Prisblad för biobränsle, torv, m.m.* 2000-2006. Quarterly publication. Eskilstuna, Sweden. Available at: www.stem.se

Swedish Energy Agency (STEM). 2006. *Prisbildning och konkurrens på elmarknaden.* Eskilstuna, Sweden. Available at: www.stem.se

UN News Centre. 2006. Annan calls for new approaches to energy efficiency. Available at: www.un.org/apps/news/story.asp?NewsID=18420&Cr =sustainable&Cr1=development

---

[53] Small- and medium-scale woodfuel consumption will presumably remain as at present, scattered over Europe where forest resources exist.

US Energy Information Administration, 2006a. Oil market basics. Available at:www.eia.doe.gov/pub/oil_gas/petroleum/analysis_publications/oil_market_basics/Trade_text.htm

US Energy Information Administration. 2006b. Petroleum prices. Available at: www.eia.doe.gov/emeu/steo/pub/fsheets/petroleumprices.xls

World Coal Institute. 2005. *Coal: Secure Energy.* Available at: www.worldcoal.org/pages/content/index.asp?PageID=294

Chapter 10

Public procurement policies driving certification: certified forest products markets, 2005-2006[54]

Highlights

- Certified forest area increased by 12% from 2005, reaching 270 million hectares by mid-2006, which is 7% of the global forest area.

- Certification remains largely confined to the northern hemisphere's temperate and boreal forests, and to developed countries: 87% of certified forest is in the UNECE region (58% in North America and 29% in western Europe).

- Roundwood production from certified forests represents approximately 25% of global production but only a tiny amount of this is labelled as being of certified origin.

- Only 2.7% of the commercially accessible forests in Russia were certified by mid-2006, making Russia's vast forests the prize for certification schemes: the Forest Stewardship Council (FSC) certified 9 million hectares in 2005, while a Russian certification scheme may apply for endorsement by the Programme for the Endorsement of Forest Certification (PEFC).

- Chain-of-custody certificates increased by approximately 20%, reaching 7,200 certificates worldwide, which still covers only a fraction of overall trade.

- In Asia, markets for certified forest products (CFPs) are rising in Japan, but China is producing CFPs mainly for export to North America and Europe.

- Public procurement policies for wood and paper products are increasingly specifying CFPs for assurance of sustainable forest management.

- Except in the Netherlands, there is a lack of demand from final consumers for CFPs.

- Procurement policies accounted for the origin of forest products, as well as the EU Action Plan for Forest Law Enforcement, Governance and Trade, may increase demand for CFPs.

- By May 2006, Canada accounted for over half of PEFC and almost one quarter of FSC worldwide certifications: the PEFC umbrella now covers more than two thirds of the total certified forest area worldwide, with FSC accounting for another 28%.

- Certification of non-wood forest products is gaining importance in developing countries as well as in the developed world.

---

[54] By Mr. Florian Kraxner, International Institute for Applied Systems Analysis, Dr. Eric Hansen, Oregon State University, and Dr. Toshiaki Owari, University of Tokyo.

Secretariat introduction

Certified forest products (CFPs) have received attention from Governments in new procurement policies for wood and paper products, which aim to ensure that purchases come from sustainably managed legal sources. Certification of sustainable forest management is also receiving more international attention as Governments develop policies on forest law enforcement and governance issues.

Private companies who want to project a "green" image in line with their corporate responsibility strategies are increasingly adopting similar responsible purchase policies in all sectors and not just in the forest sector. The UNECE Timber Committee monitors markets for CFPs, while the FAO European Forestry Commission follows developments in forest certification. They have jointly published a series of UNECE/FAO *Geneva Timber and Forest Discussion Papers* on certification issues.[55]

Following the 2005 market discussions, the Timber Committee and European Forestry Commission held a policy forum, Forest Certification: Do Governments Have a Role?[56] This showed that the level of government involvement varies considerably between countries: some take an active role in national certification, while others consider it a market responsibility and therefore avoid direct involvement. One outcome from 2005 was the decision to organize another policy forum in October 2006, Public Procurement Policies for Wood and Paper Products and their Impacts on Sustainable Forest Management and Timber Markets.

There are currently no official statistics for trade in CFPs, as confirmed by the FAO/UNECE Working Party on Forest Economics and Statistics in May 2006, reflecting the fact that CFPs do not feature in the Harmonized Commodity Description and Coding System (HS) maintained by the World Customs Organization. Therefore, the analysis presented here has been based on other sources, including responses from a survey of the UNECE Timber Committee and the network of country correspondents on certification of sustainable forest management and certified forest products markets of the FAO European Forestry Commission in the UNECE region. In addition, the authors interviewed key producers, retailers of CFPs, Global Forest and Trade Networks[57], auditing bodies and certification systems. The secretariat thanks all those who responded to these surveys, especially the country correspondents. Unless

otherwise attributed, all estimates and opinions in this chapter are from the authors' interpretations and analysis of the results of these surveys.

We sincerely appreciate the role of Mr. Florian Kraxner,[58] expert in CFPs, International Institute for Applied Systems Analysis, Laxenburg, Austria, who again led the production of this chapter. Dr. Eric Hansen,[59] Professor, Oregon State University, US, who wrote the first chapter on CFPs in 1998, contributed again to this analysis. He also presented CFP markets at the last Timber Committee Market Discussions. We welcome the new perspective on Asia provided by Prof. Toshiaki Owari,[60] University of Tokyo, Japan.

10.1 Introduction

The UNECE region's CFP markets have been analysed in a chapter in the UNECE/FAO *Forest Products Annual Market Review* since 1998. This year's chapter provides an overview of the market and trade of CFPs and concentrates on policy-related aspects of certification in the forest sector. CFPs bear labels demonstrating, in a manner verifiable by independent bodies, that they come from forests that meet standards for sustainable forest management (SFM). Consumers might find labels on furniture and wood products, while manufacturers can verify the sources through the certification scheme's chain-of-custody (CoC) procedures. Non-independently certified forests and their CFPs and process certification schemes such as ISO 14001 are not included in this analysis.

10.2 Supply of CFPs

By May 2006, the area of certified forest worldwide totalled 270 million hectares, approximately 7% of the world's forests (3.9 billion hectares) (FAO, 2005), a relatively steep increase since the first third-party certification of forest area took place in 1993 by the Forest Stewardship Council (FSC). However, compared

---

[55] Available at: www.unece.org/trade/timber/mis/cfp.htm

[56] Available at: www.unece.org/trade/timber

[57] WWF-led partnerships for responsible forest management and trade between non-governmental organizations, companies and communities.

[58] Mr. Florian Kraxner, expert in certified forest products markets, International Institute for Applied Systems Analysis, A-2361 Laxenburg, Austria, tel: +43 2236 807 233, fax: +43 2236 807 599, email: kraxner@iiasa.ac.at, website: www.iiasa.ac.at/Research/FOR.

[59] Dr. Eric Hansen, Professor, Forest Products Marketing, Forest Business Solutions Program, Department of Wood Science and Engineering, Oregon State University, 108 Richardson Hall, Corvallis, Oregon 97331-5751, US, tel: +1 541 737 4240, fax: +1 541 737 3385, e-mail: Eric.Hansen2@oregonstate.edu, website:
www.woodscience.oregonsate.edu/faculty/hansen/hansene.htm.

[60] Dr. Toshiaki Owari, Professor, Forest Business and Management, University Forest in Hokkaido, Graduate School of Agricultural and Life Sciences, University of Tokyo, Yamabe, Furano 079-1561, Japan, tel: +81 167 42 2111, fax: +81 167 42 2689, e-mail: owari@uf.a.u-tokyo.ac.jp

with the previous survey period (May 2004 – May 2005), the annual rate of increase in certified area has fallen by half to some 12% during the last 12 months. Approximately 1.5 million hectares in Sweden and another 0.8 million hectares in Canada are double certified by two different systems (graph 10.2.1).

- American Tree Farm System (ATFS);
- Canadian Standards Association Sustainable Forest Management Program (CSA, endorsed by PEFC in 2005);
- FSC;
- PEFC, formerly known as the Pan European Forest Certification System;
- Sustainable Forestry Initiative (SFI, endorsed by PEFC in 2005) in the US and Canada.

GRAPH 10.2.1

Forest area certified by major certification schemes, 1998-2006

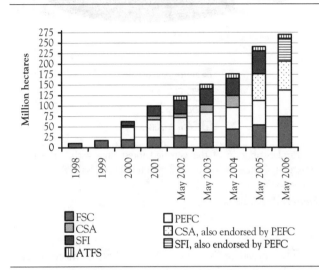

Notes: As of mid-2006 approximately 2.3 million hectares have been certified by more than one scheme. These are not deducted from one or the other scheme. The graph therefore shows a slightly higher amount of total forest area certified than exists in reality. FSC=Forest Stewardship Council. PEFC=Programme for the Endorsement of Forest Certification Schemes. CSA=Canadian Standards Association system (endorsed by PEFC in 2005). SFI=Sustainable Forestry Initiative (endorsed by PEFC in 2005). ATFS = American Tree Farm System.

Sources: Individual certification systems, country correspondents and Canadian Sustainable Forestry Certification Coalition, 2006.

Forest industry and consumers alike desire mutual recognition by two or more certification systems. However, this is not feasible between FSC and the Programme for the Endorsement of Forest Certification schemes (PEFC) in the near future due to controversies between them. Hence, there is a tendency in forest and CoC certification towards "dual-certification" or "double certification", i.e. the certification by two or multiple third-party schemes at the same time for the same forests and the same products (figure 10.2.1).

Since 2000 the certified forest area has risen sharply every year, mainly due to certification by:

FIGURE 10.2.1

Certification logos

Source: Certification systems, 2006.

In addition, the international Dutch Keurhout System has approved approximately 4.4 million hectares in Malaysia and some 1.2 million hectares of independently certified forests in Gabon.

PEFC endorsed the CSA system at the beginning of 2005, as well as SFI, the second largest certification scheme in North America, by the end of 2005. Allowing SFI to bear the PEFC label means including another 69 million hectares under the PEFC umbrella, which now totals 187 million hectares of certified forest area worldwide. Nevertheless, compared with the exponential growth of previous years, the increasing development of PEFC has slowed in terms of hectares added to the globally certified forest area.

FSC listed a total of 74 million hectares in May 2006, an increase of more than 20 million hectares, or one third by this scheme during the last 12 months. With SFI, PEFC has been able to include another big certification scheme in its system, but the resulting consortium could only increase its total certified area by some ten million hectares, or by 5%, from May 2005 to May 2006.

The third major system of North America is ATFS, which has remained relatively stable throughout the last five survey periods. Of the 11.7 million hectares in the ATFS, 10 million are certified. ATFS is seeking endorsement by PEFC and might join within the next year.

In terms of share of certified forest area, the market seems relatively equally divided (graph 10.2.2). FSC is slightly ahead, accounting for 28% of the area certified globally. With a share of 26%, CSA is the second largest scheme, slightly ahead of PEFC, with 23%, followed by SFI, with 20%. The smallest market share among the five major schemes is still held by ATFS, with 3% as of May 2006. As the CSA scheme and the SFI scheme were endorsed by PEFC in 2005, the total market share of the combined systems that are allowed to use the PEFC label on their CFPs has increased to more than two-thirds (69%).

GRAPH 10.2.2

Share of certified forest area by major schemes, 2006

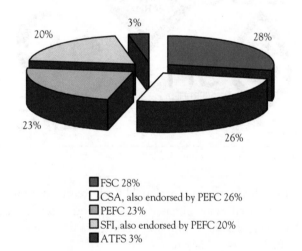

■ FSC 28%
□ CSA, also endorsed by PEFC 26%
■ PEFC 23%
□ SFI, also endorsed by PEFC 20%
■ ATFS 3%

Notes: If a forest area has been certified to more than one standard, the respective area has been counted to each of the certifying schemes involved; hence the grand total of certified forest area in this graph shows a higher amount (approximately 2.3 million hectares more) than exists in reality. ATF=9 million ha. CSA endorsed by PEFC=69 million ha. FSC=74 million ha. PEFC=63 million ha. SFI endorsed by PEFC=54 million ha. As of mid-2006.

Sources: Individual certification systems, Forest Certification Watch and Canadian Sustainable Forestry Certification Coalition, 2006.

Most of the PEFC-certified forest area lies in the northern hemisphere, i.e. non-tropical zones, with two thirds of it outside Europe (graph 10.2.3). The share in the tropics is less than 1%, but Gabon will soon be the first African country producing wood under the PEFC label. There is no PEFC-certified forest area in Asia or in European countries outside EU/European Free Trade Association (EFTA).

GRAPH 10.2.3

Regional distribution of certified forest area by PEFC (and PEFC - endorsed systems), 2006

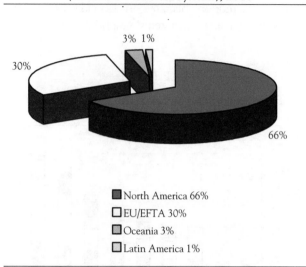

■ North America 66%
□ EU/EFTA 30%
▨ Oceania 3%
□ Latin America 1%

Notes: Distribution of the certified forest area within the PEFC system, including the endorsed CSA and SFI in North America. As of mid-2006.
Source: PEFC, 2006.

The spread of forests certified by FSC is more diverse than PEFC, but the overwhelming majority still lies in the northern hemisphere (graph 10.2.4).

GRAPH 10.2.4

Regional distribution of certified forest area by FSC, 2006

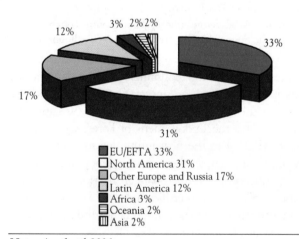

■ EU/EFTA 33%
□ North America 31%
□ Other Europe and Russia 17%
□ Latin America 12%
■ Africa 3%
▤ Oceania 2%
▥ Asia 2%

Note: As of mid-2006.
Source: FSC, 2006.

TABLE 10.2.1

Certified forest area and certified roundwood production by region, 2005-2006

Region	Total forest area (million ha)	Total certified forest area (million ha)		Area certified (% of total forest)		Estimated industrial roundwood produced from certified forest (million m³)		Estimated % of global industrial roundwood from certified forests	
		2005	2006	2005	2006	2005	2006	2005	2006
North America	470.6	140.2	157.7	29.8	33.5	180.6	201.8	11.38	12.71
EU/EFTA	155.5	78.5	78.9	50.5	50.7	160.1	162.5	10.09	10.23
EECCA	907.4	8.8	13.0	1.0	1.4	1.6	2.3	0.1	0.82
Oceania	197.6	3.4	6.4	1.7	3.3	0.9	1.6	0.05	0.10
Africa	649.9	6.2	2.1	1.0	0.3	0.7	0.2	0.04	0.01
Latin America	964.4	2.3	11.1	0.2	1.1	0.4	1.9	0.03	0.12
Asia	524.1	0.8	1.1	0.2	0.2	0.4	0.5	0.02	0.03
World total	3869.5	240.2	270.3	6.2	7.0	344.6	370.8	21.71	24.02

Notes: The source of the forest area (excluding "other wooded land") and industrial roundwood production from certified forests is FAO's *State of the World's Forest 2005* data. Roundwood production has been estimated by multiplying annual roundwood production from "forests available for wood supply" by the percentage of the regions' certified forest area (i.e. it has been assumed that the removals of industrial roundwood from each hectare from certified forests is the same as the average for all forest available for wood supply). However, not all certified roundwood is sold with a label. EECCA represents Eastern Europe, Caucasus and Central Asia, the new UNECE term for the 12 Commonwealth of Independent States (CIS) countries.

Sources: Individual certification systems, Forest Certification Watch, the Canadian Sustainable Forestry Certification Coalition, 2006, FAO, 2005 and the authors' compilation. As of mid-2006.

More than half (58%) of the world's certified forest is in North America, with around one third (29%) in the EU/EFTA region. North America's share of the certified forest area has remained almost unchanged since 2005, while the proportion in EU/EFTA is falling relative to increases in the share of other European countries, Russia, Latin America and Oceania. Nevertheless, even with this change, the area certified outside EU/EFTA and North America still only accounts for 12% of the global total (graph 10.2.5).

While the original driver for certification might have been uncontrolled deforestation in the tropics, in practice, its adoption has been far more successful in the northern than in the southern hemisphere, in the temperate and boreal regions than in the tropical zone, and in the developed than in the developing world. This trend still appears to be increasing. The ambitious certification efforts that are currently under way in the world's most forest-rich country, Russia, are likely only to serve to emphasize these disparities.

In western Europe, approximately half of the total forest area is certified, compared with one third in North America. The proportions in all other regions are much smaller, reaching a maximum of 1%, except for Oceania, with 3% of its forest area currently certified. In all regions except Africa, where there has been a decrease, the proportion of certified forest has increased since 2005 (graph 10.2.6 and table 10.2.1). The slight decrease in

Africa was caused by certified areas which, when audited, could not obtain an extension of their certification due to mismanagement or other problems.

GRAPH 10.2.5

Geographical distribution of total certified forest area, 2005-2006

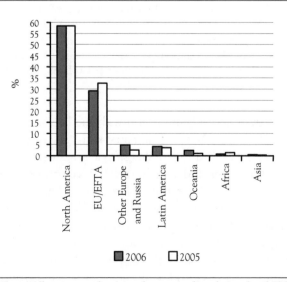

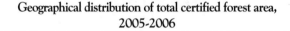

Notes: All major certification schemes combined. As of mid-2006.
Sources: Individual certification systems, Forest Certification Watch and Canadian Sustainable Forestry Certification Coalition, 2006.

The potential roundwood supply from the world's certified forests in 2006 is estimated at approximately 370 million m³, 8% more than in 2005 (table 10.2.1). This equates to approximately 25% of the world's production of industrial roundwood, or about 40% of the industrial roundwood production of North America and Europe (without Russia) where 87% of certified forests are situated. To estimate roundwood production from certified forest area, the regions' average annual removals on "forests available for wood supply" are multiplied by the percentage of the regions' certified forest area. According to the UNECE/FAO definition, roundwood is composed of industrial roundwood and fuelwood; however, the latter was not considered in this estimation.

GRAPH 10.2.6

Certified forest as a percentage of total forest area by regions, 2005-2006

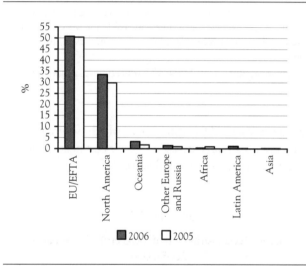

Notes: The forest area is based on the FAO *State of the World's Forests 2005* data, excluding the category "other wooded land." As of mid-2006. Asia is 0.2%.

Sources: Individual certification systems, Forest Certification Watch, Canadian Sustainable Certification Coalition 2006 and FAO, 2005.

North America is the region with the largest area of certified forest. Canada dominates with 120.7 million hectares of certified forest, almost four times that of the US (34.6 million ha) (graph 10.2.7). Even though the rate of increase in certified forest area has slowed, Canada's certified area grew by almost 20% in 2005. By May 2006, over half of PEFC-certified forest and almost one quarter of FSC-certified area were in Canada. The certified area in the US decreased by one million hectares. There were no significant increases in certified forest area in Finland (22.1 million ha), Sweden (15.6 million ha) and Norway (9.2 million ha). The same was true for Germany (7.7 million ha) and Poland (6.2 million ha). The newcomers in the top ten are Russia,

ranked sixth (9 million ha), followed by Australia (5.6 million ha) and Brazil (4.3 million ha). Russia and Australia showed growth rates over 100%.

In most of the top ten countries there is a clear tendency towards a single certification scheme. Canada, Finland, Norway, Germany, Australia and France are clearly dominated by PEFC or PEFC-endorsed systems. In Russia, Poland and Brazil, FSC is the predominant system. The US and Sweden have several schemes certifying almost equal amounts of forest.

Australia and Brazil have become the first countries from outside the UNECE region to feature among the top ten, but there are more countries that might enter the stage in the near future, such as Bolivia (1.9 million ha) and South Africa (1.6 million ha).

There are seven new countries that have certified forest area, two of which are within the UNECE region: Bulgaria (21,000 ha by FSC) and Luxembourg (17,088 ha by PEFC). Outside the region there is an increment of tropical and sub-tropical forest area certified totalling approximately 700,000 hectares in Guyana, Laos, Cameroon, Mozambique, the Republic of Korea and Viet Nam. FSC has issued the first certificates in all of these tropical countries.

GRAPH 10.2.7

Top 10 countries' certified forest area, 2005-2006

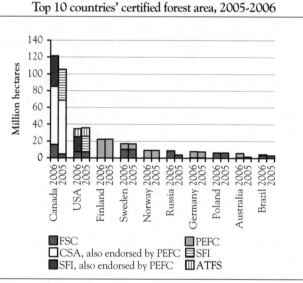

Notes: The graph contains no overlap owing to double certification. Areas are as of mid-2006 and mid-2005.

Sources: Individual certification systems, country correspondents, Forest Certification Watch and Canadian Sustainable Forestry Certification Coalition, 2006.

10.3 Demand for Certified Forest Products

Some European wood-producing countries such as Finland and Austria are close to reaching or have already reached 100% certification of their forests. This means that the entire roundwood production could bear a certification label from one of the major approving schemes. However, due to the frequent lack of demand by final consumers, on the one hand, and lack of incentive for the producer (i.e. a market advantage such as a price premium), on the other, the vast majority of these products, as in previous years, are marketed without any reference to certification. Netherlands is an exception, where the consumer is seen as the driving force for CFPs in the market. Downstream industries do not usually ask for commodity products to be certified, hence potential supply of CFPs exceeds actual demand in many markets, especially of PEFC-certified CFPs. An additional constraint impeding awareness of CFPs among the public is that most companies did not communicate that their products were certified (Owari *et al.*, 2006).

FSC CFPs from tropical wood are increasingly appearing in the shelves of do-it-yourself retailers and even supermarket chains selling garden furniture from tropical wood in western and central Europe, including the United Kingdom.

CFPs remain difficult to quantify due to the lack of official figures and trade classifications. One practicable tool for describing market characteristics such as the amount of CFPs in business-to-business markets is the number and type of CoC certificates.

Since 1998 the number of such certificates has increased tremendously. Between May 2005 and May 2006 the rate of increase was 20%, slightly lower than in previous years (graph 10.3.1). By mid-2006 the number of certificates worldwide totalled 7,200, of which 64% were by FSC and 36% by PEFC. These proportions are identical to those from the last survey, which indicates that both systems have increased at the same rate (20%) over the last year in terms of certificates issued. Prior to that, PEFC had enjoyed a significantly higher rate than FSC.

With some exceptions, the rate of increase in individual countries has been fairly evenly distributed. PEFC mainly gained in France (+207) and the United Kingdom (+102), as well as in the Czech Republic (+57), Belgium (+50), Canada (+48) and Germany (+45). During the past 12 months, the PEFC system has issued the first CoC certificates in Chile (nine) and China (two). On the other hand, FSC grew mostly in the United Kingdom (+118), as well as in the US (+87), the Netherlands (+55), China (+52), Japan (+42) and Germany (+46). FSC has approved the first CoC

certificates in Hong Kong S.A.R. (six) and New Zealand (one).

Both the SFI and CSA systems in North America have developed logos, licensing procedures and on-product labelling, but have not yet issued CoC certificates. FSC and PEFC remain the only schemes on the market, offering full CoCs for CFPs. FSC certificates have so far been issued in 73 (two new) countries and PEFC certificates in 22 (two new) countries.

GRAPH 10.3.1

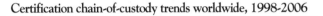

Certification chain-of-custody trends worldwide, 1998-2006

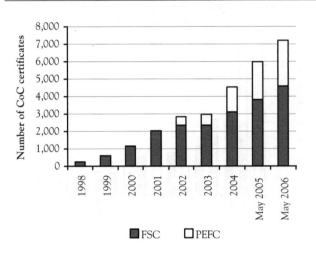

Notes: The numbers denote CoC certificates irrespective of the size of the individual companies, or of volume of production or trade. As of May 2006.
Sources: FSC and PEFC, 2006.

Using the total number of CoC certificates issued per country as an indicator for business-to-business demand for CFPs, France has taken the lead position from Germany within the UNECE region (graph 10.3.2). France had certificates from both schemes, PEFC accounting for 90% of all certificates issued in the country and FSC accounting for 10%. Germany is now rated second, with 62% of its certificates issued by the PEFC system, which is growing at the same rate as FSC certification. In third position is the United Kingdom, ahead of the US and Poland. Switzerland lost its position to the US because of the interim suspension of the Swiss Q-label system due to a non-conformity with the PEFC regulations. This ranking illustrates that in most countries' markets, with the exception of Germany, Belgium and Spain, there is an obvious dominance of one system, tending to converge toward one of the certification schemes.

In countries outside the UNECE region, almost all companies holding a CoC certificate obtained their certificates from FSC (graph 10.3.3). Japan leads with 310 certificates and is followed by Brazil, with 181 certificates, and China, with 148 certificates in mid-2006. The important market growth for CFPs for Asia is illustrated over the last year by the dominant position of Japan, the 50% growth in CoC certificates in China and the large number of certificates issued in Viet Nam, Malaysia and Indonesia. Growth in Asia is rising in parallel to South America. However, these companies are most often exporting to North America and Europe, rather than supplying their domestic markets, which have not yet demanded certified products.

GRAPH 10.3.2

Chain-of-custody certificate distribution within the UNECE region, 2006

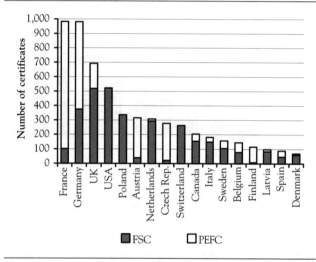

FSC   PEFC

Notes: Countries with less than 50 CoC certificates are not shown. The numbers denote CoC certificates irrespective of the size of the individual companies as of May 2006.

Sources: FSC, PEFC and authors' compilation, 2006.

The distribution of CoC certificates across the product range illustrates that companies from all wood-based industries and trade sectors hold CoC certificates. Companies holding CoC certificates of FSC (64%) cover a relatively wide product range (graph 10.3.4). Generally, the distribution of CoC certificates among industry sectors did not change over the last year. Wood manufacturing and sawnwood producers hold approximately half of the CoC certificates, with equal shares of 26%. Roundwood sellers hold approximately 14% of the certificates, 10% of which are in the furniture sector. PEFC CoC certificates (36% of the total) are mainly issued for timber trade and sawmilling, with almost the same shares, approximately one-third of the total. These two PEFC CoC main sectors are followed by other primary forest industries (13%). In contrast to last year's statistics, the timber trade sector lost some 13% to the benefit of the sawmilling industry and secondary wood manufacturing (graph 10.3.5). Due to non-comparable information and lack of data, one cannot conclude that FSC is the preferred scheme by the wood

manufacturing industry, while PEFC is preferred by the wood trading sector.

GRAPH 10.3.3

Chain-of-custody certificate distribution outside the UNECE region, 2006

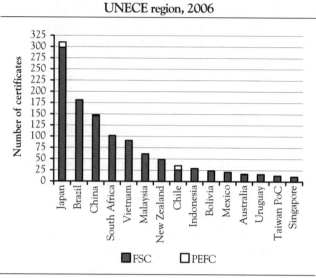

FSC   PEFC

Notes: The graph only includes countries with 10 or more CoC certificates. The numbers denote CoC certificates irrespective of the size of the individual companies as of May 2006. As of mid-2006, neither SFI, CSA nor ATFS have CoC.

Sources: FSC, PEFC and authors' compilation, 2006.

GRAPH 10.3.4

FSC chain-of-custody distribution by industry sector, 2006

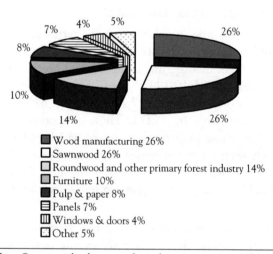

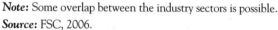

- Wood manufacturing 26%
- Sawnwood 26%
- Roundwood and other primary forest industry 14%
- Furniture 10%
- Pulp & paper 8%
- Panels 7%
- Windows & doors 4%
- Other 5%

Note: Some overlap between the industry sectors is possible.
Source: FSC, 2006.

GRAPH 10.3.5

PEFC chain-of-custody distribution by industry sector, 2006

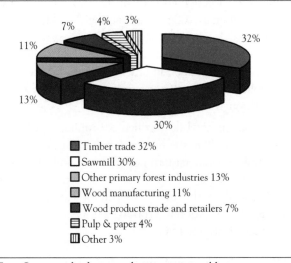

- ■ Timber trade 32%
- ☐ Sawmill 30%
- ▨ Other primary forest industries 13%
- ▨ Wood manufacturing 11%
- ■ Wood products trade and retailers 7%
- ▤ Pulp & paper 4%
- ▥ Other 3%

Note: Some overlap between the sectors is possible.
Source: PEFC, 2006.

10.4   Policy issues

10.4.1   *Public procurement, governance and illegal logging*

Public wood procurement policies continue to receive international attention and major developments have occurred in the past year. The emergence of NGO initiatives is very important, especially those concerning green building.

Heightened awareness of illegal logging and the trade of illegally derived wood products has led to an urgent need for better governance. Public procurement policies are increasingly being established as part of the solution to these problems (UNECE/FAO, 2006). During the last three years, major efforts have been taken to establish "green purchase" regulations for public entities by Governments and also by environmental non-governmental organizations (ENGOs) of European countries including Belgium, Denmark, France, Germany, Italy, Netherlands, Spain and Switzerland and the United Kingdom, as well as countries outside Europe, including the US and Japan. In many cases, public procurement officers satisfy the new requirements by purchasing only CFPs, which are seen by many procurement offices as guarantees of legally and sustainably sourced wood and paper products.

This development of the public procurement process for promoting sustainable forest management and giving preference to certified timber is, on the one hand, seen as an opportunity and as one of the driving forces for enhanced worldwide forest and CoC certification. Conversely, the broad public discussion on illegal practices and deforestation might also affect consumer trust in the certification schemes, or at least reduce the effectiveness of campaigns, communication, information and promotional activities to support forest certification.

At their March 2005 meeting, G8 Environment and Development Ministers outlined a number of steps to combat illegal logging, including public purchasing policies that help ensure that Governments do not contribute to illegal logging. Following the meeting, during the 2005 Gleneagles Summit, G8 leaders agreed to a number of measures to promote sustainable forest management. This action has spurred further development of purchasing policies, although treatment of the issue is inconsistent, with some countries reporting implementation of policies, and others with no developments to report. Several country correspondents reported continued ENGO pressure on Governments to adopt purchasing policies specifying that forest products should come only from sustainably managed forests. The Forestry Agency of Japan recently developed its *Guidelines for Verification of Legality and Sustainability of Wood and Wood Products*, which recognizes the main certification systems active in the UNECE region. According to the PEFC Council Newsletter of May 2006, Belgium recognizes PEFC in its public procurement guidelines.

In the United States, NGO initiatives are having the most significant impact in the marketplace. According to one industry analyst, green building is the main factor driving demand for CFPs, especially those that are FSC certified. The Leadership in Energy and Environmental Design (LEED) green building certification system from the US Green Building Council (USGBC) is growing quickly and maintains its exclusive commitment to FSC certification. Concentrated efforts by forest industry representatives to have the standard broadened have resulted in proposed changes to the system (USGBC, 2006). The Materials and Resources Credit 6 may change from "rapidly renewable" to "bio-based." This would allow entry for use of CFPs from non-FSC systems within LEED. Materials and Resources Credit 7 may also become "bio-based", but still require products from a certified source. It has been suggested that FSC is the only system that would satisfy the certification requirement at this time. If implemented, wood products could earn two of the 69 potential points in the LEED system. The proposed changes will be fully considered after a period of time for public comment. Green Globes, a green building certification system initially funded by the US forest industry (WSJ, 2006), recognizes the main forest certification systems operating in the UNECE region (Green Globes, 2006). Another noteworthy green building effort comes from the National Association of Homebuilders (NAHB). In 2006, the Association published its Model Green Home Building Guidelines, which recognize the main certification systems in the UNECE (NAHB, 2006).

Illegal logging is responsible for vast environmental damage in both developing and developed countries. But the damage is also economic, i.e. through reduced prices for legal timber, which must compete with illegal timber in a distorted marketplace. For example, timber prices in 2004 were between 7% and 16% less than they would have been if there had not been illegal logging, depending on the different product categories (AF&PA, 2006). The global annual loss has been estimated at approximately $15 billion, taking account of losses to Governments and to legal competitors (World Bank, 2006).

Timber is traded internationally and affected by procurement regulations. Hence, a highly desirable next step in the public procurement and governance procedure is harmonization of different national approaches. This step is also required to avoid artificial trade barriers, especially in the EU countries where most procurement policies are currently being developed. It is expected that harmonizing their national procurement policies will help prevent the same certified timber from being recognized as legal and sustainable in one country while considered inadequate in another. These kinds of market and trade distortions might also put at risk the efforts and achievements of civil society in developing certification as a tool to promote sustainable forest management. The EU Action Plan for Forest Law Enforcement, Governance and Trade (FLEGT) partly responds to this criticism by aiming at an innovative approach to tackle illegal logging. In the plan, the push for good governance in developing countries is linked with the legal instruments and leverage offered by the EU's own internal market.

Participants in the Timber Committee and European Forestry Commission Policy Forum in 2005 in Geneva, Switzerland, pointed out that Governments should try to remain neutral regarding competing schemes when considering their public procurement policies. Governments and other stakeholders should refocus on the commonly shared objective of promoting sustainable forest management, especially combating deforestation. They agreed further that certification is only one tool for achieving this objective and that the lack of information on production, consumption and trade of CFPs constrains decision-making of policy-makers, analysts and market actors.

10.4.2 Certification in the Russian Federation

In 1997, when the new Forest Code of the Russian Federation was published, an obligation in Article 71 was to certify the entire productive Russian forest area and to provide only certified wood to western markets by 2007. Since this government-driven decision, two third-party certification systems have been established in Russia. FSC started its direct certification process with the help of the

Working Group of the Russian National Council on Voluntary Forest Certification in 1999, and issued its first certificate for forest management in 2005. PEFC started its process later in 2004. The National Working Group has been developing the Russian State Forest Certification System since 2001, which aims at acceptance by mid-2006 in order to further proceed with the application for the assessment and endorsement process through PEFC.

FSC has meanwhile certified 8.9 million hectares of forest area mainly in the European part of Russia, but also in central Siberia, easternmost Siberia and the Altai Region. Also, the 27 CoC certificates by FSC were mainly issued in the European part of Russia and the Altai Region (National Working Group on Voluntary Forest Certification – FSC, 2005).

10.4.3 Developments on the Japanese and Chinese markets for certified forest products

Mainly because of their importance on the global wood market, Japan and China are the driving economies for the regional CFP market in Eastern and Southeast Asia. In Japan, a national certification scheme, Sustainable Green Ecosystem Council (SGEC), was introduced in 2003, and major paper manufacturers and house-building companies in Japan have decided to apply for this certificate. The dominating scheme in both Japan and China is FSC. The paper and tissue industries are the majority of CoC certificate holders in these countries.

Of surveyed respondents from the Japanese forest sector and paper industry, 77% had sold CFPs in 2004. The sales value of certified products reported by 84 respondents totalled $228 million, of which paper products accounted for 90%. The main certified products sold were paper for plain paper copy (PPC) and printing, wood chips as raw material for paper, and printed material such as environmental reports and calendars. Certified wood products such as sawnwood represented only a small proportion of sales. As with companies in Europe and North America, it was not possible for most Japanese companies to receive premium prices for CFPs (Owari and Sawanobori, 2006).

Major paper manufacturers in Japan have procurement policies which increasingly require the use of certified wood as raw material. In addition, the Japanese Government is aiming to tackle the serious problem of illegal logging. The new Law on Promoting Green Purchasing, public procurement requires the use of wood and wood-based products from legal sources. Forest area certification and CoC certification is seen as one appropriate tool to prove and promote legality and sustainability (Owari and Sawanobori, 2006).

In China, a National Forest and Trade Network (FTN) was launched in 2005 (White, 2006). Among the members there are eight companies representing some 425,000 hectares of FSC-certified forests and 753,000 m^3 (roundwood equivalent) of certified products in trade as of June 2006 (GFTN, 2006). Among the members of this fast growing network, the main drivers for the supply with CFPs are seen in two different areas. On the one hand, the export market, particularly in Europe, is seen as a main driver; on the other, due to the growing standard of living and related awareness of environmental issues such as the origin of forest products, green products' potential can be seen in the domestic market (White, 2006).

10.4.4   Non-wood forest products certification

Forests produce many non-wood forest products (NWFPs) that play an important role for millions of people worldwide, providing food, fodder, and other products and materials. Their trade provides employment as well as income, particularly for rural people and especially women (FAO, 2004). The total value of world trade in NWFP is approximately $13 billion.

While most NWFPs are used for subsistence and in support of small-scale, household-based enterprises, others provide raw materials for large-scale industrial processing for products such as foods and beverages, confectionery, flavourings, perfumes, medicines, paints and polishes. At least 150 NWFPs are of major significance in international trade. NWFPs may come from natural forests, forest plantations or agroforestry systems, and require special management and monitoring in order to ensure the long-term viability of species and to minimize adverse social and ecological impacts. NWFP harvesting is considered to have fewer negative impacts on forest ecosystems than timber harvesting and can provide an array of social and economic benefits. These benefits include carbon sequestration, watershed and soil conservation functions, diversification of income opportunities, and income benefits often yielded more quickly than timber. NWFP harvest and management is present in most forest management systems worldwide, for both commercial and subsistence purposes (Rainforest Alliance, 2006).

The positive development proves that after FSC permitted certification of NWFP management systems in 1998 and approved the first NWFP certification in Mexico in 1999, certification of NWFPs has steadily gained in importance. Many products such as palm hearts, maple syrup, medicinal, plants, forest tea and venison have been certified in developing countries and many others are in process, including herbal teas, pine nuts, cork, rubber and brazil nuts.

In Europe, PEFC has recently issued a CoC certificate for pine oil (mugolio), derived from Pinus mugo, a traditional forest product from northern Italy used to scent and purify air and for medical applications. The local tourism authorities also use this and other CFPs for internationally promoting the uniqueness of the region and its specialities, which shows additional benefit from a certification label.

10.4.5   *"Avoided Deforestation", Degradation and Forest Management Certification*

Approximately 13 million hectares of forests are lost every year due to deforestation activities. The net change in forest area from 2000 to 2005 is estimated at a loss of 7.3 million hectares per year (an area about the size of Sierra Leone or Panama), down from 8.9 million hectares per year from 1990 to 2000 (FAO, *Forest Resources Assessment 2005*, 2006).

Even though forest planting, landscape restoration and natural expansion of forests have significantly reduced the net loss of forest area, Africa, South America, Oceania, and North and Central America continued to have a net loss of forests. In Europe, the forest area continued to expand, although at a slower rate. Asia, which had a net loss in the 1990s, reported a net gain of forests during 2000 to 2005, primarily due to large-scale afforestation in China. This tendency again shows that deforestation mainly takes place in tropical forests while forest area is increasing in the North hemisphere.

These dimensions of forest loss indicate that deforestation is caused by conversion to agricultural land, fire, urban expansion, oil exploitation and mining. Forest degradation is due to legal and illegal logging, biofuel extraction and lack of forest management activities. Not only is biodiversity destroyed, but also the livelihoods of many of the world's poorest people. Deforestation is also a major source of greenhouse gas emissions. Hence, it has been proposed to include "Avoided Deforestation" in the Clean Development Mechanisms (CDMs) in the second commitment period of the Kyoto Protocol (post-2012), so that developing countries where deforestation has been taking place could be compensated for taking action to avoid deforestation, thus reducing carbon emissions (Fort and Iglesias, 2006).

In May 2006, participants in a workshop by the Joanneum Research Center and the Center for International Forestry Research (CIFOR) on avoided deforestation in Austria agreed that one major strategy to tackle deforestation and degradation is to ensure sustainable forest management, in addition to combating illegal logging, forest fires, forest degradation, and poverty in rural areas. An appropriate tool to confirm the application of sustainability criteria and indicators while combining them with economic and social topics might be third-party certification of the endangered forest area. Nevertheless, current arrangements under the United

Nations Framework Convention on Climate Change and the Kyoto Protocol were considered too cumbersome and costly to be applied by a large part of the business community, and are thus effective deterrents for participation in a scheme. More user-friendly schemes would be necessary; forest certification schemes might be one option.

10.5 References

American Forest & Paper Association (AF&PA). 2006. Available at: www.afandpa.org

AF&PA. 2006. *Sustainable Forestry Initiative.* Available at: www.afandpa.org/Content/NavigationMenu/Environment_and_Recycling/SFI/SFI.htm

American Tree Farm System (ATFS). 2006. Available at: www.treefarmsystem.org

Canadian Sustainable Forestry Certification Coalition. 2006. Available at: www.sfms.com

Canadian Standards Association (CSA). 2006. Available at: www.csagroup.org

Center for International Forestry Research (CIFOR). 2006. Available at: www.cifor.cgiar.org

FAO. 2005. *State of the World's Forest 2005.* Rome, Italy. Available at: www.fao.org/forestry

FAO. 2005. *Global Forest Resources Assessment.* Forestry Department. Rome, Italy. Available at: www.fao.org/forestry

FAO. 2004: *Trade and Sustainable Forest Management – Impacts and Interactions. Analytic Study of the Global Project GCP/INT/775/JPN: Impact Assessment of Forest Products Trade in the Promotion of Sustainable Forest Management.* Rome, Italy. Available at: www.fao.org/forestry

Forest Code of the Russian Federation. 1997. *Article 71. Mandatory Certification of Forest Resources.*

Forest Stewardship Council (FSC). 2006. Available at: www.fscoax.org/coc/index.htm

Forest Stewardship Council (FSC), Germany. 2006. Available at: www.fsc-info.org

Fort B. & Iglesias S. (editors). 2006. The Jakarta 12: Asia-Europe Agendas for Sustainable Development. Workshop 12. The Roles of Improved Tropical Forest Management in Climate Change Mitigation and Sustainable Development.

Global Forest and Trade Network (GFTN). 2006. Available at:www.panda.org/about_wwf/what_we_do/forests/our_solutions/responsible_forestry/certification/gftn/members/gftn_participants/index.cfm

Green Globes. 2006. Available at: www.greenglobes.com

International Tropical Timber Organization (ITTO). 2005. *Annual Review and Assessment of the World Timber Situation, 2005.* Yokohama, Japan. Prepared by the Division of Economic Information and Market Intelligence. Available at: www.itto.or.jp/live/Live_Server/377/E-AR05-Text.pdf

International Tropical Timber Organization (ITTO). 2006. Available at: www.itto.or.jp

Joanneum Research Center. 2006. *Reducing Emissions from Deforestation in Developing Countries. A Workshop to Discuss Methodological and Policy Issues.* Bad Blumau, Austria. 10-12 May 2006. Available at: www.joanneum.at/REDD/, www.joanneum.at/REDD/REDD-BOG1.pdf

Keurhout System. 2006. Available at: www.keurhout.nl

Leadership in Energy and Environmental Design (LEED). 2006. Available at: www.usgbc.org/DisplayPage.aspx?CategoryID=19&

National Association of Homebuilders (NAHB). 2006. Available at www.nahb.org/gbg

National Working Group on Voluntary Forest Certification – FSC. 2005. Russian National Framework on the National Standard for Voluntary Forest Certification – FSC. (In Russian).

Orsa Florestal. 2006. *Mercado de Madeira Certificada.* Powerpoint Presentation by R. Waack, A. Tacon & C. Graça. (in Portuguese).

Owari, T., Juslin, H., Rummukainen, A. & Yoshimura, T. 2006. Strategies, Functions and Benefits of Forest Certification in Wood Products Marketing: Perspective of Finnish Suppliers. *Forest Policy and Economics* (in press).

Owari, T. & Sawanobori, Y. 2006. *Analysis of the Certified Forest Products Market in Japan.* Berlin / Heidelberg, Germany, Springer, Holz als Roh- und Werkstoff (in press).

Programme for the Endorsement of Forest Certification Schemes (PEFC). 2006. Available at www.pefc.org

PEFC Czech Republic. 2006. Available at: www.pefc.cz/register

Russian Federal Forest Service. 2006. *Major Indicators of Forest Management Activities in Russia.* Moscow. 198 pp. (in Russian).

Rainforest Alliance. 2006. Available at: www.rainforest-alliance.org

Royal Institute of International Affairs (RIIA). 2006. Sustainable Development Programme. Available at: www.illegal-logging.info

UNECE Timber Committee and FAO European Forestry Commission. 2006. *UNECE Timber Committee and FAO European Forestry Commission Officially Nominated Country Correspondents on CFPs and Certification of Sustainable Forest Management* (unpublished survey).

UNECE/FAO. 2006. *Forest Certification: Do Governments have a Role?* by M. Koleva. UNECE Timber Section. Geneva Timber and Forest Discussion Paper 44. Proceedings and Summary of Discussions at the UNECE Timber Committee Policy Forum, 2005. Geneva, Switzerland. Available at: www.unece.org/trade/timber/docs/dp/dp-44.pdf

US Green Building Council. 2006. Available at: www.usgbc.org/ShowFile.aspx?DocumentID=1425

Wall Street Journal (WSJ). 2006. Timber Business Backs a New "Green" Standard. March 29.

White, G.. 2006. Responsible approach. Timber Trade Journal (TTJ). 13/20 May 2006, Available at Forest and Trade Asia website: www.forestandtradeasia.org

World Wildlife Fund. 2006. Available at: www.wwf.org

Chapter 11

Trade policies playing a major role in value-added wood products trade: Value-added wood products markets, 2005-2006[61]

Highlights

- Public procurement policies may change trade flows of value-added wood products at the cost of some regions in favour of others; UNECE region's benefits are uncertain.

- Asian furniture exporters' rapid penetration continued in all major markets; US imports grew rapidly while European markets remained flat.

- There is considerable controversy in the US bedroom furniture market over imports – furniture retailers and domestic manufacturers are on a collision course.

- Canadian furniture manufacturers filed a petition against Chinese furniture imports but lost, while US tariffs continue on some Chinese furniture.

- Facing lower cost imports, European furniture manufacturers have been trying to find ways to maintain competitivity without trade policy measures.

- In 2005 Europe's profiled wood imports were dominated for the first time by Brazil, China and Indonesia.

- Strong housing markets in the United States and Canada in 2004 and 2005 continued to drive demand for engineered wood products (EWPs).

- Glulam production reached another North American record in 2005, reversing the trend of increasing European imports, owing to the strong housing and non-residential markets.

- I-beam manufacturers gained market share in 2005 over solid sawn floor beams, open web wood trusses and steel, although a 5% drop in sawnwood prices constrained I-beam share growth.

- Laminated Veneer Lumber (LVL) production, following a dramatic increase in 2004, increased again in 2005, driven by the robust single-family housing market where open concept designs and customization by utilizing beams and headers create opportunities for EWPs.

- Life cycles for wood products such as sawnwood and sheathing plywood are well past their prime – EWPs are the wood products of the future because of their predictable performance, design efficiencies and effective use of wood resources.

---

[61] By Mr. Tapani Pahkasalo, Savcor Indufor Oy; Mr. Craig Adair, APA — The Engineered Wood Association and Dr. Al Schuler, USDA Forest Service.

Secretariat introduction

This chapter's analysis of the trade flows of value-added wood products (VAWPs) and engineered wood products (EWPs) complements our primary products market analysis. VAWPs indicate the demand for primary products, and are increasingly produced from commodity products driven by effective national economic development policies. These policies are changing the market flows; for example, more and more tropical VAWPs are being imported into the UNECE region.

The chapter is divided into two sections: value-added furniture and joinery products, and EWPs. As some of the production of primary products is not accounted for in statistics when integrated processing occurs, the chapter gives an indication of production and consumption through the trade statistics.

Mr. Tapani Pahkasalo,[62] Market Analyst, Savcor Indufor Oy, produced the value-added markets section. He assisted in this chapter's analysis last year and presented the findings at the Timber Committee Market Discussions. He is a member of the UNECE/FAO Team of Specialists on Forest Products Markets and Marketing and was a marketing assistant on the Forest Products Annual Market Review in 2003. Mr. Jukka Tissari, Head, Business Inteligence and Market Research, Savcor Indufor Oy, provided a technical review of the chapter. The analysis focuses on the top five countries' imports to capture the changes of trade flows between importing countries and supplier regions. Intra-regional trade is nevertheless important in VAWPs. The VAWPs section covers both market developments and policy developments.

The section on North American EWPs is provided once again thanks to Mr. Craig Adair,[63] Director, Market Research, APA–The Engineered Wood Association, and Dr. Al Schuler,[64] Research Economist, USDA Forest Service. Dr. Schuler is a member of the UNECE/FAO Team of Specialists on Forest Products Markets and Marketing. Innovations and new market applications for EWPs are part of the solution to the "sound use of wood" policy, as recommended by the UNECE Timber Committee and FAO European Forestry Commission.

---

[62] Mr. Tapani Pahkasalo, Market Analyst, Savcor Indufor Oy, Töölönkatu 11 A, FIN-00100 Helsinki, tel. +358 9 684 01115, fax +358 9135 2552, e-mail: tapani.pahkasalo@savcor.com, www.savcor.com/forest.

[63] Mr. Craig Adair, Director, Market Research, APA–The Engineered Wood Association, P.O. Box 11700, Tacoma, Washington, USA 98411-0700, tel. +1 253 565 7265, fax +1 253 565 6600, e-mail: craig.adair@apawood.org, www.apawood.org.

[64] Dr. Al Schuler, Research Economist, Northeast Forest Experiment Station, USDA Forest Service, 241 Mercer Springs Road, Princeton, West Virginia, USA 24740, tel. +1 304 431 2727, fax +1 304 431 2772, e-mail: aschuler@fs.fed.us, www.fs.fed.us/ne.

11.1 Introduction

VAWPs are used in the construction sector as EWPs and in builders joinery and carpentry (BJC) and profiled woods. In addition, the furniture industry's wooden products included in VAWPs. Demand drivers for VAWP consumption are housing and decoration activity, and increasingly, renovation, maintenance and improvement (RMI). North American demand comes in large part from new housing construction, while western European demand concentrates increasingly on RMI.

International division of labour deepens as production shifts increasingly eastwards and southwards. European trade has boomed over the years, not showing any signs of slowdown. However, the UNECE region has lost its comparative advantages of advanced technology, superior quality and design, effective distribution and networking. Industry associations in the UNECE countries have chosen to implement different competitiveness strategies; some actively pursue trade sanctions against ever-increasing imports while others seek to enhance the industry's competitiveness via diverse policy measures. US bedroom furniture imports from China were sanctioned for dumping, with almost no effect on imported quantities. Canadian furniture manufacturers lost a case against Chinese imports and European furniture manufacturers propose lowering the cost of work in Europe.

Several leading exporting countries of VAWPs are being accused of illegal logging. Governments' public procurement policies could have an impact on trade flows of VAWP in favour of some regions if they restricted imports from other ones. The obvious beneficiaries would be plantation-rich countries that produce standardized BJC products from similar raw materials; benefits for the UNECE region's national manufacturers are uncertain. Competitiveness can hardly be obtained by curtailing imports from more competitive regions. UNECE region's customers would be obvious losers of protective trade measures.

11.2 Imports of value-added wood products in 2004 and 2005

11.2.1 Wooden furniture imports in major markets

11.2.1.1 Market developments

The rapid growth in imports of the world's top five furniture importers (United States, Germany, United Kingdom, France and Japan) somewhat levelled off during 2005 (table 11.2.1 and graph 11.2.1). The world furniture market imports grew by $1.6 billion in 2005, the growth concentrating entirely in US import markets. US imports from Asia grew by the same figure, $1.6 billion, or 11%, compared to the year earlier. US furniture imports

TABLE 11.2.1

Wooden furniture imports for the top five importing countries, 2004-2005

(% of national imports)

Exporting regions	United States		Germany		France		United Kingdom		Japan	
	2004	2005	2004	2005	2004	2005	2004	2005	2004	2005
Asia	57.5	61.7	11.1	12.8	13.5	16.6	28.4	35.1	80.1	82.3
North America	19.4	17.6	0.2	0.1	0.4	0.4	1.5	1.9	2.1	1.7
Europe	14.1	11.8	87.2	85.4	81.4	78.6	66.1	59.7	17.6	15.8
Latin America	8.7	8.5	0.7	0.8	3.3	3.1	2.2	2.1	0.0	0.0
Others	0.3	0.4	0.9	0.9	1.4	1.3	1.9	1.3	0.2	0.1
Total imports in billion $	14.5	16.1	4.7	4.4	3.5	3.7	4.7	4.6	2.2	2.4
Of which furniture parts, billion $	1.6	1.9	0.8	0.9	0.5	0.5	0.7	0.7	0.4	0.5

Sources: Eurostat, Trade Statistics of Japan by Ministry of Trade and Customs, International Trade Administration (ITA), Under-Secretary for International Trade of the US Government, 2006.

totalled $16.1 billion, which is already more than the remaining four of the top five importers' furniture imports together. Housing construction activity has remained at record levels, which also boosts furniture demand. Population growth, due to immigration and high fertility, and larger homes combined with affordable furniture has increased furniture consumption and imports to record levels. Chinese furniture exports to the United States are now eight times higher than Italian imports. Canada is the second largest exporter and Italy is still the third largest exporter to the United States, although Italy's exports decreased by 14% to under $1 billion. Vietnamese wooden furniture exports to the United States grew 88% in 2005, while Chinese and Malaysian exports grew by 20%.

Total wooden furniture imports by Germany and the United Kingdom decreased by 5.6% and 2.5% respectively in 2005, dropping to $4.4 billion and $4.6 billion. Japanese and French furniture imports increased by 7.7% and 8% respectively, to $2.4 billion and $3.7 billion. Double-digit growth rates in total imports were not seen in Europe in 2005, partly due to slow economic growth in the area and to a weaker US dollar in past years' statistics.

Asian penetration in the European markets has nevertheless continued, mainly at the cost of intra-European trade. UK imports from Asia increased by an impressive 24%, French imports by 23% and the German imports from Asia also grew by 15%. Although total imports decreased in some markets, the Asian-originated furniture trade has continued to increase rapidly. UK imports from Italy slipped by over 15%, while imports from China expanded by 42%. Italy still maintains a narrowing lead as the world's largest furniture exporter (graph 11.2.2). German imports from China increased by 25%, but imports from Poland still have a clear lead. Romanian wooden furniture exports are rising slowly, in

part due to foreign direct investment from liberalized economic development policies.

Latin American exports, especially to Germany, have also increased, albeit at a low level. UK and German imports from other European sources suffered a significant decline, 12% and 8% respectively; however, intra-European trade to France increased slightly. This reflects the strong overall import growth in France. Italy is the largest exporter to France, although China's exports to France increased by 58% from 2004.

GRAPH 11.2.1

Furniture imports for the top five importing countries, 2001-2005

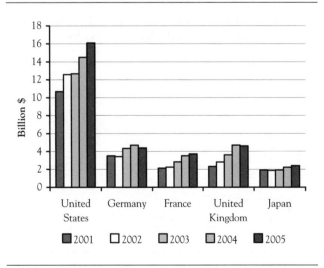
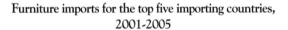

Sources: Eurostat, Trade Statistics of Japan by the Ministry of Trade and Customs, International Trade Administration (ITA), Under-Secretary for International Trade of the US Government, 2006.

TABLE 11.2.2

Builders joinery and carpentry imports for the top five importing countries, 2004-2005

(% of national imports)

	United States		Germany		France		United Kingdom		Japan	
Exporting regions	*2004*	*2005*	*2004*	*2005*	*2004*	*2005*	*2004*	*2005*	*2004*	*2005*
Asia	11.1	12.7	6.3	10.2	9.7	11.5	19.3	20.8	50.7	54.9
North America	67.3	67.4	0.4	0.3	1.2	1.1	9.3	10.0	10.1	8.1
Europe	6.0	5.8	92.4	88.4	85.4	83.1	57.9	57.0	33.2	30.5
Latin America	13.9	12.5	0.2	0.1	2.4	3.2	4.6	5.1	0.1	0.1
Others	1.7	1.5	0.7	1.0	1.2	1.1	8.8	7.1	5.9	6.4
Total imports in billion $	2.5	2.7	0.9	0.7	0.3	0.4	0.7	0.7	0.7	0.8

Sources: Eurostat, Trade Statistics of Japan by Ministry of Trade and Customs, USDA Foreign Agricultural Service, 2006.

TABLE 11.2.3

Profiled wood imports for the top five importing countries, 2004-2005

((% of national imports)

	United States		Germany		France		United Kingdom		Japan	
Exporting regions	*2004*	*2005*	*2004*	*2005*	*2004*	*2005*	*2004*	*2005*	*2004*	*2005*
Asia	21.3	28.7	13.1	20.3	10.1	13.5	35.3	38.1	71.8	75.7
North America	23.2	20.3	1.3	1.2	0.5	0.5	9.3	6.4	7.6	6.7
Europe	4.3	4.7	83.6	74.8	70.5	60.3	53.4	53.1	15.0	12.0
Latin America	47.8	43.5	0.7	1.8	14.9	23.0	1.0	1.8	4.2	4.6
Others	3.4	2.7	1.3	1.8	4.0	2.8	1.0	0.5	1.5	1.1
Total imports in billion $	1.5	1.6	0.2	0.2	0.2	0.2	0.3	0.3	0.3	0.3

Sources: Eurostat, Trade Statistics of Japan by Ministry of Trade and Customs, USDA Foreign Agricultural Service, 2006.

GRAPH 11.2.2

Wooden furniture exports from China, Italy, Poland and Romania to selected countries, 2000-2005

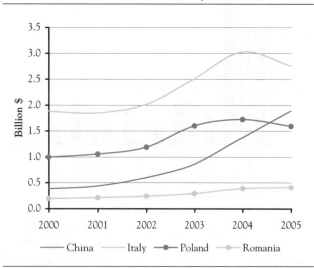

Note: Selected importing countries are France, Germany and the United Kingdom.

Source: Eurostat, 2006.

11.2.1.2 Policy development

The furniture sector is going through structural changes and the employment in the industry is falling in many of the UNECE countries. The German and Italian furniture industry were preparing an anti-dumping complaint against the Chinese furniture industry, but the European Furniture Manufacturers Federation decided not to get involved in such a petition for several political, financial and economic reasons (Press Release by the Union Européenne de l'Ameublement [UEA], March 2006). In addition, the UEA stated that the way towards "the solution to the loss of competitiveness of the European furniture industry does not lie in thinly veiled protectionist efforts but in the improvement of the competitive position of the EU industry. That means in the first place reduce its labour cost". The UEA proposes lowering the cost of work, without touching the workers' established system of benefits, by cutting social costs borne by the employer. Taxing consumption instead of labour and production would enhance the European industry's competitiveness. According to the UEA, this would not mean less revenue for Governments or higher prices for consumers.

In mid-2004, the US Department of Commerce (DoC) imposed anti-dumping duties ranging from 2.32% to 198% on Chinese bedroom furniture, depending on the degree of alleged "unfair pricing". In January 2006, the DoC began an administrative review of import duties, which is expected to be completed within one year (North American Lumber Market, January 2006). Despite facing duties, US imports of Chinese bedroom furniture also continue to increase in 2006.

The bedroom furniture trade dispute continues on the national level in the United States, with members of the Furniture Retailers of America and of the American Furniture Manufacturers Committee for Legal Trade on a collision course. The retailers are alleging that the anti-dumping complaint was motivated by the possibility of significant personal gains by furniture manufacturers. Some national manufacturers might receive tens of millions of dollars as a result of the so-called Byrd Amendment. The Byrd Amendment allows companies that filed successful anti-dumping petitions to receive the duties collected by the US Government from foreign competitors instead of earmarking those proceeds for the general treasury. In 2003, the World Trade Organization ruled that the Byrd Amendment violated global trade law. Now it seems likely that national manufacturers might lose these "anti-dumping dividends" (*Wood & Wood Products*, April 2006).

FIGURE 11.2.1

Wooden furniture using OSB frame

Source: APA – The Engineered Wood Association, 2006.

The Canadian Council of Furniture Manufacturers (CCFM), consisting of three regional associations (Quebec Furniture Manufacturers' Association, Ontario Furniture Manufacturers Association and Furniture West) filed a complaint with the Canadian International Trade Tribunal (CITT) requesting an investigation into home furniture imported from China (*Wood & Wood Products*, November 2005). In October 2005, the Canadian Trade

Tribunal dismissed the petition made by the CCFM and refused to initiate an anti-dumping investigation against Chinese household furniture imports (North American Lumber Market, March 2006). CITT said the products in question could not be categorized into a single product group but into a number of different ranges of products. CITT added that no information had been provided by CCFM on these separate products. Information was also missing on the proportion of local manufacturers affected and the losses per product incurred as a result of the Chinese imports.

To cope with the new reality, the Canadian furniture industry has created tools to improve its position in the domestic and international markets. The CCFM said that the formation of R&D and technology transfer investment funds, as well as the furniture industry research partnership, have been adopted to increase the industry's competitiveness.

The World Furniture Congress, held in May 2006, was to discuss the possible creation of a World Furniture Organization. Already more than 40 presidents of national furniture manufacturers organizations have indicated their participation, including from China. The organizers hope to be able to promote better international relations in the sector.

11.2.2 Builders joinery, carpentry and profiled wood markets

11.2.2.1 Market developments

Overall imports of BJC by the largest importers grew slightly from 2004 (graph 11.2.3 and table 11.2.2). However, the US imports continued a rapid growth trend, 8.6% in 2005, while German imports dropped over 20% and UK imports decreased a little, 2%. French and Japanese BJC imports grew moderately, 6.8% and 4.6%, respectively.

European and North American BJC markets continued subregional trade with neighbouring countries supplying some 60% to 90% of imported BJC products. The United Kingdom has the highest share of non-European imports; 43% of BJC products are imported from other regions. Asian imports continued to gain market share in Europe, Indonesia has appeared as a strong exporter in the past year. Indonesian exports to Germany grew impressively, by 43%, and exports to UK, by 15%. US markets continue to be dominated by the Canadian imports, followed by China and Brazil, with nearly equal shares, accounting for almost 50% of other than North American imports. Notable, however, is the 50% increase in Chinese BJC exports to the United States.

GRAPH 11.2.3

Builders' joinery and carpentry imports for the top five importing countries, 2001-2005

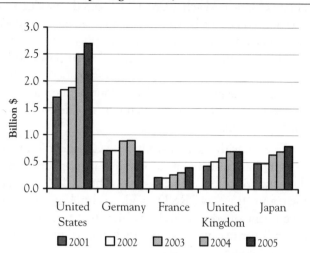

Sources: Eurostat, Trade Statistics of Japan by Ministry of Trade and Customs, USDA Foreign Agricultural Service, 2006.

Profiled wood imports by the largest importers did not experience significant growth in 2005. Total imports by the largest importers were $2.6 in 2005, 2.8% higher than in 2004. US imports represent 62% of total imports, totalling $1.6 billion in 2005 (graph 11.2.4 and table 11.2.3). There was a mere 3.4% growth compared with nearly 55% in 2004. German and Japanese imports declined, by 4.3% and 3.1% respectively, while French imports grew by 18% and UK imports increased slightly, by 2.1%. More interesting is that non-European (inter-regional) exporters have taken the lead in Europe in all markets, Indonesia being the largest supplier to Germany, China to the United Kingdom and Brazil to France. Also noteworthy is the 211% growth of Chinese exports to France. European profiled wood imports are quickly being replaced by cheaper exports from the emerging world. In the US import markets, Brazil continues to be the largest supplier, followed by China, Chile and Canada.

Plantation-rich countries such as Brazil and Chile, countries with abundant cheap labour combined with imported raw material such as China, and countries with cheap labour combined with large natural wood reserves such as Indonesia, have been successful in implementing strategies of moving into further processed products. This has created an enormous export-oriented wood processing industry in many countries, with China referred to as the "world's largest wood shop". Customers in the consuming countries, mainly in the UNECE region, are largely unaware of the products' origin, as doors, mouldings and profiled wood are sold without brands and labels through large retailers and chains.

Since the cost of wood in the mechanical forest industry, including VAWP manufacturing, represents a significant part of the production costs, the shift towards cheaper plantation timber is obvious. However, the vast softwood resources in Russia and natural hardwood forests in tropical Asia and parts of Africa are being harvested currently too. Natural forests' higher harvesting costs, combined with long transportation distances, have been set off by using cheap labour. Illegal logging, undermining the true cost of timber, has also kept the raw material cost down. Illegal loggers do not typically pay stumpage prices, royalties or any taxes for their profits. Modern plantations are managed sustainably to produce high quality raw material at minimum environmental and social disturbance. However, currently, the lack of economic opportunities for VAWP processing limits plantations mainly to fibre production for wood pulp. Plantation-owning companies, usually operating in the pulp and paper industry, rarely see solid wood manufacturing as sufficiently economically attractive.

GRAPH 11.2.4

Profiled wood imports for the top five importing countries, 2001-2005

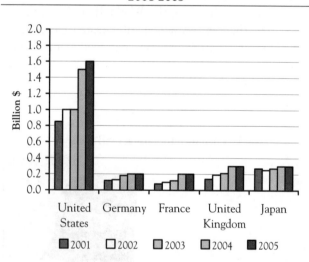

Sources: Eurostat, Trade Statistics of Japan by Ministry of Trade and Customs, USDA Foreign Agricultural Service, 2006.

Governments' public purchasing policies (PPPs) could change the trade pattern if the rules are also adopted by the private sector. Environmentally strict PPPs, requiring legality and sustainability of all wood products, would favour plantation-based countries, as they are usually better prepared to prove the origin of wood. Additionally, many plantations have been either PEFC or FSC certified to prove sustainability, and equipped with the necessary chain-of-custody certificates to prove legality. Illegal logging is a common problem in many of VAWP-producing countries. Illegal wood is relatively easy to "launder" into VAWPs and hard to retrace, even with chain-of-custody through certification systems.

11.3 North American engineered wood product markets

Strong housing markets in the United States and Canada in 2004 and 2005 continue to drive demand for EWPs as builders insist on products to satisfy knowledgeable homebuilders and buyers with good value. EWPs have improved predictable performance (over conventional sawnwood), which means fewer "callbacks" (for example, for squeaky floors or bowed walls) from dissatisfied customers. The following EWP analysis is based on North American data because it is the only information available in the UNECE region. The bulk of EWP production occurs in North America, due primarily to the prevalence of wood-frame residential construction.

Nevertheless, there is increasing usage of EWPs elsewhere. For example, Japan is using increasing volumes of EWPs (glulam and laminated sawnwood) for pre-cut, standard-sized post and beams. Post and beam construction, which is a labour-intensive technology, is the prevalent wood frame construction method in Japan. However, growing skilled labour shortages and stricter building standards are forcing the trend to factory-made, pre-cut technology.

11.3.1 Glulam timber

Glulam production reached another North American record of 720,000 m³ in 2005 (graph 11.3.1). The strong housing market, and a rebounding non-residential market, where exposed glulam has popular visual appeal, are major drivers. The 37% increase in production in North America between 2003 and 2005 reversed the trend of increasing imports from Europe – in fact, the small volume of imports fell by 21% between 2004 and 2005 (table 11.3.1).

FIGURE 11.3.1

Glulam beam used for garage door header

Source: APA – The Engineered Wood Association, 2006.

New home construction and remodelling together account for approximately two-thirds of the glulam consumption with the bulk used as floor beams and garage door headers (figure 11.3.1 and graph 11.3.2). The other major end use is non-residential, at 26%. New technology and product development will provide a basis for modest increased market share in the future. New generation beams with higher design strengths will increase opportunities in residential and non-residential applications. For example, LVL is being used as a tension laminate to strengthen beams and a thin layer of fibre reinforced polymers placed between wood laminations are being used to strengthen glulam and expand end-use applications.

GRAPH 11.3.1

Glulam production in North America, 2000-2006

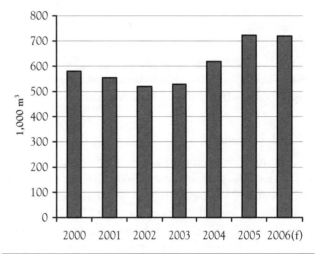

Notes: f = forecast. Conversion factor: 650 board feet per cubic metre.
Source: APA – The Engineered Wood Association, 2006.

GRAPH 11.3.2

Glulam end uses in North America, 2005

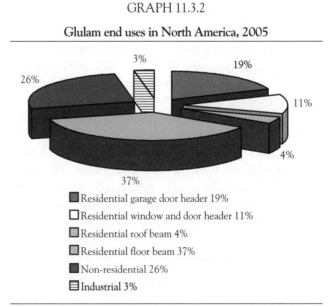

■ Residential garage door header 19%
☐ Residential window and door header 11%
▨ Residential roof beam 4%
▨ Residential floor beam 37%
■ Non-residential 26%
▤ Industrial 3%

Source: APA – The Engineered Wood Association, 2006.

TABLE 11.3.1

Glulam consumption and production in North America, 2002-2006

(1,000 m³)

	2002	2003	2004	2005	2006ᶠ	% change 2002-2006
United States						
Consumption						
Residential	324.6	332.3	415.4	466.2	453.8	40%
Non-residential	135.4	138.5	146.2	176.9	172.3	27%
Industrial, other	18.5	18.5	20.0	33.8	33.8	83%
Total	478.5	489.2	581.5	676.9	660.0	38%
Exports	21.5	15.4	10.8	15.4	29.2	36%
Imports	6.2	7.7	13.8	10.8	10.8	75%
Production	493.8	496.9	578.5	681.5	678.5	37%
Canada						
Consumption	15.4	18.5	21.5	24.6	23.1	50%
Exports	10.8	12.3	18.5	16.9	18.5	71%
Production	26.2	30.8	40.0	41.5	41.5	59%
Total North American production	520.0	527.7	618.5	723.1	720.0	38%

Notes: Conversion factor: 650 board feet per cubic metre. f = forecast.

Source: APA – The Engineered Wood Association, 2006.

11.3.2 I-beams.

I-beams are gaining market share, and in 2005 enjoyed a 44% share compared with 42% for solid sawn floor beams, 13% for open web wood trusses, and less than 1% for steel floor joists (graph 11.3.3). However, share growth in this key market is slowing (graph 11.3.4). This is to be expected as market share approaches 50%. I-beams compete with solid sawnwood; a 5% drop in sawnwood prices in 2005 may have affected I-beam share growth. However, it is believed that lower production in 2005 was a result of inventory adjustment from excess production in late 2004 and early 2005 (graph 11.3.5).

I–beams still have the advantages of predictable performance and quality with less waste compared to solid sawn floor joists (figure 11.3.2). With the continued consolidation in home building (the top ten builders now build over 20% of single-family homes in the United States compared to 10% a decade ago), growth prospects for I-beams, and EWPs in general, are good. The large builders are leading the transition from "site built" homes to more efficient, higher quality homes built with more factory-built components. The advantages of factory-built components (e.g. roof trusses, engineered wall panels, and EWPs) include less site waste, reduced labour content, and better quality control, which reduces possible "callbacks" from unhappy customers.

GRAPH 11.3.3

New residential raised floors in North America, 2005

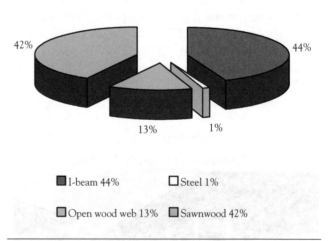

42%   44%

13%   1%

■ I-beam 44%   □ Steel 1%

□ Open wood web 13%   ■ Sawnwood 42%

Note: Types of beams supporting raised floors (as opposed to concrete slabs).

Source: APA – The Engineered Wood Association, 2006.

I-beam construction is changing due to economics. For example, in 1994, 74% of I-beams used LVL for flanges, but today, that number is closer to 50%. More manufacturers are substituting less expensive solid sawnwood and oriented strand lumber[65] to better target I-beam products to the most appropriate end-use applications.

---

[65] Lumber is used synonymously with sawnwood.

Most of the I-beams are consumed in residential construction, with 74% in new residential floors, 9% in renovation, and 3% in new residential roofs and walls (graph 11.3.6 and table 11.3.2). Only 14% goes to markets other than residential. However, the non-residential end uses are growing the fastest, in percentage terms – 171% between 2002 and 2006, compared with 16% in new residential end uses. Another significant part of the I-beam story is the rapid growth in production in Canada – 111% between 2002 and 2006 versus 17% in the United States. Canadian production now accounts for 34% of North American production compared to 23% just five years ago.

GRAPH 11.3.4

I-beam market share in the United States, 1999-2006

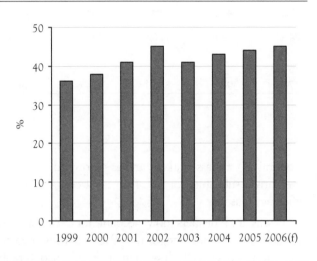

Notes: f = forecast. Wooden I-beam market share percentage of total raised floor area, single-family homes.
Sources: NAHB builder surveys, APA forecast, 2006.

GRAPH 11.3.5

I-beam production in North America, 2000-2006

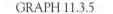

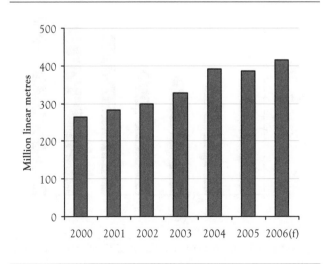

Notes: f = forecast. Conversion factor: 3.28 linear feet per metre.
Source: APA – The Engineered Wood Association, 2006.

GRAPH 11.3.6

I-beam end uses in North America, 2005

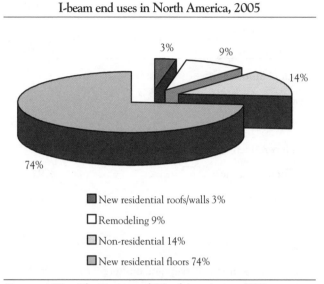

- ■ New residential roofs/walls 3%
- □ Remodeling 9%
- ■ Non-residential 14%
- ■ New residential floors 74%

Source: APA – The Engineered Wood Association, 2006.

FIGURE 11.3.2

I–beams used for raised residential floors

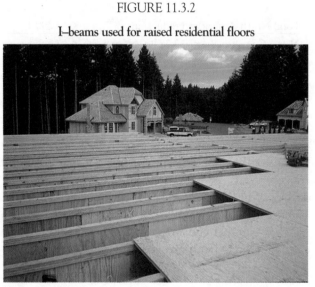

Source: APA – The Engineered Wood Association, 2006.

11.3.3 LVL

LVL production increased again in 2005 following the dramatic increase in 2004, driven by the robust single-family housing market (graph 11.3.7, figure 11.3.3 and table 11.3.3). In addition, homeowners' demand for higher ceilings, bay windows, three car garages, and open concept designs create opportunities for EWPs that facilitate innovative design options. Today's homebuyer wants (and can afford) more individuality or customization in home design, which favours design-friendly products with predictable performance properties like LVL. Incidentally, the same trends are apparent in furniture, kitchen cabinets, automobiles, and appliances – towards more customization. Along these same lines,

TABLE 11.3.2

Wooden I-beam consumption and production in North America, 2002-2006

(Million linear metres)

	2002	2003	2004	2005	2006ᶠ	% change 2002-2006
United States						
Demand - domestic markets						
New residential	247.6	232.0	263.4	291.2	286.6	16%
Non-residential, other	32.0	56.1	74.4	81.4	86.9	171%
Total domestic	279.6	288.1	337.8	372.6	373.5	34%
Production	230.5	243.3	268.3	258.2	269.8	17%
Canada						
Demand - domestic markets and offshore	36.0	39.3	41.8	40.5	41.2	14%
Production	68.6	84.1	122.6	126.8	144.8	111%
Total North American production	299.1	327.4	390.9	385.1	414.6	39%

Notes: Conversion factor: 3.28 linear feet per metre. *f* = forecast.
Source: APA – the Engineered Wood Association, 2006.

more independent construction managers can be observed in the residential markets – they are similar to "fabricators" in non-residential markets where steel and concrete are more prevalent. In addition, the development and availability of design/build/cost software – bringing homebuyers, homebuilders and vendors together – further enhances the market opportunities for customization in home building.

FIGURE 11.3.3

LVL beam and flanges for I–beams with OSB webs

Source: APA – The Engineered Wood Association, 2006.

Growth in demand for beams and headers is much faster than LVL for use as I-beam flanges. This trend is expected to continue as customization becomes more economical for mass markets, and as sawnwood and other alternatives substitute for LVL flanges for cost and design efficiency reasons.

Beams and headers now account for 55% of LVL demand and I-beam flanges for 39% – flanges used to account for over 70% less than a decade ago (graph 11.3.8).

GRAPH 11.3.7

LVL production in North America, 2000-2006

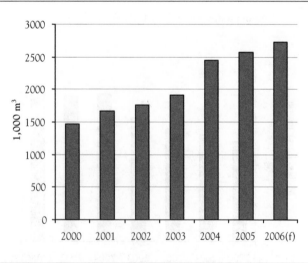

Notes: f = forecast. Conversion factor: 35.3137 cubic feet per cubic metre.
Source: APA – The Engineered Wood Association, 2006.

TABLE 11.3.3

LVL consumption and production in North America, 2002-2006

(1,000 m³)

	2002	2003	2004	2005	2006ᶠ	% change 2002-2006
Demand						
I-beam flanges	792.9	869.4	962.8	909.0	911.9	15%
Beams, headers, others	968.5	1042.1	1481.1	1656.6	1806.7	87%
Total demand (and production)	1761.4	1911.5	2443.9	2565.6	2718.6	54%
Production						
Total production US	1588.7	1744.4	2223.0	2347.6	2395.7	51%
Total production Canada	172.7	167.1	220.9	218.1	322.8	87%

Notes: Conversion factor: 35.3137 cubic feet per cubic metre. *f* = forecast.
Source: APA – The Engineered Wood Association, 2006.

GRAPH 11.3.8

LVL end uses in North America, 2005

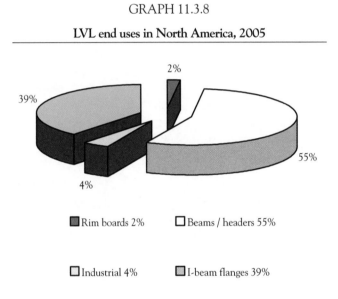

Rim boards 2% □ Beams / headers 55%

□ Industrial 4% ■ I-beam flanges 39%

Source: APA – The Engineered Wood Association, 2006.

GRAPH 11.3.9

Wood products and competitors life cycles, 2006

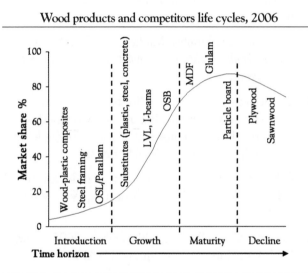

Note: OSL and Parallam are oriented strand lumber (sawnwood).
Source: USDA Forest Service, 2006.

11.3.4 Other composite products

Life cycles for wood products (as with most products) follow a predictable evolution from development, expansion, rapid growth, maturity, and finally, decline (graph 11.3.9). Key wood products such as sawnwood and sheathing plywood are well past their prime, and if wood products are going to flourish and remain competitive, they need new innovative products to compete with alternative building materials such as steel, concrete, and plastic. For example, Nucor, a major steel manufacturer in the United States, recently teamed up with Lennar Corporation, one of the nation's biggest homebuilders, to produce light gauge steel framing for the residential construction market.

There is no guarantee that wood will continue to be the preferred residential building material. We need to continually innovate to develop new products and systems that meet consumers' needs and solve customers' problems. EWPs are the products of the future, because of their predictable performance, design efficiencies and effective use of wood resources. New products being developed include oriented strand lumber, Steam-pressed Scrim Lumber[66] and composites of wood and non-wood materials. Steam-pressed Scrim Lumber uses small-diameter logs that are crushed into long strands and then pressed with an adhesive into a mat that can be sawn into final products for uses such as wooden beams. As these products come to market, they will be included in future

---

[66] www.cfr.msstate.edu/timtek

market analyses. Furthermore, innovations in building design software together with computer innovations (faster computation time, reduced cost, etc.) facilitate the customization in home building. Design-friendly EWPs are consistent with these trends.

11.4 References

APA – The Engineered Wood Association. 2006. *Market Outlook, Structural Panels and Engineered Wood, 2006 – 2011.* A publication for APA members only. Tacoma, Washington, USA.

EUROSTAT. 2006. External Trade. Available at www.epp.eurostat.cec.eu.int

International Trade Administration, Office of Trade and Industry Information. Available at www. ita.doc.gov/td/industry/otea/

North American Lumber Market. January 2006. *Global Wood Trade Network. Review of duties on Chinese bedroom furniture.*

North American Lumber Market. March 2006. *Global Wood Trade Network. Canada rejects anti-dumping application.*

Trade Statistics of Japan, Ministry of Finance and Customs. 2006. Japan Imports of Commodity by Country. Union Européenne de l'Ameublement (UEA) Press Release, 31 March, Brussels.

USDA Forest Service. 2006. Chart produced by Al Schuler. Northern Station, Princeton, West Virginia, USA.

Wood & Wood Products. November 2005. Vance Publishing, Lincolnshire, Illinois, USA.

Wood & Wood Products. April 2006. Vance Publishing, Lincolnshire, Illinois, USA. Editorial by Rich Christiansson.

Chapter 12

Public procurement policies affecting tropical timber exports: Tropical timber markets, 2004-2006[67]

Highlights

- Public procurement policies in importing countries are beginning to affect tropical timber exports.

- With less than 5% of tropical forests managed sustainably, countries are moving towards certification of sustainable forest management as a means to maintain exports to environmentally sensitive markets.

- China remains the world's top log importer: tropical log imports have almost tripled since the mid-1990s, but fell in 2005 as imports of non-tropical logs continue to boom.

- Tropical log production increased in 2005 by 2%, although log exports fell 8% as economic development policies take effect for more domestic value-added processing.

- Producer countries log exports fell again in 2005 to a level well under half the level exported just over a decade ago.

- Sawnwood exports from Malaysia increased by 10% to 2.8 million m³, benefiting from an Indonesian export ban.

- Log prices for some Southeast Asian species rose to eight-year highs in 2005 due to tighter supply of Asian logs heightened by crackdowns on illegal logging, restrictions on log exports and active buying from China and India.

- Malaysia and particularly Indonesia and Brazil are facing formidable competition from Chinese plywood exporters and losing market share in Europe and the United States.

- Prices of Brazilian plywood spiked in 2005 due to reconstruction following Hurricane Katrina in the southern United States.

- Brazil became the largest supplier of softwood plywood to the huge US market (well ahead of Canada) and lost its duty-free status in mid-2005.

- Chinese plywood imports remain at only around one-quarter of mid-1990s levels as authorities continue policies, including tariffs, to increase domestic plywood production from imported logs to boost employment and offset reduced domestic log supplies.

---

[67] By Dr. Steven E. Johnson, Dr. Jairo Castaño and Mr. Jean-Christophe Claudon, all from the International Tropical Timber Organization.

Secretariat Introduction

This analysis is possible thanks to continued close cooperation with our colleagues in the International Tropical Timber Organization (ITTO), whose *Annual Review and Assessment of the World Timber Situation 2005* and bi-weekly *Market Information Service* (MIS) reports serve as the basis for this chapter. We once again thank Dr. Steve Johnson,[68] Statistician and Economist, Dr. Jairo Castaño, MIS Coordinator, and Mr. Jean-Christophe Claudon, Statistical Assistant, for contributing this analysis.

Some of the terminology in this chapter differs slightly from the rest of the *Review*. In addition, due to unavailable data for several countries, 2004 is the base year for analysis in this chapter. Where possible, information for 2005 and 2006 has been included. ITTO categorizes its 59 members into producer (tropical) and consumer (non-tropical) countries, which together constitute 95% of all tropical timber trade.

For a complete analysis of trends in the production, consumption and trade of primary and secondary tropical timber products in relation to global timber trends, see the *Annual Review and Assessment of the World Timber Situation – 2005* prepared by the ITTO, which is available on the ITTO website (www.itto.or.jp).

12.1 Overview

The actual size of the tropical forest is estimated to be 814 million hectares, but the ITTO estimates that only 34 million hectares (approximately 4.4% of the total of the tropical forest) are managed in a sustainable way. Deforestation remains an important issue. In 2006, an alliance of developing countries led by Papua New Guinea and Costa Rica proposed a mechanism in which industrial nations would pay producing countries for avoiding deforestation in exchange for "carbon credits" to meet the requirements of the Kyoto protocol. Big producers of tropical timber such as Malaysia are moving to sustainable forest management practices. In 2007 Malaysia is going to impose a logging ban in the large forests of Sabah State on Borneo Island in order to protect the home of many wildlife species.

The production of tropical industrial roundwood ("logs") in ITTO producer member countries fell to 128.3 million m³ in 2004 (down from 130.2 million m³ in 2003), before rebounding to almost 131 million m³ in

2005 (figure 12.1.1). In 2005, Malaysia was still the number one exporter of all tropical timber products in the world.

_____

[68] Dr. Steven E. Johnson, Statistician and Economist, Dr. Jairo Castaño, Market Information Service Coordinator and Mr. Jean-Christophe Claudon, Statistical Assistant, Division of Economic Information and Market Intelligence, International Tropical Timber Organization (ITTO), International Organizations Center, 5th Floor, Pacifico-Yokohama, 1-1-1 Minato-Mirai, Nishi-ku, Yokohama 220-0012, Japan, tel: +81 45 223 1110, fax +81 45 223 1111, website: www.itto.or.jp, e-mail: itto@itto.or.jp.

FIGURE 12.1.1

Tropical timber harvesting

Source: FAO, 2006.

China remains the biggest importer of tropical logs and sawnwood. China's imports continued to drive the tropical log market despite falling back in 2004. Many of China's imported tropical logs are converted to plywood, with the country now being the world's third largest exporter of plywood.

In 2004 and 2005, Japan remained by far the biggest tropical plywood importer. Its imports increased by 38% in 2004 and remained stable in 2005 (+0.9%). However, domestic production is plummeting along with tropical log imports, while coniferous plywood imports and production steadily increase.

Many producer countries continued their shift from primary to secondary processed wood products exports in 2004, with trade in these products continuing to rival that of primary tropical timber products trade.

One issue that is starting to have an impact on the trade of tropical timber products is public procurement policies (PPPs) in major consumer markets. This issue was discussed in the annual ITTO Market Discussion in June 2006, which focused on *Timber Markets and Procurement Policies*. Some opportunities arising from PPPs were identified: stronger demand for certified wood; improved returns from investment in certification; reduced unfair competition from illegal wood; and market opportunities for timber certified by a variety of certification systems (as opposed to only one certification scheme).

However, some threats were also acknowledged, including: inconsistent policies at the national level creating a barrier to trade; major beneficiaries likely to be forest owners in wealthy northern countries; single-issue environmental group (ENGO) campaigns leading to an unbalanced approach; procurement requirements reflecting media-inspired perception of forestry issues; non-sustainable development needs of supplying countries; goal posts constantly shifted to satisfy ENGOs; and green requirements on timber not matched by equivalent requirements on substitutes. It was noted that some EU member governments (the United Kingdom, Belgium, the Netherlands, France, Germany and Denmark) were developing their own PPPs with little evidence of coordination, let alone harmonization. Furthermore, formal efforts to develop PPPs were only at the level of the national government, which was a less significant timber buyer than local and regional government (estimated at 200,000 authorities). Influencing local governments was considered a challenge as their procurement policies were often driven by public preconceptions and the media rather than objective assessment.

However, most speakers agreed that the ongoing trend among European countries to increase PPPs for tropical forest products was a reality that was expected to persist. It was concluded that producers should engage themselves in the process of the development of PPPs to avoid being excluded from the market. Some producers expressed the hope that the EU Forest Law Enforcement, Governance and Trade (FLEGT) initiative would provide common requirements applicable to all EU member countries as well as to domestic and imported timbers. The possibility was emphasized that wood could be substituted by other materials not subject to the strict requirements facing the wood sector.

TABLE 12.1.1

Production and trade of primary tropical timber products, ITTO total, 2004-2005

(Million m³)

	2004	2005	% Change
Logs			
Production	131.1	133.9	2.1
Imports	15.6	15.8	1.2
Exports	12.1	11.0	-9.1
Sawnwood			
Production	42.5	43.3	1.8
Imports	11.1	10.6	-4.5
Exports	10.9	11.0	0.9
Veneer			
Production	3.7	3.9	2.7
Imports	1.3	1.5	15.3
Exports	1.1	1.4	27.2
Plywood			
Production	20.6	20.7	0.4
Imports	10.9	11.1	1.8
Exports	10.4	10.7	2.8

Source: ITTO *Annual Review and Assessment of the World Timber Situation* – 2005, 2006.

This chapter provides details of trends in trade and prices of major primary tropical timber products by all 59 ITTO members (table 12.1.1). For trends in secondary products, see chapter 11.

12.2 Export trends

ITTO producer countries exported nearly 12 million m³ of logs worth $1.6 billion in 2004. Producer log exports in 2004 were down 8% from 2003 levels and fell further to 10.9 million m³ in 2005, well under half the level exported just over a decade ago. Malaysia continues to dominate the trade in tropical logs with 5.1 million m³ exported in 2004, constituting 42.8% of ITTO producer member exports (graph 12.2.1). Malaysia's log trade in 2004 decreased in volume by 6.4% from 2003 levels, and a further 12.1% to 4.5 million m³ in 2005. Malaysia's major log customers are all in Asia, with China, Taiwan Province of China (PoC), India and Japan being the major markets.

GRAPH 12.2.1

Major tropical log exporters, 2003-2005

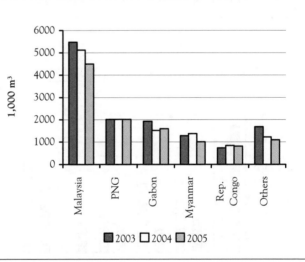

Note: PNG = Papua New Guinea.
Source: ITTO, 2006.

Sawnwood exports by producer members appeared to jump by nearly 31% to 10.5 million m³ (worth $2.2 billion) in 2004, remaining stable in 2005. However, this large apparent increase in 2004 was due to an adjustment in Indonesian figures in line with trading partner reports (graph 12.2.2). Exports from the Latin American and Asia-Pacific regions fluctuated in 2004 and 2005, with African exports following a steady upward trend. ITTO members account for most global exports of tropical sawnwood, with Singapore and Paraguay the only significant non-member exporters in 2004. Malaysia continues to lead the trade in tropical sawnwood, with the 2.8 million m³ exported in 2004 constituting 27% of total ITTO producer member exports. Malaysia's sawnwood trade rose by 10% in 2004 as its major markets of China, Taiwan PoC, Thailand and the Netherlands increased their consumption.

GRAPH 12.2.2

Major tropical sawnwood exporters, 2003-2005

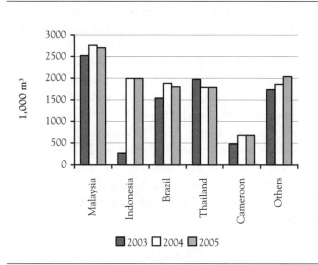

Note: Indonesia's large apparent increase in 2004 was due to an adjustment of export statistics in line with trading partner reports.
Source: ITTO, 2006.

GRAPH 12.2.3

Major tropical veneer exporters, 2003-2005

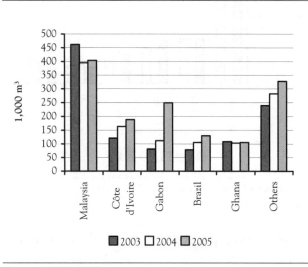

Source: ITTO, 2006.

Veneer exports from ITTO producer countries increased by 8.1% in 2004 to slightly over 1 million m³, worth $491 million, increasing a further 25.1% in 2005. Malaysia continues to be the dominant tropical veneer exporter, with exports of 396,000 m³ in 2004 accounting for 38.4% of the ITTO producer member total (graph 12.2.3) Malaysian exports are mainly directed to China, Japan, Taiwan PoC, the Philippines, and the Republic of Korea. The EU accounted for 57.6% of total consumer country tropical veneer exports in 2004. Italy, Spain and

Germany are the largest EU tropical veneer exporters. Total exports by ITTO consumer countries were stable in 2005.

GRAPH 12.2.4

Major tropical plywood exporters, 2003-2005

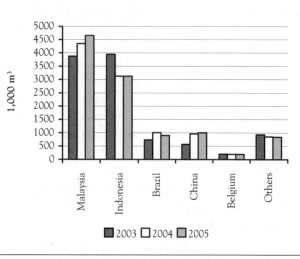

Source: ITTO, 2006.

Tropical plywood exports by producer members in 2004 declined by 1.8% to just under 9 million m³, worth nearly $3.1 billion, with Malaysia (4.3 million m³) and Indonesia (3.1 million m³) accounting for 71% of this total (graph 12.2.4). As for production, 2004 marked the first year when Malaysia's plywood exports exceeded those of its neighbour. Indonesia's exports remained stable in 2005, but Malaysia's increased by 7% to almost 4.7 million m³. Its exports are mainly to Japan, the Republic of Korea and the United States. Indonesia was traditionally Malaysia's major competitor in the tropical plywood trade, but its exports slumped by 21% to 3.1 million m³ in 2004 and remained at around that level in 2005. Indonesian exports are down from highs of around 10 million m³ (or 85% of total ITTO producer exports) in the early 1990s. This decrease is mainly due to stronger logging controls in Indonesia, which have resulted in a fall in production of tropical logs, from 35 million m³ in 2001 to 23 million m³ in 2005. Indonesia wants to restructure and reduce its own wood industry as well and increase imports to supplement domestic log supplies. The Indonesian wood industry has been facing stronger government controls and restructuring in the recent years.

Growth of China's tropical plywood exports has been rapid and notable, reaching 959,000 m³ in 2004 (up 69% from 2003 levels), and increasing a further 4% in 2005 to over 1 million m³. Brazil remained the third largest exporter of tropical plywood in 2004, but China overtook it in 2005.

Tropical plywood exports from the EU grew by 2% to 488,000 m³ in 2004, when it accounted for slightly more than 32% of consumer exports. EU exports were mainly from Belgium and France in 2004. Total consumer country exports of tropical plywood were stable at just over 1.5 million m³ in 2005.

12.3 Import trends

Total imports of tropical hardwood logs by ITTO members decreased 3% to 15.6 million m³ in 2004, about 29% (or 3.5 million m³) greater than total tropical log exports reported by all members. The gap between reported imports and exports increased to 44% (just over 4.8 million m³) in 2005.

Differences between reported ITTO imports and exports are to some extent made up by reported log exports from the Solomon Islands and Equatorial Guinea, the two largest non-ITTO tropical log exporters with exports averaging around 400,000 m³ each in recent years. Other non-member tropical log exporters are less significant (all under 100,000 m³ per year) and include Mozambique, Laos, Singapore, Guinea, Guinea-Bissau, Benin, Vietnam and Madagascar. The reported sum of all log exports by non-ITTO tropical countries in 2004 was 1.5 million m³, which leaves 2 million m³ or more tropical imports by non-ITTO members (estimated to be around 500,000 m³) to be accounted for by unrecorded or under-reported exports and/or over-reported imports from both members and non-members.

GRAPH 12.3.1

Major tropical log importers, 2003-2005

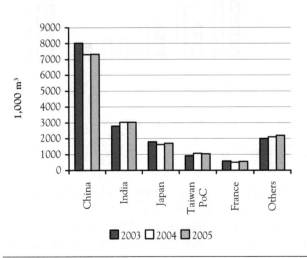

■ 2003 □ 2004 ■ 2005

Source: ITTO, 2006.

Tropical log imports by ITTO consumer countries declined by 6% to 11.9 million m³ in 2004 due to a 9% reduction in China's imports, which fell for the first time in over a decade (graph 12.3.1). However, log imports by ITTO consumer countries increased by 1.2% in 2005 to

nearly 12 million m³ due primarily to an increase in Japanese tropical log imports. China, still the world's top tropical log importer, maintained imports at 7.3 million m³ in 2005.

China's tropical log imports, which accounted for almost half of total ITTO imports in 2004-2005, have almost tripled since the mid-1990s, with Malaysia, Papua New Guinea, Gabon, Myanmar and the Republic of Congo the main sources. China's import of non-tropical logs continues to boom, with Russia providing the bulk of the 19 million m³ imported in 2004. China's total log imports from all sources remained at 26 million m³ in 2005, exceeding by far those of all other countries.

Japan's imports of tropical logs decreased 9% to 1.6 million m³ in 2004, but rose 5% in 2005. Despite this increase, Japan's imports have still nearly halved in the past decade due to: the contracting economy during most of the period; reduced supplies from Malaysia; competition from China for available log supplies; increasing reliance on softwood logs for plywood manufacture; and higher imports of sawnwood and plywood.

India, on the other hand, is now the world's second largest importer of tropical logs with imports up by 9% to over 3 million m³ in 2004. This strong increase is explained by the fact that import duties in India are generally higher for processed wood products (15% in 2005 for plywood and veneer) than they are for logs (5% in 2005). This policy is set to promote downstream processing in the country. In 2004, India increased plywood production by 10% and veneer production by 4.8%.

EU countries imported over 1.3 million m³ of tropical logs in 2004, down 2% from 2003. European log imports rebounded to almost 1.4 million m³ in 2005. Most EU tropical log imports continue to come from African producers. Imports by France, the largest EU tropical log importer, decreased by 13% to 506,000 m³ in 2004 as log export restrictions in some of its main suppliers (Cameroon, Gabon, Liberia and the Republic of Congo) were imposed or strengthened. French imports increased to 550,000 m³ in 2005.

Total ITTO imports of tropical sawnwood increased 11% to over 11.1 million m³ in 2004, but declined to 10.6 million m³ in 2005. With 2004 imports of almost 3 million m³, China is by far the top tropical sawnwood importer (graph 12.3.2). China's imports increased by 4.3% in 2004, and a further 7% in 2005 to offset reduced log imports from Indonesia. China's tropical sawnwood imports are mainly from Indonesia (32%), Thailand (28%) and Malaysia (14%). China, Hong Kong Special Administrative Region and Taiwan PoC together account for over 50% of ITTO consumer imports in

2004. Taiwan PoC's reported imports were sharply down in 2005.

GRAPH 12.3.2

Major tropical sawnwood importers, 2003-2005

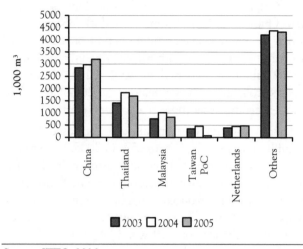

Source: ITTO, 2006.

Thailand's imports (which more than halved in the Asian financial crisis of 1998) also increased by 30% to 1.8 million m³ in 2004, returning to pre-crisis levels. Japan's imports of tropical sawnwood decreased 23% to 378,000 m³ in 2004, but increased 15% to 434,000 m³ in 2005. Imports of tropical sawnwood by all consumer countries increased by 5.9% in 2004 to 7.7 million m³ and remained stable in 2005.

GRAPH 12.3.3

Major tropical veneer importers, 2003-2005

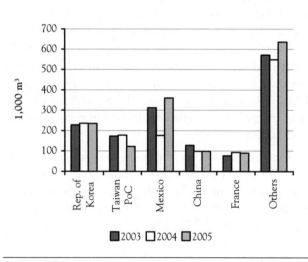

Source: ITTO, 2006.

Total ITTO tropical veneer imports decreased 11% to 1.3 million m³ in 2004, followed by an increase of 16% in 2005. With a 3.5% increase in 2004, the Republic of

Korea remained the largest tropical veneer importer at 236,000 m³ (graph 12.3.3). Tropical veneer imports by the Republic of Korea were stable in 2005. Taiwan PoC is the second largest tropical veneer importer, at around 177,000 m³ in 2004 and 122,000 m³ in 2005. Mexico, ITTO's third largest tropical veneer importer in 2004 at 175,000 m³, passed Taiwan PoC and the Republic of Korea in 2005 when its reported imports doubled to 361,000 m³. Meanwhile, China's imports (previously ITTO's largest) dropped by 23% to 98,000 m³ in 2004 and remained the same in 2005 as it increasingly met its veneer needs via production from imported tropical logs.

EU imports of tropical veneer increased in 2004 to 357,000 m³ (up by 17.4%) before decreasing in 2005 to 345,000 m³ (down by 3.3%), accounting for over one-fifth of total ITTO imports. The majority of European imports are from African producers (mainly Cameroon, Côte d'Ivoire, Gabon and Ghana). Japan imported 44,000 m³ of tropical veneer in 2004, a 10% increase from 2003 levels, but reduced imports by 4.5% in 2005 to 42,000 m³. Formerly a major tropical veneer importer, Japan is now a less significant importer than producer countries such as Malaysia and the Philippines.

GRAPH 12.3.4

Major tropical plywood importers, 2003-2005

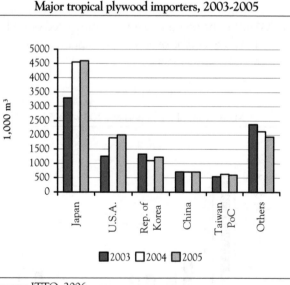

Source: ITTO, 2006.

Total ITTO imports of tropical plywood jumped by 15.6% to almost 11 million m³ in 2004, with a smaller increase to 11.1 million m³ in 2005. The majority of all tropical plywood imports are sourced from Indonesia and Malaysia (53% and 44% respectively in 2005 for the top importer, Japan).

Japan continues to replace domestic tropical hardwood plywood production with domestic softwood plywood production (mainly from imported Russian larch logs), imported plywood (tropical and non-tropical) and substitutes like OSB and MDF. Its tropical plywood imports increased by 1% to 4.6 million m³ in 2005 after a strong increase of almost 38% in 2004 when new product quality requirements began to be met in supplying countries (graph 12.3.4). The recent trend toward increasing plywood imports by Japan is partially due to its difficulty in obtaining tropical logs for domestic production in the face of competition from China. Low prices (compared to the cost of domestic production) also continue to make imported plywood more attractive than domestic production. Japan is also now importing significant quantities of low-priced tropical plywood from China.

The United States overtook the Republic of Korea as the second largest tropical plywood importer in 2004 at over 1.8 million m³, a strong increase from the depressed levels of 2003. US tropical plywood import sources were 21.1% from Indonesia, 25.7% from Malaysia and most of the rest from China and Brazil. The Republic of Korea was the third largest tropical plywood importer in 2004, at over 1.1 million m³. China's imports dropped 1.4% in 2004 to 706,000 m³ and remained stable in 2005. Chinese imports remain at only around one-quarter of mid-1990s levels as authorities continue policies to increase domestic plywood production from imported logs to boost employment and offset reduced domestic log supplies. Tariffs on imported plywood are 15%, compared to zero for logs. Taiwan PoC (628,000 m³) was also a substantial tropical plywood importer in 2004, from Malaysia (48.1%), Indonesia (42.3%), and China (7.7%).

EU imports of tropical plywood totalled nearly 1.2 million m³ in 2004, a 15.7% decrease from 2003 levels. EU imports are mostly by the United Kingdom, Belgium, the Netherlands, Germany, Italy and France. Most of the EU tropical plywood also came from Indonesia and Malaysia, with Brazil and inter-European trade also playing a fairly large role in many countries' imports. China continued to export growing amounts of tropical plywood to the EU, with quality and pricing concerns leading to anti-dumping actions against some products. European imports of tropical plywood increased slightly in 2005.

12.4 Prices

Prices for most primary tropical timber products and species kept strengthening during 2005, as supply of raw materials worsened, global economies expanded and consumer confidence improved in most markets.

African log and sawnwood prices, except sapele and wawa (obeche), held on to gains made in 2004, with some species (African mahogany or khaya) reaching new record highs in 2005 (graph 12.4.1). Wawa prices, which jumped nearly 60% in late 2004 due partially to the listing of ramin in CITES' Appendix II, lost some ground in 2005. Wawa sellers saw the reduced ramin availability,

for which wawa is a substitute, as an opportunity to raise prices. African logs and sawnwood products, which are generally priced in euros, recovered competitiveness due to a weaker euro and as prices for Southeast Asian products quoted in US dollars rose. Price gains were also due to combinations of the following factors: shortages in supply of certain species; political unrest in Côte d'Ivoire and Liberia; the ongoing UN Security Council embargo against Liberian exports[69]; bans on exports of 20 primary species in Cameroon; tax increases in several countries; shipping bottlenecks; and rising freight rates. Price increases were moderated, however, by dull demand in the European market. West African producers fear that once the Société Nationale des Bois du Gabon (SNBG) ceases its export monopoly and price leadership role in 2006, prices for okoume and ozigo logs could become volatile.

GRAPH 12.4.1

Tropical hardwood log price trends, 2004-2006

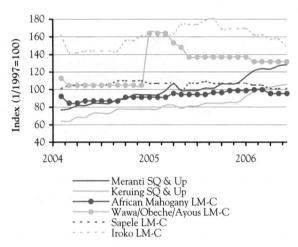

Note: SQ & up, L-MC are grade specifications.
Source: ITTO, 2006.

Log prices for some Southeast Asian species rose to eight-year (keruing) and 12-year (meranti) highs in 2005 due to tighter supply of Asian logs heightened by crackdowns on illegal logging, restrictions on log exports and reduced logging quotas in Indonesia (graph 12.4.2). These increases were also the result of active buying from China and India despite some resistance to higher prices by buyers in Japan. Prices of other Asian tropical log species have still not fully recovered to the highs of the mid-1990s. Price gains and new record highs also continued in 2005 for rubberwood logs for domestic consumption in Malaysia's export-oriented furniture

---

[69] The UN Security Council lifted its Liberian timber export ban on 21 June 2006. However Liberian President Ellen Johnson Sirleaf announced a moratorium on timber exports pending new forest sector legislation.

sector. Soaring prices of natural rubber have resulted in reduced timber supply from rubber plantations.

GRAPH 12.4.2

Tropical sawnwood price trends, 2004-2006

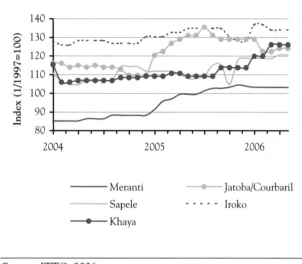

Source: ITTO, 2006.

Nominal prices for most Asian and African tropical sawnwood species were stable or rising in 2005. African mahogany (khaya), sapele, iroko, meranti and seraya reached new record highs in 2005 or early 2006. The US continued as the major market for export khaya (African mahogany) as the supply of South American mahogany, strongly favoured by US consumers, remained limited. Prices for Latin American tropical sawnwood rose to new record highs during 2005 due to a limited export quota for mahogany in Peru and price corrections in Brazil as a result of the strengthening of the real.

There was increased interest in African tropical sawnwood from major buyers in 2005, due to a switch away from Malaysia as prices for meranti sawnwood remained firm due to log shortages and an export ban on sawnwood, imposed by Indonesia in September 2004.

Iroko sawnwood prices quoted in pounds Sterling were slightly rising or relatively stable for most of 2005, while prices for this species in US dollars dropped by over 11% due to the strengthening of that currency (graph 12.4.3).

Prices for Asian plywood continued rising in 2005 and early 2006, reflecting continuous shortages in log availability and tighter control of illegal logging in Indonesia and elsewhere. Even higher prices were prevented by fierce competition from Chinese plywood. Prices were still about 10% or more below of the highs of 1996 in early 2006. Due to limited supply, Indonesian plywood continued to lose market share in Japan and Europe to Malaysian tropical plywood and Chinese "combi" plywood products with poplar or bintagor cores. Malaysian and Chinese plywood products will continue

gaining ground in major markets as the long-term trend is towards declining availability from Indonesia. In addition, several importers have been searching for alternatives to Indonesian plywood due to concerns over illegal logging, despite some improvements in controls. In late 2005 the EU was preparing to implement a licensing scheme ("FLEGT") to certify the legality of timber imported from exporting countries that volunteered to participate in the scheme.

GRAPH 12.4.3

Odum/iroko price trends, 2003-2005

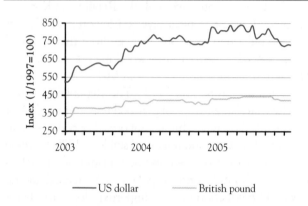

Note: Grade First & Seconds, 25 mm thickness, UK market.
Source: ITTO, 2006.

GRAPH 12.4.4

Tropical plywood price trends, 2004-2006

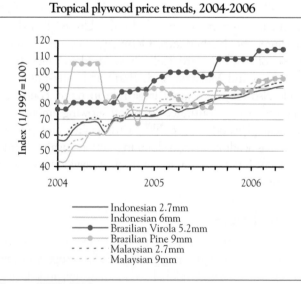

Source: ITTO, 2006.

Prices of Brazilian plywood continued rising in 2005 thanks to strong demand in the United States and the United Kingdom (graph 12.4.4). Prices of these products rose sharply from September due to reconstruction following Hurricane Katrina in the southern United States. Prices of white virola plywood, the most popular Brazilian product, reached eight-year highs in early 2006. However, the impact of Katrina on prices was expected to be short-lived.

With Brazil becoming the largest supplier of softwood plywood to the huge US market (well ahead of Canada), the product lost its duty-free status in mid-2005. Most buyers in Europe were refraining from placing additional orders for Brazilian plywood due to the substantial price increases in 2005. European buyers were sourcing alternative plywood grades from elsewhere in Europe and from China. Brazil is facing stiff competition from Chinese plywood exporters, which, with a more favourable exchange rate and low production costs, have managed to make inroads in Europe and the United States at more competitive prices.

12.5 References

ITTO. 2005a. Annual Review and Assessment of the World Timber Situation – 2005. Available at: www.itto.or.jp

ITTO. 2005b. ITTO Tropical Timber Market Report (biweekly). Available at: www.itto.or.jp

ITTO. 2006c. Status of Tropical Forest Management 2005. Available at: www.itto.or.jp

Annexes

Components of wood products groups

(Based on Joint Forest Sector Questionnaire nomenclature)

The important breakdowns of the major groups of primary forest products are diagrammed below. In addition, many sub-items are further divided into softwood or hardwood. These are all of the roundwood products, sawnwood, veneer sheets and plywood. Items that do not fit into listed aggregates are not shown. These are wood charcoal, chips and particles, wood residues, sawnwood, other pulp and recovered paper.

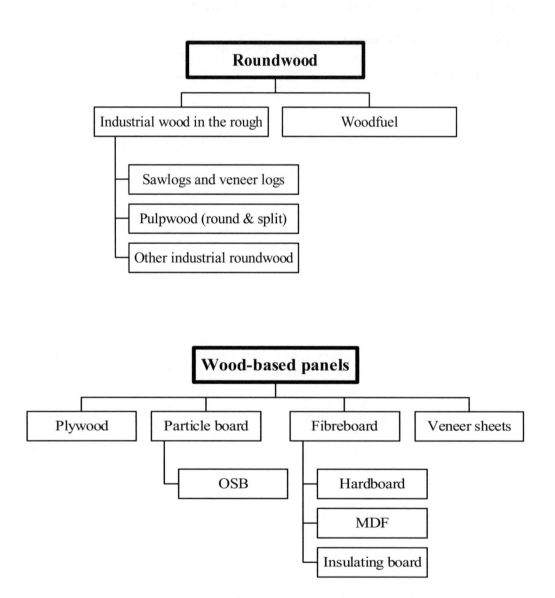

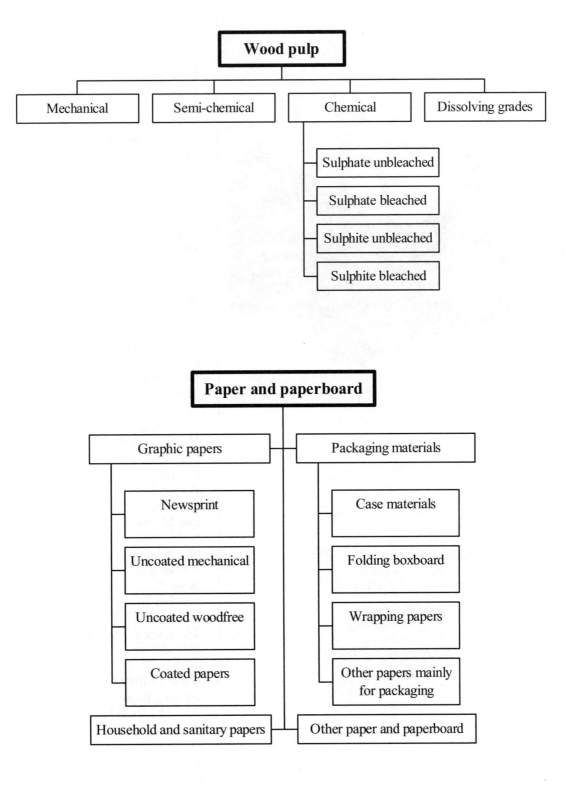

Countries in the UNECE region and its subregions

Europe subregion

Eastern Europe, Caucasus and Central Asia (EECCA)

North America subregion

Europe subregion (* = EU member)
Albania
Andorra
Austria *
Belgium *
Bosnia and Herzegovina
Bulgaria
Croatia
Cyprus *
Czech Republic *
Denmark *
Estonia *
Finland *
France *
Germany *
Greece *
Hungary *
Iceland
Ireland *
Israel
Italy *
Latvia*
Lichtenstein
Lithuania *
Luxembourg *
Malta *
Monaco
Montenegro
Netherlands *
Norway
Poland *
Portugal *
Romania
San Marino
Serbia
Slovakia *
Slovenia *
Spain *
Sweden *
Switzerland
The former Yugoslav Republic of Macedonia
Turkey
United Kingdom *

Eastern Europe, Caucasus and Central Asia (EECCA) subregion
Armenia
Azerbaijan
Belarus
Georgia
Kazakhstan
Kyrgyzstan
Republic of Moldova
Russian Federation
Tajikistan
Turkmenistan
Ukraine
Uzbekistan

North America subregion
Canada
United States

Sources of information used in the *Forest Products Annual Market Review*

- APA – The Engineered Wood Association, United States, (www.apawood.org)
- Bureau of Labor Statistics, United States, (www.stats.bls.gov)
- Canadian Standards Association, CSA International, (www.csa.ca)
- Canadian Sustainable Forestry Certification Coalition, (www.sfms.com)
- *Commerce International du Bois*, France, (www.ifrance.com/cib-ltb)
- Council of Forest Industries, Canada, (www.cofi.org)
- Ecosecurities, United Kingdom, (www.ecosecurities.com)
- European Central Bank, (www.ecb.int)
- European Federation of the Parquet Industry (FEP) (www.parquet.net)
- European Panel Federation (EPF), (www.europanels.org)
- EUROSTAT – European Union Statistical Office, (www.europa.eu.int/comm/eurostat)
- Federal Statistical Office, Germany, (www.destatis.de/e_home.htm)
- Fédération Nationale du Bois, France, (www.fnbois.com)
- Finnish Forest Industries Federation, (www.forestindustries.fi)
- Finnish Forest Research Institute (Metla), (www.metla.fi)
- Finnish Sawmills (www.finnishsawmills.fi)
- *Forest Products Journal*, United States, (www.forestprod.org/fpjover.html)
- Forest Stewardship Council (FSC), (www.fsc.org)
- *Hardwood Market Report*, United States, (www.hmr.com)
- *hardwoodmarkets.com*, United Kingdom, (www.hardwoodmarkets.com)
- *Hardwood Review Export*, United States, (www.hardwoodreview.com)
- *Hardwood Review Weekly*, United States, (www.hardwoodreview.com)
- *Holz Journal* (ZMP), Germany, (www.zmp.de/holz/index.asp)
- *Holz-Zentralblatt*, Germany, (www.holz-zentralblatt.com)
- *Import /Export Wood Purchasing News*, United States, (www.millerpublishing.com/ImportExportWoodPurchasingNews.asp)
- Infosylva (FAO), (www.fao.org/forestry/site/22449/en)
- International Monetary Fund, (www.imf.org)
- International Organization for Standardization (ISO), (www.iso.ch)
- International Tropical Timber Organisation (ITTO), (www.itto.or.jp)
- *International Woodfiber Report*, United States, (www.risiinfo.com/risi-store/do/home/…)
- *Inwood*, New Zealand, (www.nzforest.com)
- *Japan Lumber Journal*, (www.jlj.gr.jp)
- *Japan Lumber Reports*, (www.n-mokuzai.com/english.htm)
- Japan Monthly Statistics, (www.stat.go.jp/english/data/getujidb/index.htm)

- Japan Wood-Products Information & Research Center (JAWIC), (www.jawic.or.jp/english/index.php)
- *La Forêt,* Switzerland, (www.wvs.ch/topic5477.html)
- *L'Echo des Bois*, Belgium, (www.echodesbois.be)
- *Maskayu*, Malaysia, (www.mtib.gov.my/publication/publications.php)
- Ministry of Forests and Range, British Columbia, Canada, (www.gov.bc.ca/for)
- Office National des Fôrets, France, (www.onf.fr)
- *PaperTree Letter*, United States, (www.risiinfo.com/risi-store/do/home/…)
- Programme for the Endorsement of Forest Certification schemes (PEFC), (www.pefc.org)
- Pulp and Paper Products Council, Canada, (www.pppc.org)
- *Random Lengths International/Yardstick,* United States, (www.randomlengths.com/base.asp?s1=Newsletters)
- RISI (former Paperloop), United States, (www.risiinfo.com)
- Statistics Canada, Canada, (www.statcan.ca)
- Stora Enso, Finland, (www.storaenso.com)
- Swedish Energy Agency, (www.stem.se)
- Swedish Forest Industries Federation, (www.skogsindustrierna.org)
- Swiss Federal Statistical Office, (www.statistik.admin.ch)
- Timber Trades Journal Online (*TTJ*), United Kingdom, (www.ttjonline.com)
- UN Comtrade, (unstats.un.org/unsd/comtrade)
- UNECE/FAO TIMBER database, (www.unece.org/trade/timber)
- US Census Bureau, United States, (www.census.gov)
- US Energy Information Administration, United States, (www.eia.doe.gov)
- USDA Foreign Agricultural Service, United States, (www.fas.usda.gov)
- USDA Forest Service, United States, (www.fs.fed.us)
- *Wood Markets Monthly*, Canada, (www.woodmarkets.com/p_wmm.html)
- *Wood Products Statistical Roundup,* American Forest and Paper Association, United States, (www.afandpa.org/…)

Some facts about the Timber Committee

The Timber Committee is a principal subsidiary body of the UNECE (United Nations Economic Commission for Europe) based in Geneva. It constitutes a forum for cooperation and consultation between member countries on forestry, the forest industry and forest product matters. All countries of Europe, the Commonwealth of Independent States, the United States, Canada and Israel are members of the UNECE and participate in its work.

The UNECE Timber Committee shall, within the context of sustainable development, provide member countries with the information and services needed for policy- and decision-making with regard to their forest and forest industry sectors ("the sector"), including the trade and use of forest products and, when appropriate, will formulate recommendations addressed to member Governments and interested organisations. To this end, it shall:

1. With the active participation of member countries, undertake short-, medium- and long-term analyses of developments in, and having an impact on, the sector, including those offering possibilities for the facilitation of international trade and for enhancing the protection of the environment;

2. In support of these analyses, collect, store and disseminate statistics relating to the sector, and carry out activities to improve their quality and comparability;

3. Provide the framework for cooperation e.g. by organising seminars, workshops and ad hoc meetings and setting up time-limited ad hoc groups, for the exchange of economic, environmental and technical information between governments and other institutions of member countries required for the development and implementation of policies leading to the sustainable development of the sector and to the protection of the environment in their respective countries;

4. Carry out tasks identified by the UNECE or the Timber Committee as being of priority, including the facilitation of subregional cooperation and activities in support of the economies in transition of central and eastern Europe and of the countries of the region that are developing from an economic perspective;

5. It should also keep under review its structure and priorities and cooperate with other international and intergovernmental organizations active in the sector, and in particular with the FAO (Food and Agriculture Organization of the United Nations) and its European Forestry Commission, and with the ILO (International Labour Organisation), in order to ensure complementarity and to avoid duplication, thereby optimizing the use of resources.

More information about the Committee's work may be obtained by writing to:

UNECE/FAO Timber Section
Trade and Timber Division
United Nations Economic Commission for Europe
Palais des Nations
CH-1211 Geneva 10, Switzerland
Fax: +41 22 917 0041
E-mail: info.timber@unece.org
http://www.unece.org/trade/timber

UNECE/FAO

Publications

Timber Bulletin Volume LVIII (2005)   **ECE/TIM/BULL/2005/3**

    Forest Products Annual Market Review, 2004-2005

Note: *other market related publications and information are available in electronic format from our website.*

Geneva Timber and Forest Study Papers

European Forest Sector Outlook Study: 1960 – 2000 – 2020, Main Report	ECE/TIM/SP/20
Forest policies and institutions of Europe, 1998-2000	ECE/TIM/SP/19
Forest and Forest Products Country Profile: Russian Federation	ECE/TIM/SP/18

(Country profiles also exist on Albania, Armenia, Belarus, Bulgaria, former Czech and Slovak Federal Republic, Estonia, Georgia, Hungary, Lithuania, Poland, Romania, Republic of Moldova, Slovenia and Ukraine)

Forest resources of Europe, CIS, North America, Australia, Japan and New Zealand	ECE/TIM/SP/17
State of European forests and forestry, 1999	ECE/TIM/SP/16
Non-wood goods and services of the forest	ECE/TIM/SP/15

The above series of sales publications and subscriptions are available through United Nations Publications Offices as follows:

Orders from Africa, Europe and the Middle East should be sent to:

Sales and Marketing Section, Room C-113
United Nations
Palais des Nations
CH - 1211 Geneva 10, Switzerland
Fax: + 41 22 917 0027
E-mail: unpubli@unog.ch

Orders from North America, Latin America and the Caribbean, Asia and the Pacific should be sent to:

Sales and Marketing Section, Room DC2-853
United Nations
2 United Nations Plaza
New York, N.Y. 10017
United States, of America
Fax: + 1 212 963 3489
E-mail: publications@un.org

Web site: http://www.un.org/Pubs/sales.htm

* * * * *

Geneva Timber and Forest Discussion Papers *(original language only)*

Forest Certification – Do Governments Have a Role?	ECE/TIM/DP/44
International Forest Sector Institutions and Policy Instruments for Europe: A Source Book	ECE/TIM/DP/43
Forests, Wood and Energy: Policy Interactions	ECE/TIM/DP/42
Outlook for the Development of European Forest Resources	ECE/TIM/DP/41
Forest and Forest Products Country Profile: Serbia and Montenegro	ECE/TIM/DP/40
Forest Certification Update for the UNECE Region, 2003	ECE/TIM/DP/39
Forest and Forest Products Country Profile: Republic of Bulgaria	ECE/TIM/DP/38
Forest Legislation in Europe: How 23 Countries Approach the Obligation to Reforest, Public Access and Use of Non-Wood Forest Products	ECE/TIM/DP/37
Value-Added Wood Products Markets, 2001-2003	ECE/TIM/DP/36
Trends in the Tropical Timber Trade, 2002-2003	ECE/TIM/DP/35
Biological Diversity, Tree Species Composition and Environmental Protection in the Regional FRA-2000	ECE/TIM/DP/33
Forestry and Forest Products Country Profile: Ukraine	ECE/TIM/DP/32
The Development of European Forest Resources, 1950 To 2000: a Better Information Base	ECE/TIM/DP/31
Modelling and Projections of Forest Products Demand, Supply and Trade in Europe	ECE/TIM/DP/30
Employment Trends and Prospects in the European Forest Sector	ECE/TIM/DP/29
Forestry Cooperation with Countries in Transition	ECE/TIM/DP/28
Russian Federation Forest Sector Outlook Study	ECE/TIM/DP/27
Forest and Forest Products Country Profile: Georgia	ECE/TIM/DP/26
Forest certification update for the UNECE region, summer 2002	ECE/TIM/DP/25
Forecasts of economic growth in OECD and central and eastern European countries for the period 2000-2040	ECE/TIM/DP/24
Forest Certification update for the UNECE Region, summer 2001	ECE/TIM/DP/23
Structural, Compositional and Functional Aspects of Forest Biodiversity in Europe	ECE/TIM/DP/22
Markets for secondary processed wood products, 1990-2000	ECE/TIM/DP/21
Forest certification update for the UNECE Region, summer 2000	ECE/TIM/DP/20
Trade and environment issues in the forest and forest products sector	ECE/TIM/DP/19
Multiple use forestry	ECE/TIM/DP/18
Forest certification update for the UNECE Region, summer 1999	ECE/TIM/DP/17
A summary of "The competitive climate for wood products and paper packaging: the factors causing substitution with emphasis on environmental promotions"	ECE/TIM/DP/16
Recycling, energy and market interactions	ECE/TIM/DP/15
The status of forest certification in the UNECE region	ECE/TIM/DP/14
The role of women on forest properties in Haute-Savoie (France): Initial research	ECE/TIM/DP/13
Interim report on the Implementation of Resolution H3 of the Helsinki Ministerial Conference on the protection of forests in Europe (Results of the second enquiry)	ECE/TIM/DP/12
Manual on acute forest damage	ECE/TIM/DP/7

International Forest Fire News *(two issues per year)*

Timber and Forest Information Series
    Timber Committee Yearbook 2004   ECE/TIM/INF/11

The above series of publications may be requested free of charge through:

    UNECE/FAO Timber Section
    Trade and Timber Division
    United Nations Economic Commission for Europe
    Palais des Nations
    CH-1211 Geneva 10, Switzerland
    Fax: +41 22 917 0041
    E-mail: info.timber@unece.org
    Downloads are available at: http://www.unece.org/trade/timber